Lines, Angles and Triangles

☞ ‖ **Keep in mind...**
‖ **If at first you succeed, try something harder.**

Lines and Angles

A pair of points determines at least 4 geometric figures.

a line	a segment	a ray	the ray opposite XY
$\overleftrightarrow{XY}$ or $\overleftrightarrow{YX}$	$\overline{XY}$ or $\overline{YX}$	$\overrightarrow{XY}$	To name this ray with a symbol an additional point is required.

Identify the following using symbols.

1. A — B →

2. C — D

3. E — F (up/down arrows)

4. G ← H

5. I — J

6. K — L

7. A → T

8. K — V

9. ← T — V →

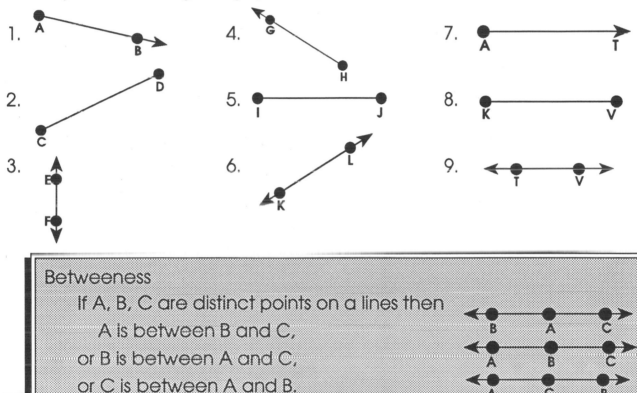

Betweeness

    If A, B, C are distinct points on a lines then

        A is between B and C,

    or B is between A and C,

    or C is between A and B.

10. Choose the appropriate symbols, (→, — or ↔) to make this statement true. LB contains points M and V, but LB contains neither M nor V. V belongs to LB but M does not. ML + LV = MV

11. Make a sketch showing the position of the four points in number 10.
12. Is M between L and B?
13. Is L between M and B?
14. Is V between L and B?

Points, Lines and Planes

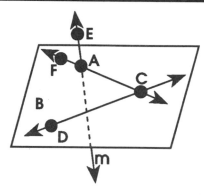

Plane E contains line *t*. Points D and O lie on line *t* and plane E. $\overleftrightarrow{PO}$ passes through plane E. $\overleftrightarrow{PO} \cap E = O$.

Any two points determines exactly one line.

Any 3 non-collinear points determine exactly one plane.

True or false.

1. $\overleftrightarrow{AC} \cap \overleftrightarrow{DC} = C$

2. E lies in B.

3. Points A, C and F are collinear.

4. Points A, C, F and E are coplanar.

5. $\overleftrightarrow{DC}$ lies in B.

6. Point A lies on m and B.

7. A line can be drawn containing points D and E.

8. A line can be drawn containing points A, C and E.

9. Any line contained in plane B intersects $\overleftrightarrow{CF}$.

10. A plane exists which contains points A, D and E.

11. m ∩ $\overleftrightarrow{FC}$ = A.

12. m ∩ B = A.

13. $\overleftrightarrow{EA}$ lies in B.

14. C, D, F, and E are coplanar.

15. $\overleftrightarrow{DC}$ and $\overleftrightarrow{EA}$ are coplanar.

Tell whether each set of points is collinear or non-collinear; coplanar or non-coplanar.

16. A, B, C   19. B, H   22. A, B, D, E

17. G, H, E, B   20. A, D, G, H 23. F, G

18. D, E, H   21. A, B, F, H 24. H, G, C, F

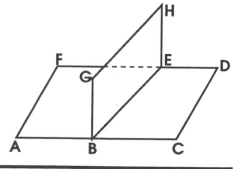

Segment Length and Midpoints

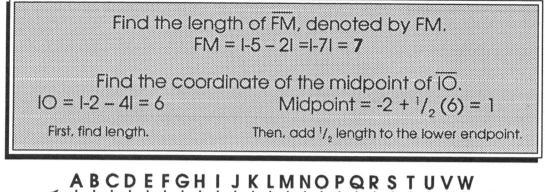

Find the length of $\overline{FM}$, denoted by FM.
$$FM = |{-5} - 2| = |{-7}| = 7$$

Find the coordinate of the midpoint of $\overline{IO}$.

$IO = |{-2} - 4| = 6$ Midpoint $= -2 + \frac{1}{2}(6) = 1$

First, find length.   Then, add $\frac{1}{2}$ length to the lower endpoint.

```
 A B C D E F G H I  J  K  L  M  N  O  P  Q  R  S  T  U  V  W
-10-9-8-7-6-5-4-3-2-1 0  1  2  3  4  5  6  7  8  9 10 11 12
```

Find the length and the coordinate of the midpoint for each segment.

1. $\overline{GW}$ 3. $\overline{PV}$ 5. $\overline{IR}$ 7. $\overline{DL}$ 9. $\overline{FR}$

2. $\overline{BN}$ 4. $\overline{AG}$ 6. $\overline{TW}$ 8. $\overline{KU}$ 10. $\overline{NT}$

11. The segment with endpoints -3 and 10.

12. The segment with endpoints -3 and $-7\frac{1}{2}$.

13. The segment with endpoints 0 and $-2\frac{5}{8}$.

14. The segment with endpoints 2 and 7.

15. The segment with endpoints -4 and 5.

16. The segment with endpoints -1 and 3.

17. The segment with endpoints 5 and 12.

18. The segment with endpoints $\frac{1}{4}$ and $2\frac{3}{4}$.

19. The segment with endpoints $-\frac{1}{2}$ and $3\frac{1}{2}$.

20. The segment with endpoints $\frac{1}{3}$ and $4\frac{2}{3}$.

21. On a number line, point Q has coordinate 1 and T has coordinate 5. A is the midpoint of $\overline{QT}$, B is the midpoint of $\overline{QA}$, C is the midpoint of $\overline{QB}$, and D is the midpoint of $\overline{QC}$. Find the coordinate of D.

Congruence of Segments and Addition Properties

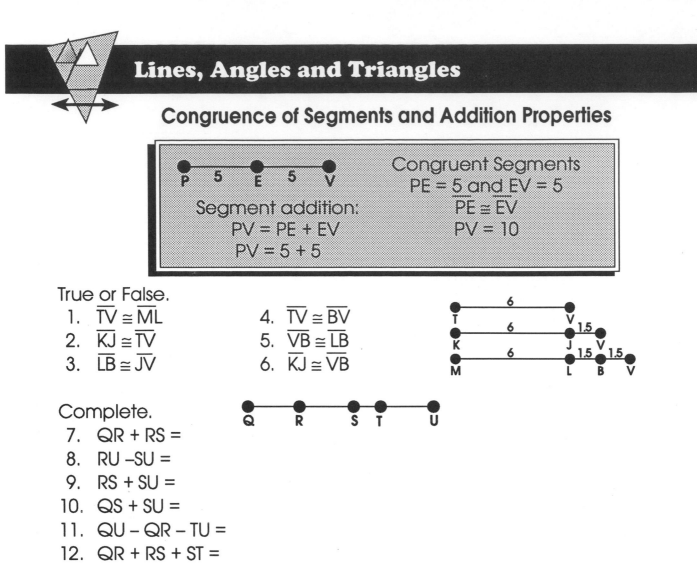

True or False.

1. $\overline{TV} \cong \overline{ML}$
2. $\overline{KJ} \cong \overline{TV}$
3. $\overline{LB} \cong \overline{JV}$

4. $\overline{TV} \cong \overline{BV}$
5. $\overline{VB} \cong \overline{LB}$
6. $\overline{KJ} \cong \overline{VB}$

Complete.

7. QR + RS =

8. RU – SU =

9. RS + SU =

10. QS + SU =

11. QU – QR – TU =

12. QR + RS + ST =

Find the length of the indicated segments.

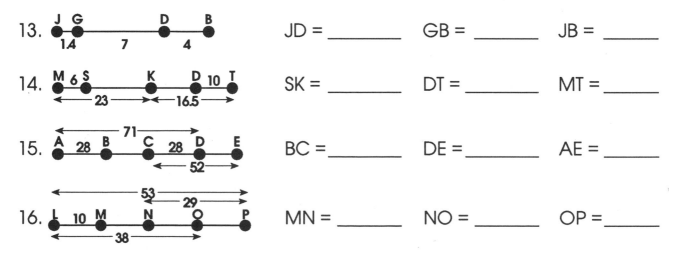

13.   JD = _____   GB = _____   JB = _____

14.   SK = _____   DT = _____   MT = _____

15.   BC = _____   DE = _____   AE = _____

16.   MN = _____   NO = _____   OP = _____

17. Which segments are congruent in #15?

Angles (∠)

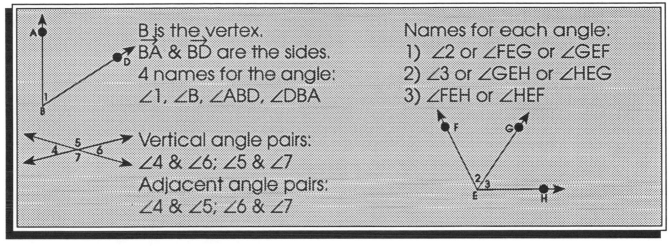

B is the vertex.
$\vec{BA}$ & $\vec{BD}$ are the sides.
4 names for the angle:
∠1, ∠B, ∠ABD, ∠DBA

Vertical angle pairs:
∠4 & ∠6; ∠5 & ∠7
Adjacent angle pairs:
∠4 & ∠5; ∠6 & ∠7

Names for each angle:
1) ∠2 or ∠FEG or ∠GEF
2) ∠3 or ∠GEH or ∠HEG
3) ∠FEH or ∠HEF

Name the indicated angle.

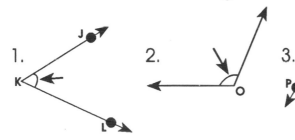

1.

2.

3.

4.

5.

6. Name 2 pairs of vertical angles.

7. Name 4 pairs of adjacent angles.

8. How many pairs of vertical angles are pictured?

9. How many pairs of adjacent angles are pictured?

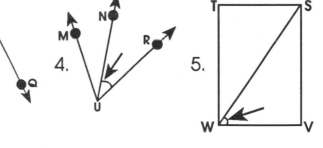

(#6-7)

(#8-9)

10. Name 2 angles adjacent to ∠RES.

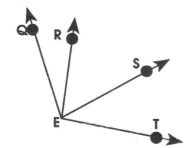

5

Congruence of Angles and Addition Properties

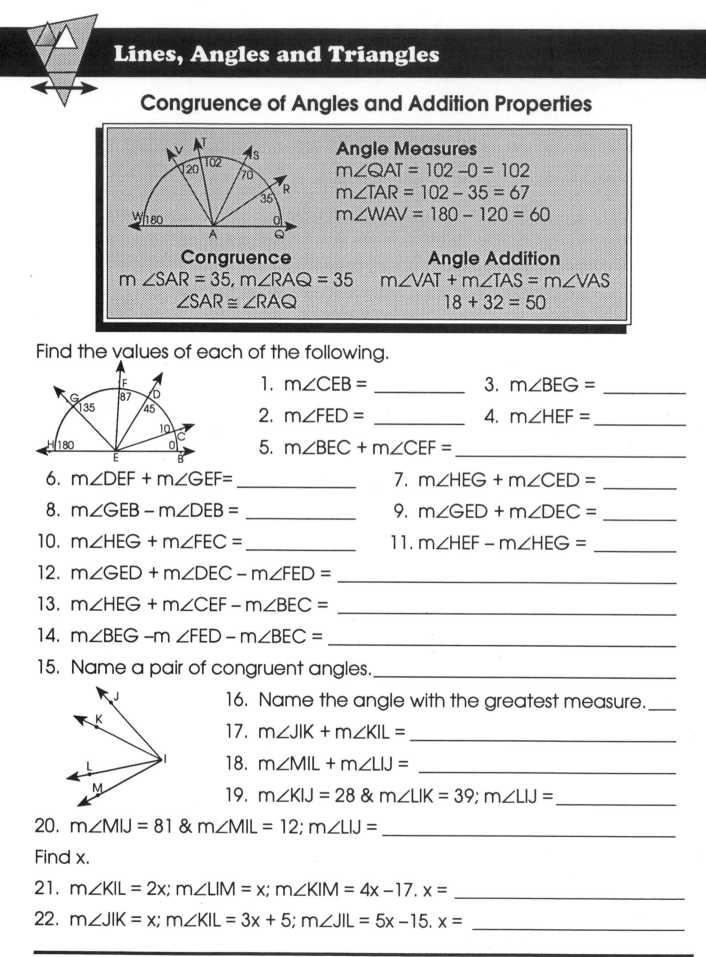

Angle Measures
m∠QAT = 102 –0 = 102
m∠TAR = 102 – 35 = 67
m∠WAV = 180 – 120 = 60

Congruence
m ∠SAR = 35, m∠RAQ = 35
∠SAR ≅ ∠RAQ

Angle Addition
m∠VAT + m∠TAS = m∠VAS
18 + 32 = 50

Find the values of each of the following.

1. m∠CEB = _____   3. m∠BEG = _____

2. m∠FED = _____   4. m∠HEF = _____

5. m∠BEC + m∠CEF = _____

6. m∠DEF + m∠GEF= _____   7. m∠HEG + m∠CED = _____

8. m∠GEB – m∠DEB = _____   9. m∠GED + m∠DEC = _____

10. m∠HEG + m∠FEC = _____   11. m∠HEF – m∠HEG = _____

12. m∠GED + m∠DEC – m∠FED = _____

13. m∠HEG + m∠CEF – m∠BEC = _____

14. m∠BEG –m ∠FED – m∠BEC = _____

15. Name a pair of congruent angles._____

16. Name the angle with the greatest measure.___

17. m∠JIK + m∠KIL = _____

18. m∠MIL + m∠LIJ = _____

19. m∠KIJ = 28 & m∠LIK = 39; m∠LIJ = _____

20. m∠MIJ = 81 & m∠MIL = 12; m∠LIJ = _____

Find x.

21. m∠KIL = 2x; m∠LIM = x; m∠KIM = 4x –17. x = _____

22. m∠JIK = x; m∠KIL = 3x + 5; m∠JIL = 5x –15. x = _____

6

Classifying Angles

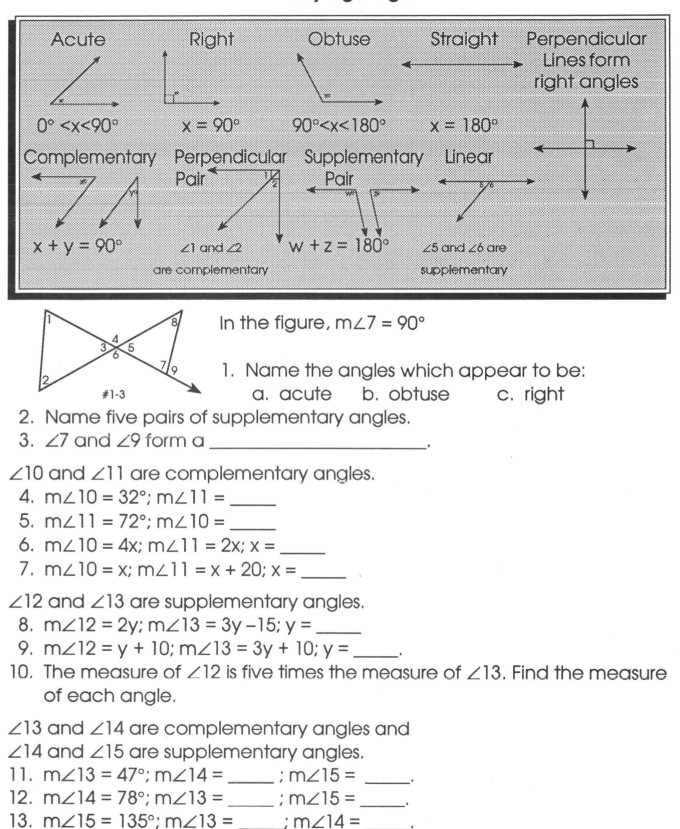

In the figure, m∠7 = 90°

1. Name the angles which appear to be:
   a. acute   b. obtuse   c. right

2. Name five pairs of supplementary angles.

3. ∠7 and ∠9 form a _____.

∠10 and ∠11 are complementary angles.

4. m∠10 = 32°; m∠11 = _____
5. m∠11 = 72°; m∠10 = _____
6. m∠10 = 4x; m∠11 = 2x; x = _____
7. m∠10 = x; m∠11 = x + 20; x = _____

∠12 and ∠13 are supplementary angles.

8. m∠12 = 2y; m∠13 = 3y –15; y = _____
9. m∠12 = y + 10; m∠13 = 3y + 10; y = _____.

10. The measure of ∠12 is five times the measure of ∠13. Find the measure of each angle.

∠13 and ∠14 are complementary angles and
∠14 and ∠15 are supplementary angles.

11. m∠13 = 47°; m∠14 = _____ ; m∠15 = _____.
12. m∠14 = 78°; m∠13 = _____ ; m∠15 = _____.
13. m∠15 = 135°; m∠13 = _____; m∠14 = _____.

Mixed Practice with Angles

Find the measure of the lettered angles.

Hatch marks indicate congruent parts.

c = 180 – 53 = **127°**

b = c = **127°**

a = 180 – b = 180 – 127 = **53°**

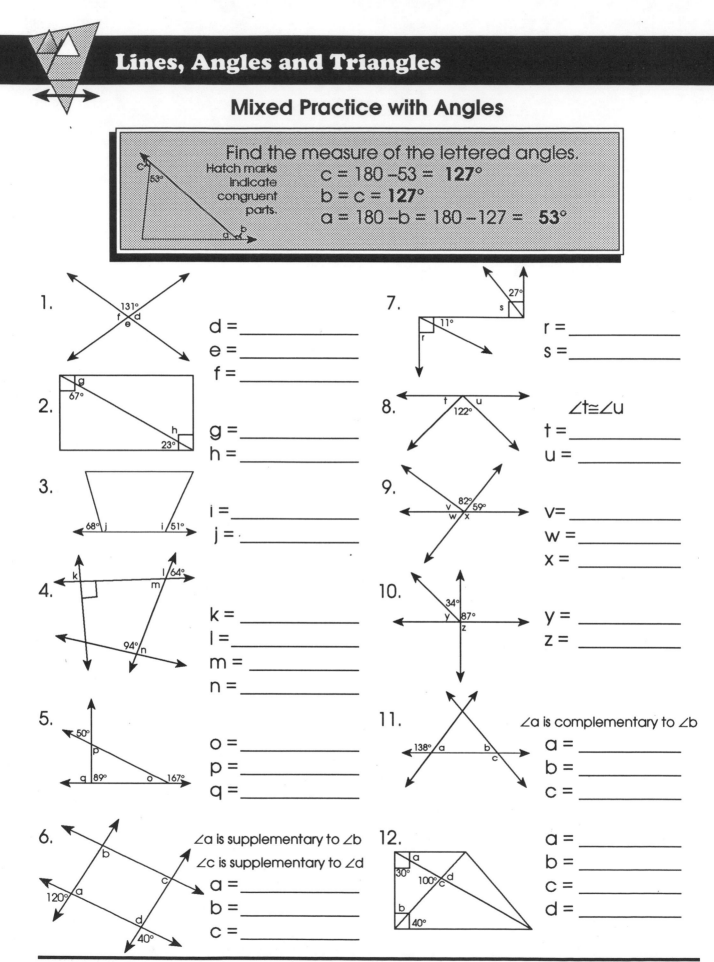

1.

d = _____

e = _____

f = _____

2.

g = _____

h = _____

3.

i = _____

j = _____

4.

k = _____

l = _____

m = _____

n = _____

5.

o = _____

p = _____

q = _____

6.

∠a is supplementary to ∠b

∠c is supplementary to ∠d

a = _____

b = _____

c = _____

7.

r = _____

s = _____

8.

∠t ≅ ∠u

t = _____

u = _____

9.

v = _____

w = _____

x = _____

10.

y = _____

z = _____

11.

∠a is complementary to ∠b

a = _____

b = _____

c = _____

12.

a = _____

b = _____

c = _____

d = _____

Algebra Applications with Angles

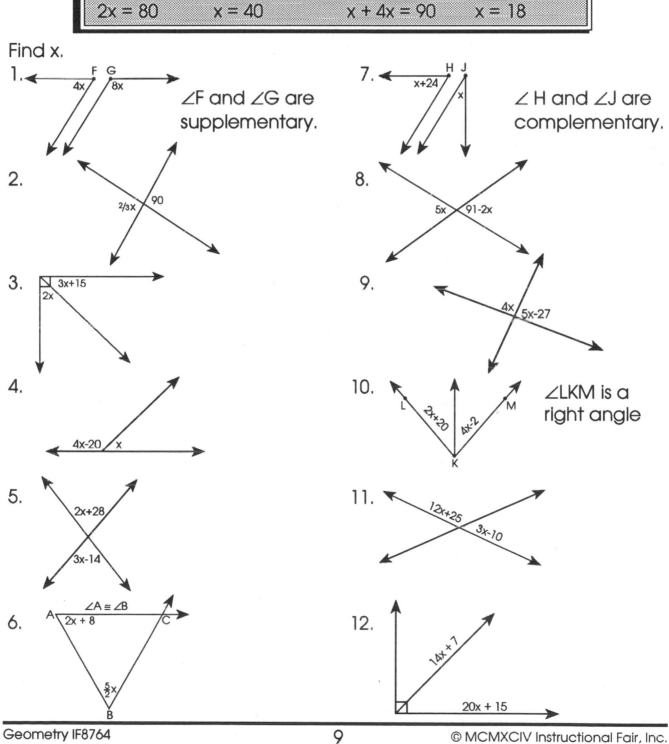

Find x.
(Note: Vertical angles are congruent.)

m∠BAD = 90

2x = 80   x = 40   x + 4x = 90   x = 18

Find x.

1. 4x 8x ∠F and ∠G are supplementary.

2. 2/3x 90

3. 3x+15 2x

4. 4x-20 x

5. 2x+28 3x-14

6. ∠A ≅ ∠B   A 2x + 8 C   5/2x   B

7. x+24 x ∠H and ∠J are complementary.

8. 5x 91-2x

9. 4x 5x-27

10. L 2x+20 4x-2 M K ∠LKM is a right angle

11. 12x+25 3x-10

12. 14x + 7 20x + 15

Triangles (△)

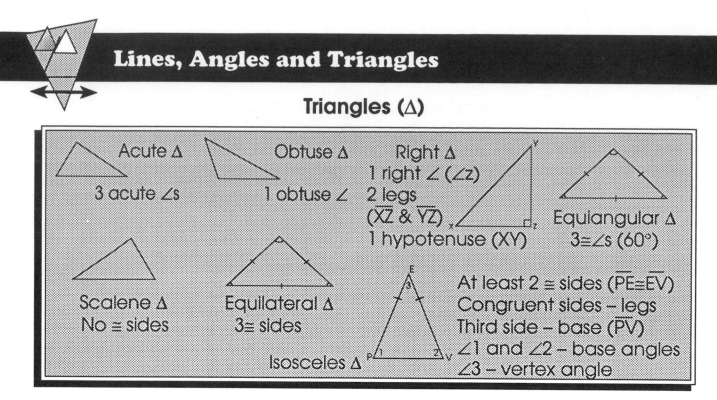

Classify each triangle by its angles and by its sides.

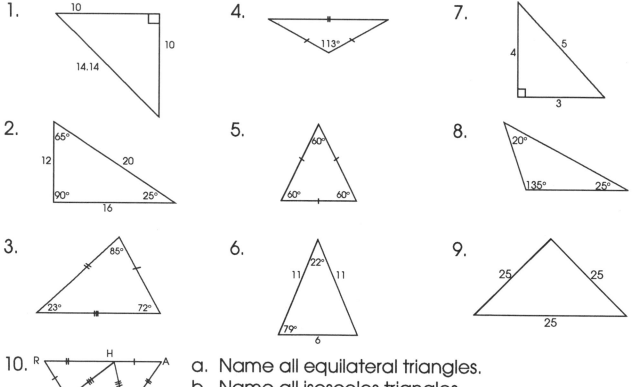

10.
a. Name all equilateral triangles.
b. Name all isosceles triangles.
c. Name all scalene triangles.

11. True or false: An equilateral triangle is always isosceles.

Congruence of Triangles

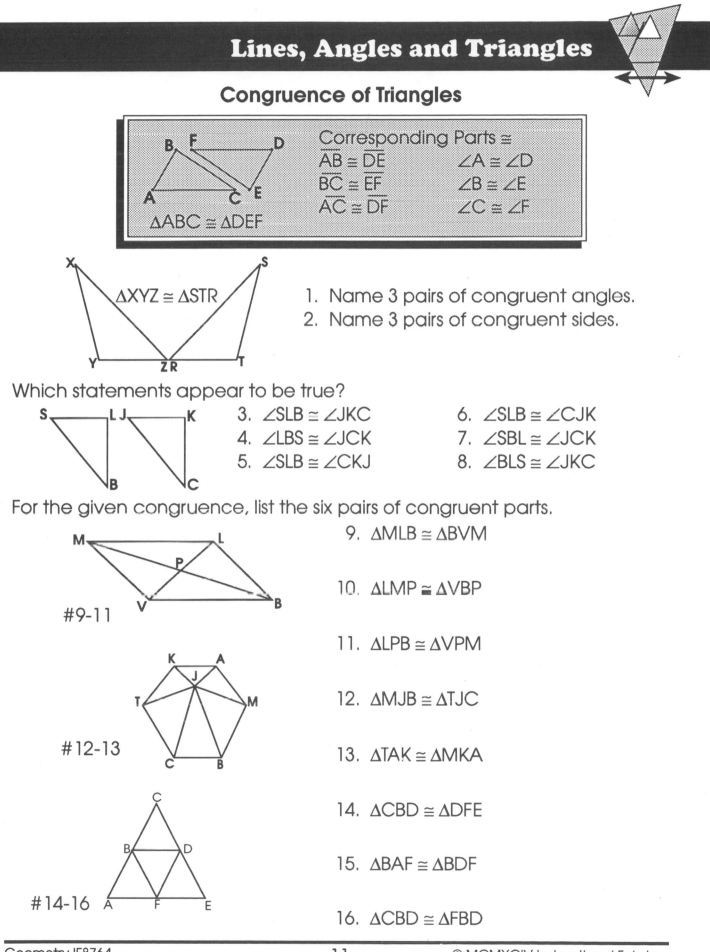

Corresponding Parts ≅
$\overline{AB} \cong \overline{DE}$ $\angle A \cong \angle D$
$\overline{BC} \cong \overline{EF}$ $\angle B \cong \angle E$
$\overline{AC} \cong \overline{DF}$ $\angle C \cong \angle F$

$\triangle ABC \cong \triangle DEF$

$\triangle XYZ \cong \triangle STR$

1. Name 3 pairs of congruent angles.
2. Name 3 pairs of congruent sides.

Which statements appear to be true?

3. $\angle SLB \cong \angle JKC$ 6. $\angle SLB \cong \angle CJK$
4. $\angle LBS \cong \angle JCK$ 7. $\angle SBL \cong \angle JCK$
5. $\angle SLB \cong \angle CKJ$ 8. $\angle BLS \cong \angle JKC$

For the given congruence, list the six pairs of congruent parts.

9. $\triangle MLB \cong \triangle BVM$

#9-11

10. $\triangle LMP \cong \triangle VBP$

11. $\triangle LPB \cong \triangle VPM$

#12-13

12. $\triangle MJB \cong \triangle TJC$

13. $\triangle TAK \cong \triangle MKA$

14. $\triangle CBD \cong \triangle DFE$

#14-16

15. $\triangle BAF \cong \triangle BDF$

16. $\triangle CBD \cong \triangle FBD$

☞ | **Keep in mind...**
Change can be beautiful: look at a cater-
pillar and think of the butterfly to come.

Symmetry

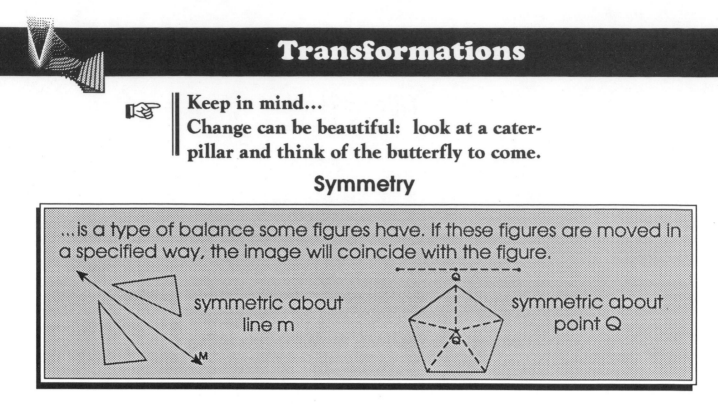

Identify the following as symmetric or not symmetric.

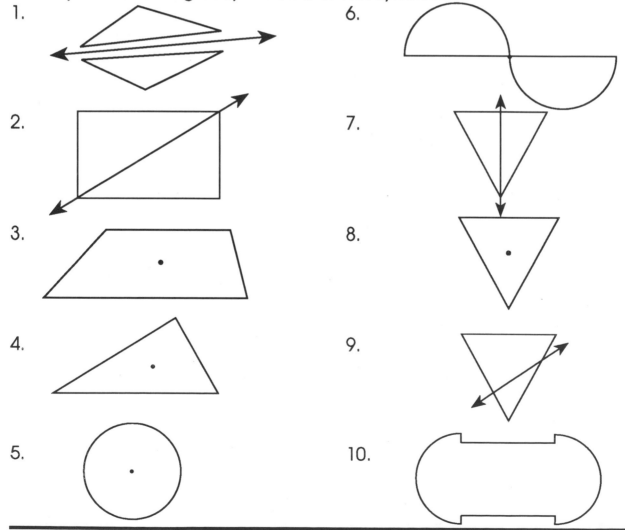

1.

2.

3.

4.

5.

6.

7.

8.

9.

10.

Orientation

These figures and their images have the same orientation.

These figures and their images have opposite orientations.

Tell whether these figures have the same or opposite orientations.

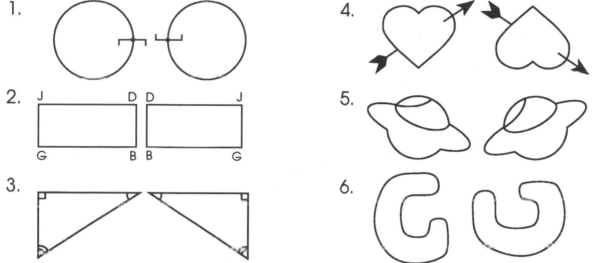

1.

4.

2. J   D D   J
   G   B B   G

5.

3.

6.

Identify the image with opposite orientation from the original figure.

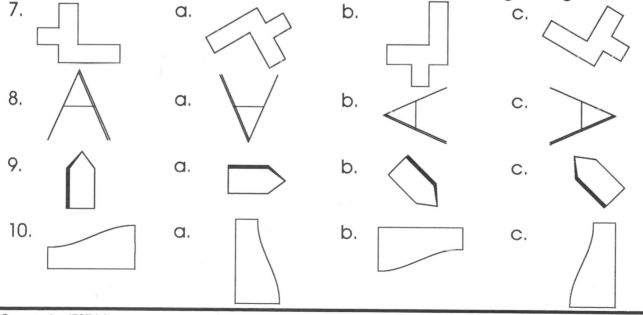

7.   a.   b.   c.

8.   a.   b.   c.

9.   a.   b.   c.

10.   a.   b.   c.

Reflections

A reflection requires a flip. The original figure and its image have opposite orientations.

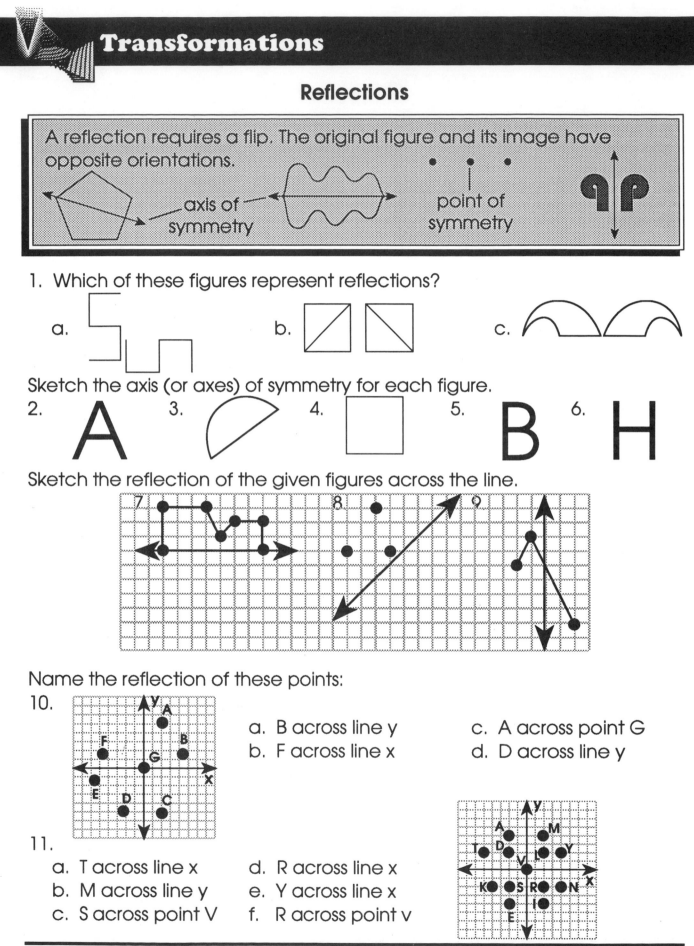

axis of symmetry

point of symmetry

1. Which of these figures represent reflections?

a.   b.   c.

Sketch the axis (or axes) of symmetry for each figure.

2. A   3.   4.   5. B   6. H

Sketch the reflection of the given figures across the line.

7   8   9

Name the reflection of these points:

10.

a. B across line y   c. A across point G
b. F across line x   d. D across line y

11.

a. T across line x   d. R across line x
b. M across line y   e. Y across line x
c. S across point V   f. R across point v

Rotations

A rotation is a turn about a point. The original figure and its image have the same orientation.

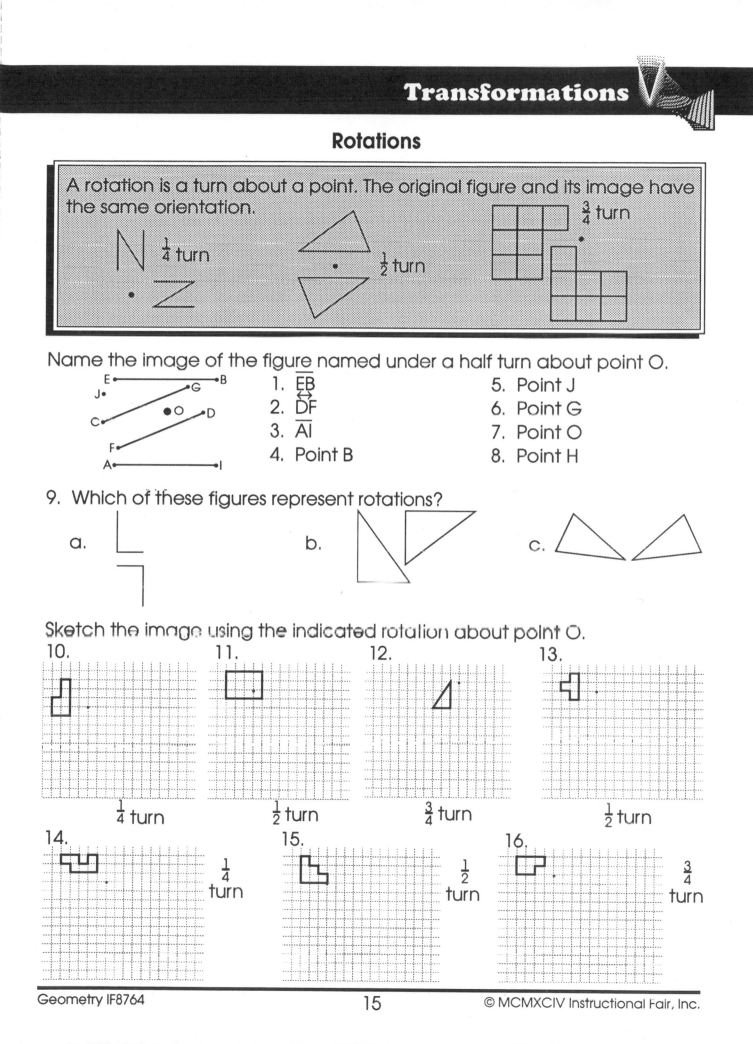

$\frac{1}{4}$ turn

$\frac{1}{2}$ turn

$\frac{3}{4}$ turn

Name the image of the figure named under a half turn about point O.

1. $\overline{EB}$
2. $\overleftrightarrow{DF}$
3. $\overline{AI}$
4. Point B

5. Point J
6. Point G
7. Point O
8. Point H

9. Which of these figures represent rotations?

a.

b.

c.

Sketch the image using the indicated rotation about point O.

10.

$\frac{1}{4}$ turn

11.

$\frac{1}{2}$ turn

12.

$\frac{3}{4}$ turn

13.

$\frac{1}{2}$ turn

14.

$\frac{1}{4}$ turn

15.

$\frac{1}{2}$ turn

16.

$\frac{3}{4}$ turn

Transformations

Translations

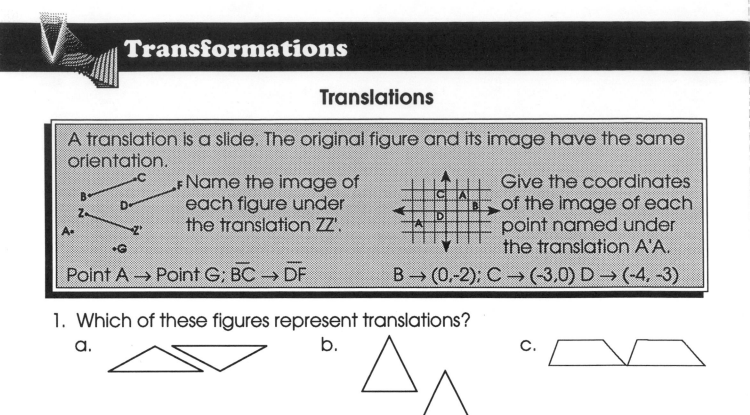

A translation is a slide. The original figure and its image have the same orientation.

Name the image of each figure under the translation ZZ'.

Point A → Point G; $\overline{BC}$ → $\overline{DF}$

Give the coordinates of the image of each point named under the translation A'A.

B → (0,-2); C → (-3,0) D → (-4, -3)

1. Which of these figures represent translations?

a.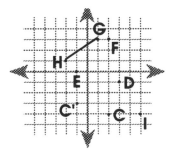

b.

c.

Name the image of each figure under the translation EE'.

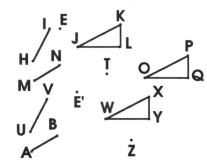

2. Point T

3. $\overline{MN}$

4. △JKL

5. Point L

6. Point N

7. $\overline{HI}$

8. △OPQ

9. Point H

Give the coordinates of the image for each point named under the translation CC'.

10. Point F

11. Point D

12. Point E

13. Point I

14. The endpoints of the segment which is the image of HG.

Mixed Practice with Transformations

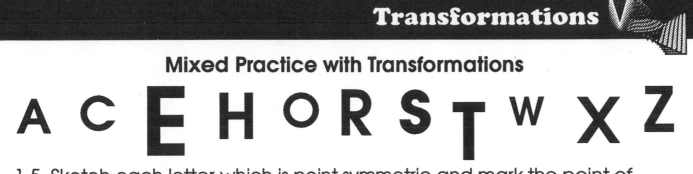

A C E H O R S T W X Z

1-5. Sketch each letter which is point symmetric and mark the point of symmetry.

6-13. Sketch each letter that is line symmetric and draw **all** lines of symmetry.

Each of these figures have been moved in a series of basic motions. Name the motion indicated by the lettered arrow.

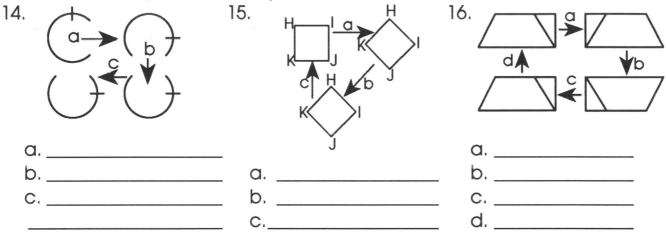

14.

a. _____
b. _____
c. _____
   _____

15.

a. _____
b. _____
c. _____

16.

a. _____
b. _____
c. _____
d. _____

Tell which single basic motion will make these figures coincide?

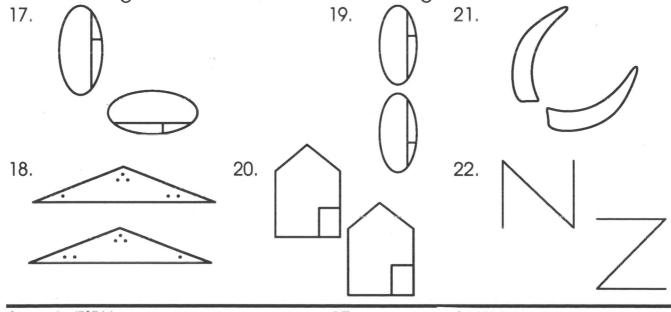

17.

18.

19.

20.

21.

22.

Transformations with Dots & Graphs

1. Draw the reflection of △MSD around line ℓ and label it M'S'D'; draw one half turn rotation around point P and label it M"S"D".

2. Find the image of each figure using the translation KK'.

More Transformations with Dots & Graphs

For each point named, give its reflection across the
   a. x-axis   b. origin   c. y-axis

1. (2,-3)

2. (-4,-1)

3. (5,5)

4. (-1,2)

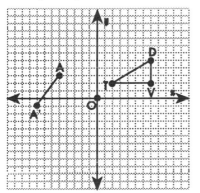

5. Find the image of ΔTDV:

   a. for the rotation of a $\frac{1}{4}$ turn counterclockwise.

   b. for the translation AA'.

   c. for the reflection across O.

6. Find the image of QRST:

   a. for the reflection across the x-axis.

   b. for the rotation about 0 of a $\frac{1}{2}$ turn clockwise.

   c. for the translation of BB'.

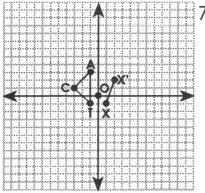

7. Find the image of ΔCAT:

   a. for the reflection across the y-axis.

   b. for the translation XX'.

   c. for the rotation about O of a $\frac{3}{4}$ turn clockwise.

Triangles

☞ **Keep in mind...**
The only ideas that will work for you
are the ones you put to work.

Included Sides and Angles

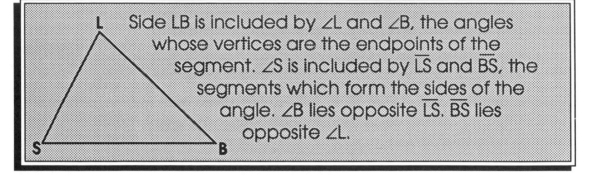

Side LB is included by ∠L and ∠B, the angles whose vertices are the endpoints of the segment. ∠S is included by $\overline{LS}$ and $\overline{BS}$, the segments which form the sides of the angle. ∠B lies opposite $\overline{LS}$. $\overline{BS}$ lies opposite ∠L.

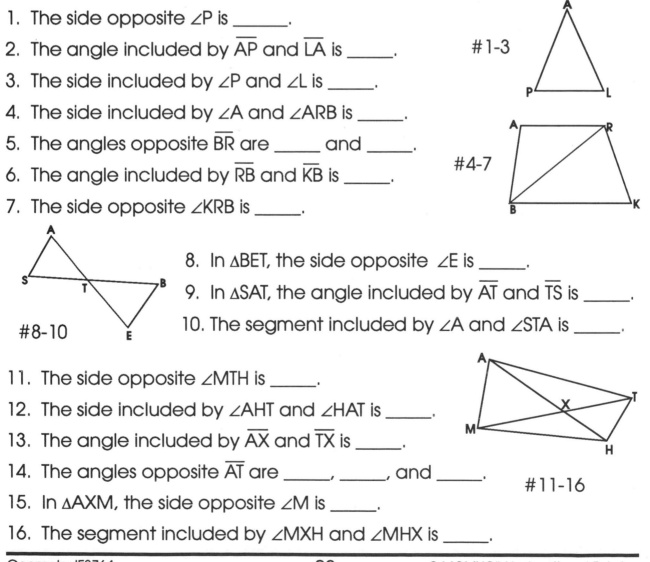

1. The side opposite ∠P is _____.

2. The angle included by $\overline{AP}$ and $\overline{LA}$ is _____.

3. The side included by ∠P and ∠L is _____.

#1-3

4. The side included by ∠A and ∠ARB is _____.

5. The angles opposite $\overline{BR}$ are _____ and _____.

6. The angle included by $\overline{RB}$ and $\overline{KB}$ is _____.

#4-7

7. The side opposite ∠KRB is _____.

8. In ∆BET, the side opposite ∠E is _____.

9. In ∆SAT, the angle included by $\overline{AT}$ and $\overline{TS}$ is _____.

10. The segment included by ∠A and ∠STA is _____.

#8-10

11. The side opposite ∠MTH is _____.

12. The side included by ∠AHT and ∠HAT is _____.

13. The angle included by $\overline{AX}$ and $\overline{TX}$ is _____.

14. The angles opposite $\overline{AT}$ are _____, _____, and _____.

15. In ∆AXM, the side opposite ∠M is _____.

#11-16

16. The segment included by ∠MXH and ∠MHX is _____.

Ways To Prove Triangles Congruent

SSS (side, side, side) = three sides of one triangle congruent to the corresponding parts of another triangle ⟹ ≅ Δs.

SAS (side, angle, side) = two sides and the included angle of one triangle congruent to the corresponding parts of another triangle ⟹ ≅ Δs.

Identify which property will prove these triangles congruent (SSS, SAS or none).

1.

2.

3.

4.

5.

6.

7.

8.

9.

10.

11.

12.

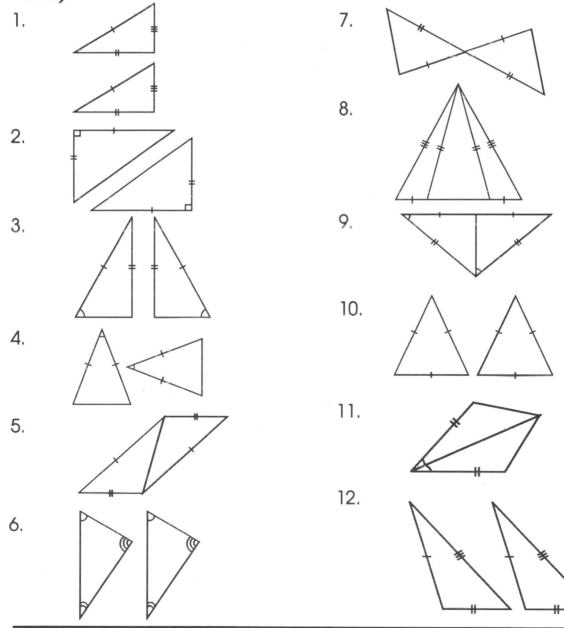

More Ways To Prove Triangles Congruent

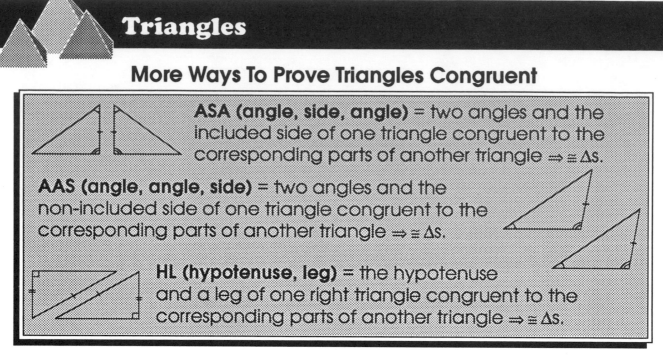

ASA (angle, side, angle) = two angles and the included side of one triangle congruent to the corresponding parts of another triangle ⇒ ≅ △s.

AAS (angle, angle, side) = two angles and the non-included side of one triangle congruent to the corresponding parts of another triangle ⇒ ≅ △s.

HL (hypotenuse, leg) = the hypotenuse and a leg of one right triangle congruent to the corresponding parts of another triangle ⇒ ≅ △s.

Identify which property will prove these triangles congruent (ASA, AAS, HL or none).

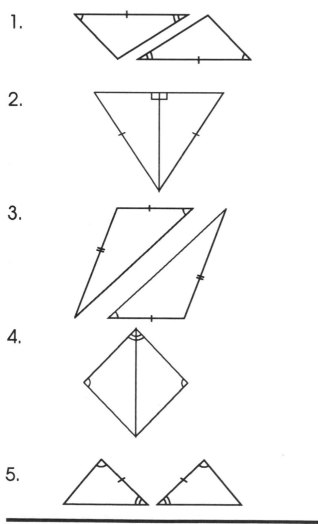

1.

2.

3.

4.

5.

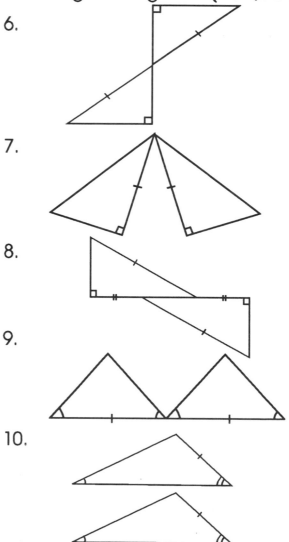

6.

7.

8.

9.

10.

More Congruent Triangles

Identify which property will prove these triangles congruent. (SSS, SAS, ASA, AAS, HL or none)

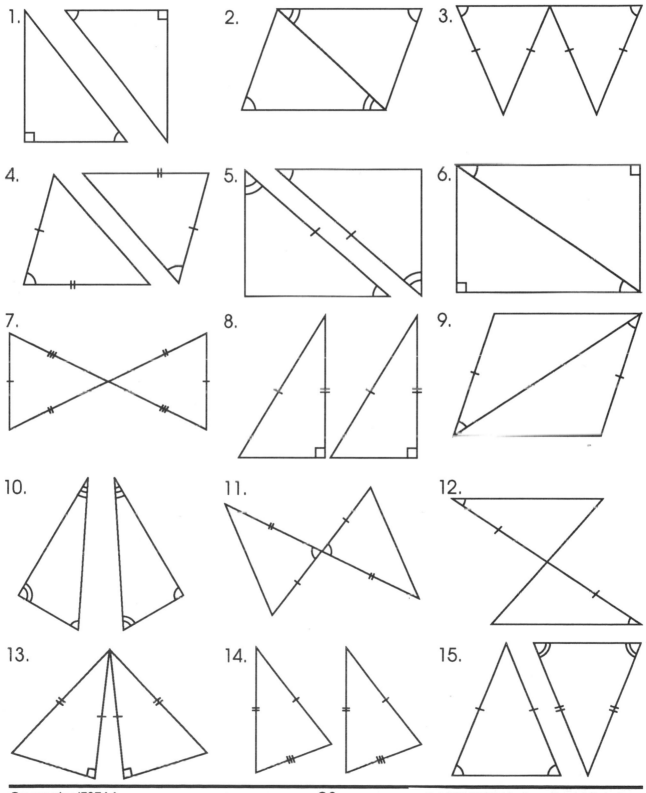

Triangle Inequality Properties

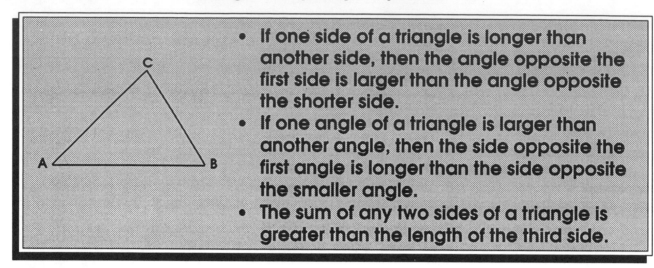

- If one side of a triangle is longer than another side, then the angle opposite the first side is larger than the angle opposite the shorter side.
- If one angle of a triangle is larger than another angle, then the side opposite the first angle is longer than the side opposite the smaller angle.
- The sum of any two sides of a triangle is greater than the length of the third side.

Is it possible for a triangle to have sides with the following lengths?

1. 20, 9, 8   2. 6, 6, 20   3. 5, 5, 10.2

4. 3, 4, 5   5. 15, 15, .03   6. 9, 12, 15

Which angle would be the largest?

7. 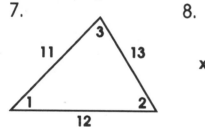   8. 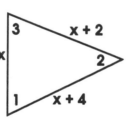   9. 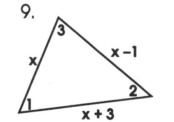   10.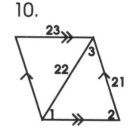

Which segment is the longest?

11. 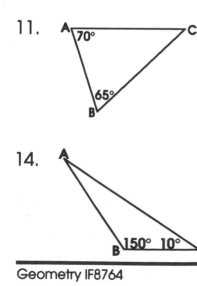   12.   13.

14.   15.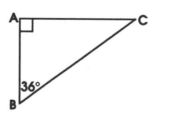

Proofs in Two Column Form

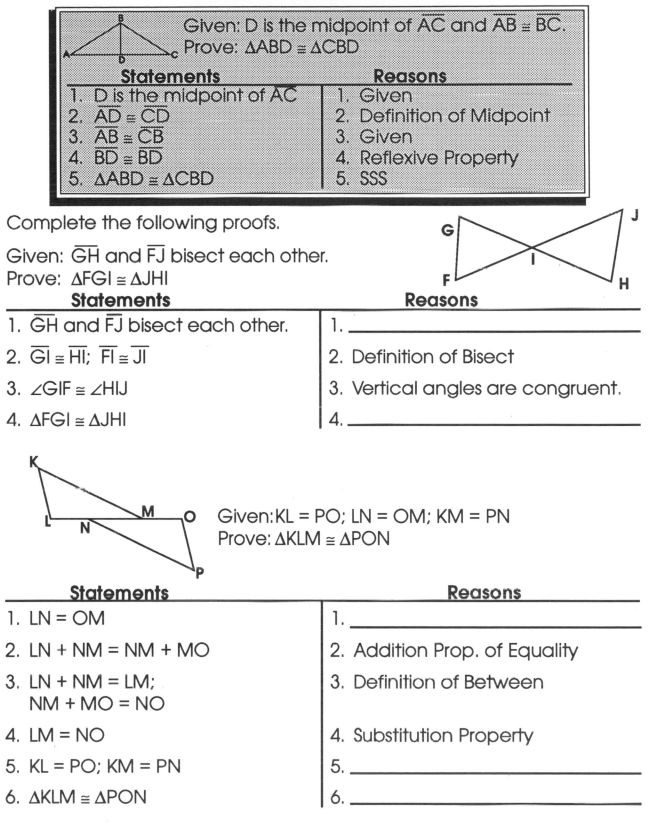

Given: D is the midpoint of $\overline{AC}$ and $\overline{AB} \cong \overline{BC}$.
Prove: $\triangle ABD \cong \triangle CBD$

Statements	Reasons
1. D is the midpoint of $\overline{AC}$	1. Given
2. $\overline{AD} \cong \overline{CD}$	2. Definition of Midpoint
3. $\overline{AB} \cong \overline{CB}$	3. Given
4. $\overline{BD} \cong \overline{BD}$	4. Reflexive Property
5. $\triangle ABD \cong \triangle CBD$	5. SSS

Complete the following proofs.

Given: $\overline{GH}$ and $\overline{FJ}$ bisect each other.
Prove: $\triangle FGI \cong \triangle JHI$

Statements	Reasons
1. $\overline{GH}$ and $\overline{FJ}$ bisect each other.	1. _____
2. $\overline{GI} \cong \overline{HI}$; $\overline{FI} \cong \overline{JI}$	2. Definition of Bisect
3. $\angle GIF \cong \angle HIJ$	3. Vertical angles are congruent.
4. $\triangle FGI \cong \triangle JHI$	4. _____

Given: KL = PO; LN = OM; KM = PN
Prove: $\triangle KLM \cong \triangle PON$

Statements	Reasons
1. LN = OM	1. _____
2. LN + NM = NM + MO	2. Addition Prop. of Equality
3. LN + NM = LM; NM + MO = NO	3. Definition of Between
4. LM = NO	4. Substitution Property
5. KL = PO; KM = PN	5. _____
6. $\triangle KLM \cong \triangle PON$	6. _____

25

More Practice with Proofs

Complete the following proofs.
Given: m ∠1 = 40°; m ∠3 = 40°; ∠2 ≅ ∠4
Prove: ΔRTQ ≅ ΔTRS

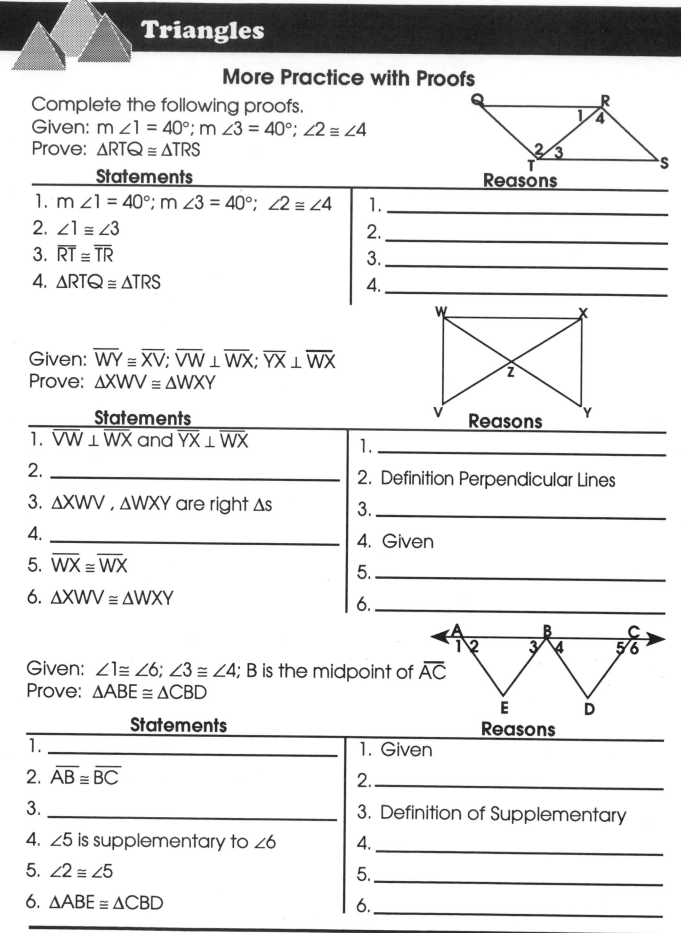

Statements	Reasons
1. m ∠1 = 40°; m ∠3 = 40°; ∠2 ≅ ∠4	1. _____
2. ∠1 ≅ ∠3	2. _____
3. $\overline{RT} ≅ \overline{TR}$	3. _____
4. ΔRTQ ≅ ΔTRS	4. _____

Given: $\overline{WY} ≅ \overline{XV}$; $\overline{VW} ⊥ \overline{WX}$; $\overline{YX} ⊥ \overline{WX}$
Prove: ΔXWV ≅ ΔWXY

Statements	Reasons
1. $\overline{VW} ⊥ \overline{WX}$ and $\overline{YX} ⊥ \overline{WX}$	1. _____
2. _____	2. Definition Perpendicular Lines
3. ΔXWV , ΔWXY are right Δs	3. _____
4. _____	4. Given
5. $\overline{WX} ≅ \overline{WX}$	5. _____
6. ΔXWV ≅ ΔWXY	6. _____

Given: ∠1≅ ∠6; ∠3 ≅ ∠4; B is the midpoint of $\overline{AC}$
Prove: ΔABE ≅ ΔCBD

Statements	Reasons
1. _____	1. Given
2. $\overline{AB} ≅ \overline{BC}$	2. _____
3. _____	3. Definition of Supplementary
4. ∠5 is supplementary to ∠6	4. _____
5. ∠2 ≅ ∠5	5. _____
6. ΔABE ≅ ΔCBD	6. _____

Try to decode these words and phrases.

> wear ⇒ long underwear
> long

1. mind matter	2. to MAN wn	3. LU CKY	4. D N A T S
5. death life	6. water swimming	7. MOmanON	8. s i t

9.
 	
stand
do   you
	10.
	
	myself I'm
		11.
		     E
		  N M
		 A P
		 M I
		 O R
		R E
			12.
			
			b JA o CK x

13. DKI	14. i i i . . .	15. T M A U H S W T	16. d o n' t s t a n d

☞ **Keep in mind . . .**
You learn by doing.

The Coordinate Plane

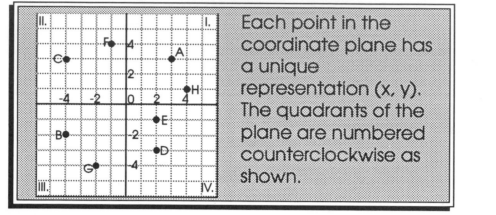

Each point in the coordinate plane has a unique representation (x, y). The quadrants of the plane are numbered counterclockwise as shown.

1. Give the coordinates of the following points.

A _____   B_____   C _____   D _____

E_____   F_____   G _____   H _____

2. Plot the following points and tell what quadrant each is in.

A _____   D _____

B_____   E_____

C _____   F_____

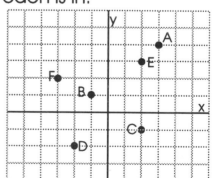

3. A line is a simple figure in the coordinate plane. Name three points on the line by giving their coordinates.

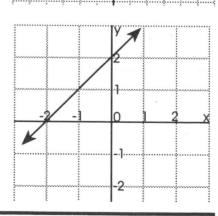

Lines and Their Equations

I. Plotting Points

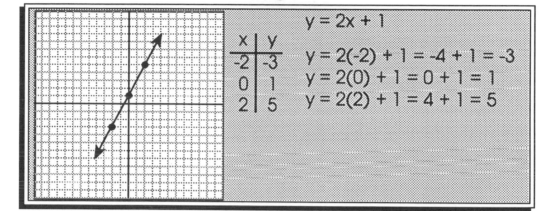

Graph the following lines by plotting points. Use your own graph paper.

1. $y = -x + 6$

2. $y = \frac{1}{2}x - 5$

3. $2x + 3y = 6$

4. $8x - 2y = -6$

5. $3x - 2y = -6$

6. $x + 6 = -3y$

II. Slope-Intercept

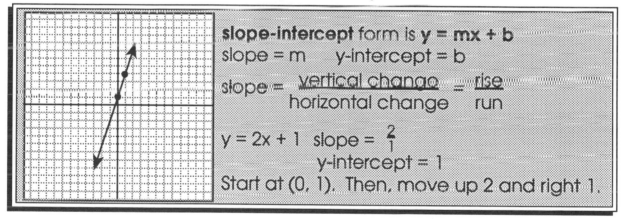

Graph the following lines by using the slope and y-intercept. Use your own graph paper.

7. $y = -2x + 3$

8. $y = \frac{2}{3}x - 1$

9. $y = 4x - 3$

10. $y = \frac{1}{3}x$

11. $y = -\frac{1}{4}x + 3$

12. $y = 2$

III. Standard Form

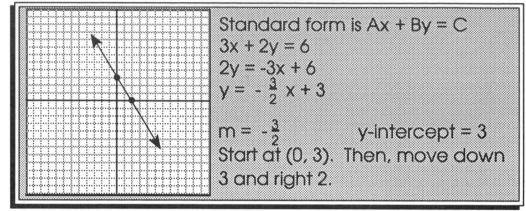

Standard form is Ax + By = C
3x + 2y = 6
2y = -3x + 6
$y = -\frac{3}{2}x + 3$

$m = -\frac{3}{2}$ y-intercept = 3
Start at (0, 3). Then, move down 3 and right 2.

Graph the following lines by using the slope and y-intercept. Use your own graph paper.

13. $2x + 5y = 10$

14. $3x - 4y = 12$

15. $-2x - 3y = 6$

16. $3x + 4y = 1$

17. $-2x + y = 4$

18. $x - 3y = 2$

IV. Segments

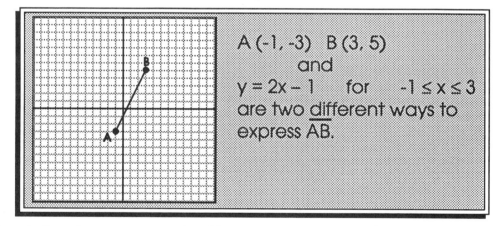

A (-1, -3) B (3, 5)
and
$y = 2x - 1$ for $-1 \leq x \leq 3$
are two <u>different</u> ways to express $\overline{AB}$.

Graph the following segments. Use your own graph paper.

19. $\overline{CD}$ C (-2, 2) D (4, -1)

20. $\overline{EF}$ E (0, -4) F (5, 2)

21. $\overline{GH}$ G (-3, -5) H (2, 5)

22. $\overline{IJ}$ $y = \frac{1}{2}x + 2$ for $-4 \leq x \leq 2$

23. $\overline{KL}$ $y = -2x + 3$ for $-1 \leq x \leq 3$

24. $\overline{MN}$ $2x - 3y = -6$ for $-3 \leq x \leq 3$

Equation of a Line in Standard Form: $Ax + By = C$

I. Given the slope and a point

$m = \frac{1}{4}$, $(-4, 3)$

Use slope-intercept form and solve for b.

$y = \frac{1}{4}x + b$ $\qquad\qquad$ $y = \frac{1}{4}x + 4$

$3 = \frac{1}{4}(-4) + b$ $\qquad\qquad$ $4y = x + 16$

$3 = -1 + b$ $\qquad\qquad\qquad$ $-x + 4y = 16$

$4 = b$ $\qquad\qquad\qquad\qquad$ $x - 4y = -16$

Find the equations of the lines with the following conditions. Write the equations in standard form.

1. $m = -2$, $(3, 1)$ $\qquad\qquad$ 2. $m = \frac{1}{3}$, $(6, 3)$

3. $m = 4$, $(\frac{1}{2}, -2)$ $\qquad\qquad$ 4. $m = -1$, $(-1, 2)$

5. $m = 2$, $(1, -2)$ $\qquad\qquad$ 6. $m = -\frac{3}{2}$, $(1, 1)$

7. $m = \frac{7}{5}$, $(0, -2)$ $\qquad\qquad$ 8. $m = -\frac{1}{2}$, $(4, 2)$

II. Given two points

$(2, 4)$, $(-1, -2)$

$m = \frac{y_2 - y_1}{x_2 - x_1} = \frac{-2 - 4}{-1 - 2} = \frac{-6}{-3} = 2$

$y = 2x + b$ $\qquad\qquad\qquad$ $y = 2x + 0$

$4 = 2(2) + b$ $\qquad\qquad\qquad$ $y = 2x$

$4 = 4 + b$ $\qquad\qquad\qquad\quad$ $2x - y = 0$

$0 = b$

Find the equations of the lines with the following conditions. Write the equations in standard form.

9. $(1, 3)$, $(-1, -1)$ $\qquad\qquad$ 10. $(2, 3)$, $(0, -3)$

11. $(3, 1)$, $(6, 0)$ $\qquad\qquad$ 12. $(4, 2)$, $(2, 4)$

13. $(-3, 0)$, $(0, 2)$ $\qquad\qquad$ 14. $(2, -1)$, $(8, 1)$

15. $(4, 0)$, $(0, 3)$ $\qquad\qquad$ 16. $(1, 2)$, $(-1, 3)$

III. Given a parallel line

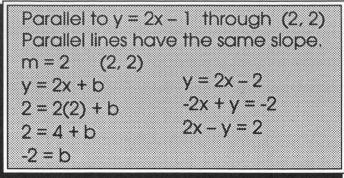

Parallel to $y = 2x - 1$ through $(2, 2)$
Parallel lines have the same slope.
$m = 2$ $(2, 2)$
$y = 2x + b$ $y = 2x - 2$
$2 = 2(2) + b$ $-2x + y = -2$
$2 = 4 + b$ $2x - y = 2$
$-2 = b$

Find the equations of the lines with the following conditions. Write the equations in standard form.

17. Parallel to $y = 3x + 4$ through $(0, -2)$

18. Parallel to $y = \frac{1}{2}x - 3$ through $(4, 2)$

19. Parallel to $2x + 3y = 6$ through $(4, -3)$

20. Parallel to $3x - 4y = 1$ through $(2, 2)$

21. Parallel to $2x - y = -3$ through $(2, -1)$

22. Parallel to $3x + 2y = 10$ through $(1, \frac{1}{2})$

23. Parallel to $7x - 3y = -5$ through $(2, 4)$

24. Parallel to $-2x + 4y = 1$ through $(-\frac{3}{2}, 1)$

IV. Given a perpendicular line

Perpendicular to $y = 2x - 1$ through $(2, 2)$
Perpendicular lines have slopes whose product is negative one.
$m = -\frac{1}{2}$, because $-\frac{1}{2} \cdot 2 = -1$
$y = -\frac{1}{2}x + b$ $y = -\frac{1}{2}x + 3$
$2 = -\frac{1}{2}(2) + b$ $2y = -x + 6$
$2 = -1 + b$ $x + 2y = 6$
$3 = b$

25. Perpendicular to $y = 3x + 4$ through $(0, -2)$

26. Perpendicular to $y = \frac{1}{2}x - 3$ through $(1, 4)$

27. Perpendicular to $3x + 2y = 6$ through $(1, 1)$

28. Perpendicular to $2x - 5y = 2$ through $(2, 3)$

Distance and Midpoint

Distance Formula	Midpoint Formula
$d = \sqrt{(x_2 - x_1)^2 + (y_2 - y_1)^2}$	$\left(\dfrac{x_1 + x_2}{2}, \dfrac{y_1 + y_2}{2}\right)$
$A(-1, -3) \qquad B(3, 5)$	$A(-1, -3) \qquad B(3, 5)$
$d(AB) = \sqrt{(3 - -1)^2 + (5 - -3)^2}$	$\left(\dfrac{-1 + 3}{2}, \dfrac{-3 + 5}{2}\right)$
$\qquad = \sqrt{(4)^2 + (8)^2}$	$\left(\dfrac{2}{2}, \dfrac{2}{2}\right)$
$\qquad = \sqrt{16 + 64}$	$(1, 1)$
$\qquad = \sqrt{80}$	
$d(AB) = 4\sqrt{5}$	

Find the distance.

1. (-2, 2)   (4, -1)

2. (-3, -5)   (2, 5)

3. (-4, 0)   (2, 3)

4. (-1, 5)   (3, -3)

5. (0, 0)   (3, 4)

6. (1, 2)   (4, 7)

7. (-2, 4)   (3, -5)

8. (2, 2)   (6, 6)

9. (3, 6)   (5, -2)

10. (-1, -4)   (3, 5)

Find the midpoint.

11. (-2, 2)   (4, -1)

12. (-3, -5)   (2, 5)

13. (-4, 0)   (2, 3)

14. (-1, 5)   (3, -3)

15. (0, 0)   (3, 4)

16. (1, 2)   (4, 7)

17. (-2, 4)   (3, -5)

18. (2, 2)   (6, 6)

19. (3, 6)   (5, -2)

20. (-1, -4)   (3, 5)

☞ **Keep in mind . . .**
You always have a lot to learn.

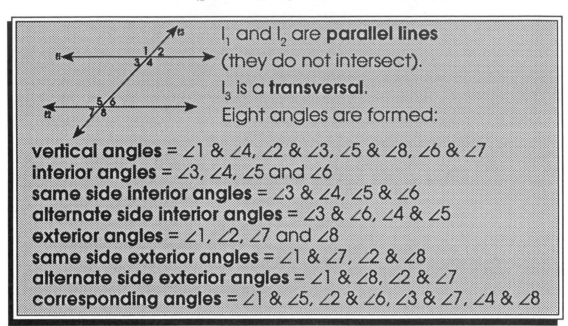

l_1 and l_2 are **parallel lines** (they do not intersect).
l_3 is a **transversal**.
Eight angles are formed:

vertical angles = ∠1 & ∠4, ∠2 & ∠3, ∠5 & ∠8, ∠6 & ∠7
interior angles = ∠3, ∠4, ∠5 and ∠6
same side interior angles = ∠3 & ∠4, ∠5 & ∠6
alternate side interior angles = ∠3 & ∠6, ∠4 & ∠5
exterior angles = ∠1, ∠2, ∠7 and ∠8
same side exterior angles = ∠1 & ∠7, ∠2 & ∠8
alternate side exterior angles = ∠1 & ∠8, ∠2 & ∠7
corresponding angles = ∠1 & ∠5, ∠2 & ∠6, ∠3 & ∠7, ∠4 & ∠8

Given two parallel lines, same side interior angles are supplementary. Fill in the blanks with the correct answers.

1. Vertical angles are _____ .
2. Same side exterior angles are _____ .
3. Alternate side interior angles are _____ .
4. Alternate side exterior angles are _____ .
5. Corresponding angles are _____ .

Find the measures of the designated angles.

l_1 is parallel to l_2.

m ∠a = _____   m ∠e = _____
m ∠b = _____   m ∠f = _____
m ∠c = _____   m ∠g = _____
m ∠d = _____

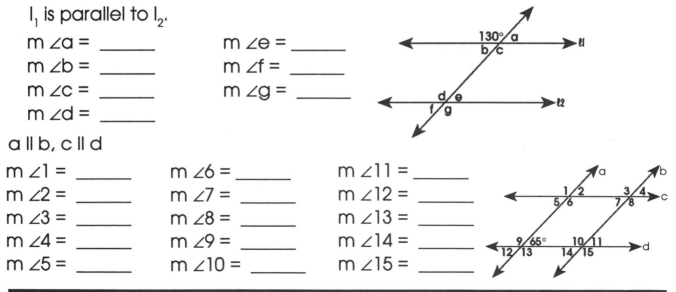

a ‖ b, c ‖ d

m ∠1 = _____   m ∠6 = _____   m ∠11 = _____
m ∠2 = _____   m ∠7 = _____   m ∠12 = _____
m ∠3 = _____   m ∠8 = _____   m ∠13 = _____
m ∠4 = _____   m ∠9 = _____   m ∠14 = _____
m ∠5 = _____   m ∠10 = _____   m ∠15 = _____

More Parallel Lines

Find the missing values.

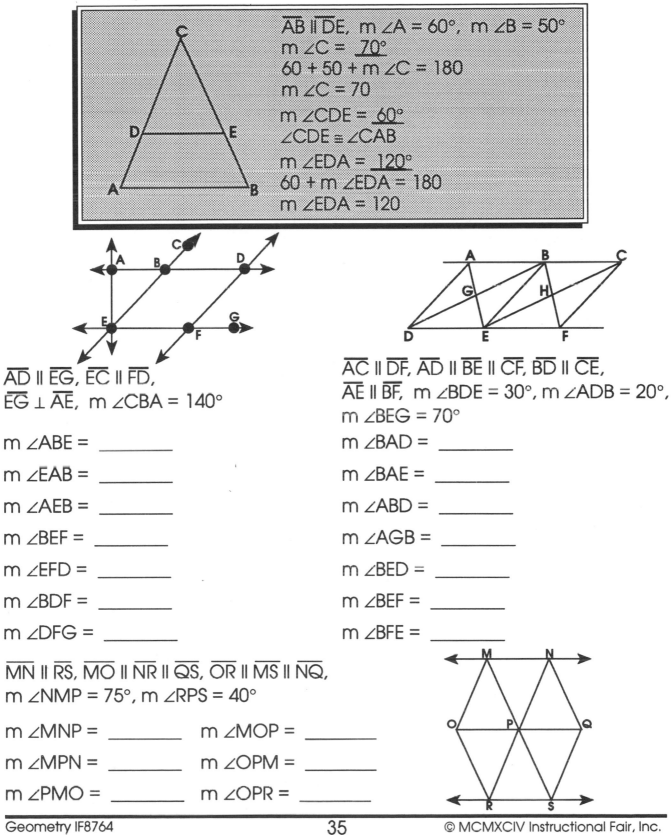

$\overline{AB} \parallel \overline{DE}$, m ∠A = 60°, m ∠B = 50°

m ∠C = __70°__
60 + 50 + m ∠C = 180
m ∠C = 70

m ∠CDE = __60°__
∠CDE ≅ ∠CAB

m ∠EDA = __120°__
60 + m ∠EDA = 180
m ∠EDA = 120

$\overline{AD} \parallel \overline{EG}$, $\overline{EC} \parallel \overline{FD}$,
$\overline{EG} \perp \overline{AE}$, m ∠CBA = 140°

m ∠ABE = _____

m ∠EAB = _____

m ∠AEB = _____

m ∠BEF = _____

m ∠EFD = _____

m ∠BDF = _____

m ∠DFG = _____

$\overline{AC} \parallel \overline{DF}$, $\overline{AD} \parallel \overline{BE} \parallel \overline{CF}$, $\overline{BD} \parallel \overline{CE}$,
$\overline{AE} \parallel \overline{BF}$, m ∠BDE = 30°, m ∠ADB = 20°,
m ∠BEG = 70°

m ∠BAD = _____

m ∠BAE = _____

m ∠ABD = _____

m ∠AGB = _____

m ∠BED = _____

m ∠BEF = _____

m ∠BFE = _____

$\overline{MN} \parallel \overline{RS}$, $\overline{MO} \parallel \overline{NR} \parallel \overline{QS}$, $\overline{OR} \parallel \overline{MS} \parallel \overline{NQ}$,
m ∠NMP = 75°, m ∠RPS = 40°

m ∠MNP = _____   m ∠MOP = _____

m ∠MPN = _____   m ∠OPM = _____

m ∠PMO = _____   m ∠OPR = _____

Proofs Using Parallel Lines

Complete the following proofs.

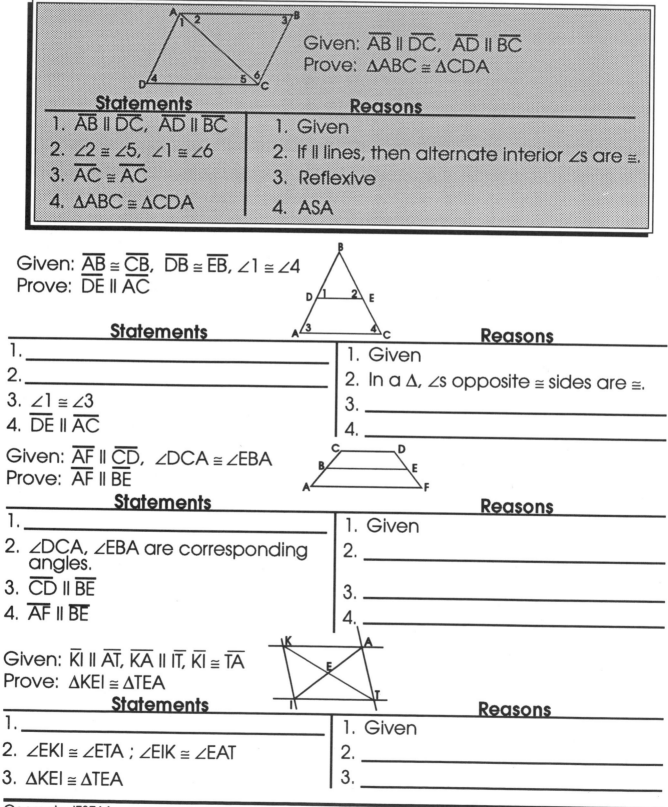

Given: $\overline{AB} \parallel \overline{DC}$, $\overline{AD} \parallel \overline{BC}$
Prove: $\triangle ABC \cong \triangle CDA$

Statements	Reasons
1. $\overline{AB} \parallel \overline{DC}$, $\overline{AD} \parallel \overline{BC}$	1. Given
2. $\angle 2 \cong \angle 5$, $\angle 1 \cong \angle 6$	2. If ∥ lines, then alternate interior ∠s are ≅.
3. $\overline{AC} \cong \overline{AC}$	3. Reflexive
4. $\triangle ABC \cong \triangle CDA$	4. ASA

Given: $\overline{AB} \cong \overline{CB}$, $\overline{DB} \cong \overline{EB}$, $\angle 1 \cong \angle 4$
Prove: $\overline{DE} \parallel \overline{AC}$

Statements	Reasons
1. _____	1. Given
2. _____	2. In a △, ∠s opposite ≅ sides are ≅.
3. $\angle 1 \cong \angle 3$	3. _____
4. $\overline{DE} \parallel \overline{AC}$	4. _____

Given: $\overline{AF} \parallel \overline{CD}$, $\angle DCA \cong \angle EBA$
Prove: $\overline{AF} \parallel \overline{BE}$

Statements	Reasons
1. _____	1. Given
2. $\angle DCA$, $\angle EBA$ are corresponding angles.	2. _____
3. $\overline{CD} \parallel \overline{BE}$	3. _____
4. $\overline{AF} \parallel \overline{BE}$	4. _____

Given: $\overline{KI} \parallel \overline{AT}$, $\overline{KA} \parallel \overline{IT}$, $\overline{KI} \cong \overline{TA}$
Prove: $\triangle KEI \cong \triangle TEA$

Statements	Reasons
1. _____	1. Given
2. $\angle EKI \cong \angle ETA$; $\angle EIK \cong \angle EAT$	2. _____
3. $\triangle KEI \cong \triangle TEA$	3. _____

More Proofs

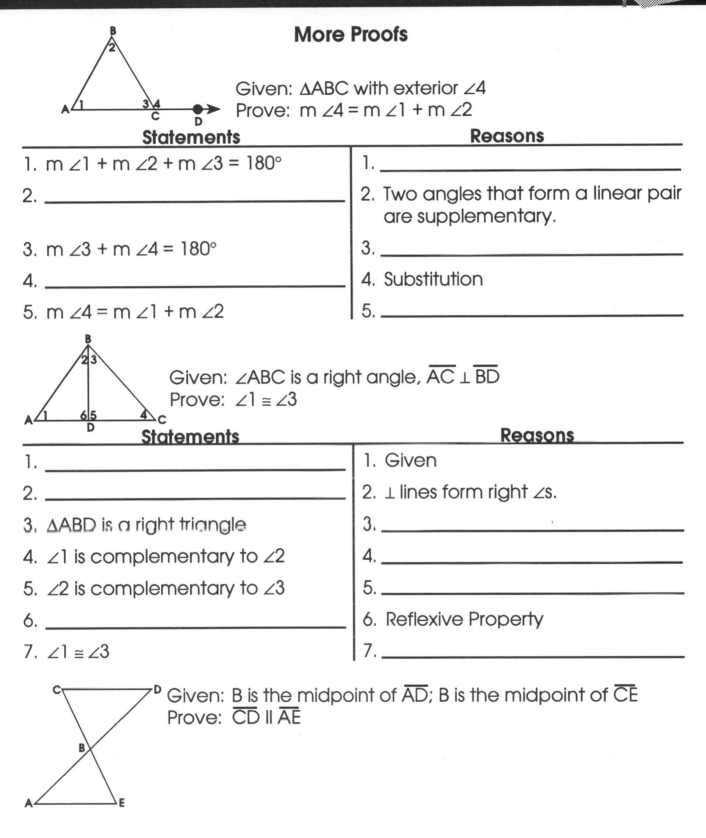

Given: △ABC with exterior ∠4
Prove: m ∠4 = m ∠1 + m ∠2

Statements	Reasons
1. m ∠1 + m ∠2 + m ∠3 = 180°	1. _____
2. _____	2. Two angles that form a linear pair are supplementary.
3. m ∠3 + m ∠4 = 180°	3. _____
4. _____	4. Substitution
5. m ∠4 = m ∠1 + m ∠2	5. _____

Given: ∠ABC is a right angle, $\overline{AC} \perp \overline{BD}$
Prove: ∠1 ≅ ∠3

Statements	Reasons
1. _____	1. Given
2. _____	2. ⊥ lines form right ∠s.
3. △ABD is a right triangle	3. _____
4. ∠1 is complementary to ∠2	4. _____
5. ∠2 is complementary to ∠3	5. _____
6. _____	6. Reflexive Property
7. ∠1 ≅ ∠3	7. _____

Given: B is the midpoint of $\overline{AD}$; B is the midpoint of $\overline{CE}$
Prove: $\overline{CD} \parallel \overline{AE}$

More Fun

> 10 = T. on the F.
> 10 = Toes on the Feet

Each equation below contains the initials of words that will make it correct. Find the missing words.

1. 26 = L. of the A. _____

2. 7 = W. of the W. _____

3. 1001 = A. N. _____

4. 12 = S. of the Z. _____

5. 54 = C. in a D. (with the J.) _____

6. 32 = D. F. at which W. F. _____

7. 90 = D. in a R. A. _____

8. 8 = S. on a S. S. _____

9. 4 = Q. in a G. _____

10. 200 = D. for P. G. in M. _____

11. 10 = D. in a D. _____

12. 2 = C. in a P. _____

13. 5 = F. on a H. _____

14. 29 = D. in F. in a L. Y. _____

15. 100 = P. in a D. _____

16. 5 = T. on a F. _____

17. 12 = M. in a Y. _____

18. 5 = D. in a Z. C. _____

19. 3 = D. in an A. C. _____

20. 24 = H. in a D. _____

38

Fun with Graphing

Draw the segments with the following endpoints on the graphs on page 40.

I. What does this figure look like? _____

1. (15, 0), (0, 1)
2. (14, 0), (0, 2)
3. (13, 0), (0, 3)
4. (12, 0), (0, 4)
5. (11, 0), (0, 5)
6. (10, 0), (0, 6)
7. (9, 0), (0, 7)
8. (8, 0), (0, 8)
9. (7, 0), (0, 9)
10. (6, 0), (0, 10)

11. (5, 0), (0, 11)
12. (4, 0), (0, 12)
13. (3, 0), (0, 13)
14. (2, 0), (0, 14)
15. (1, 0), (0, 15)
16. (-15, 0), (0, -1)
17. (-14, 0), (0, -2)
18. (-13, 0), (0, -3)
19. (-12, 0), (0, -4)
20. (-11, 0), (0, -5)

21. (-10, 0), (0, -6)
22. (-9, 0), (0, -7)
23. (-8, 0), (0, -8)
24. (-7, 0), (0, -9)
25. (-6, 0), (0, -10)
26. (-5, 0), (0, -11)
27. (-4, 0), (0, -12)
28. (-3, 0), (0, -13)
29. (-2, 0), (0, -14)
30. (-1, 0), (0, -15)

II. What does this figure look like? _____

1. (12, 12), (12, -12)
2. (12, -12), (-12, -12)
3. (-12, -12), (-12, 12)
4. (-12, 12), (12, 12)
5. (12, 12), (-12, 11)
6. (10, 12), (-12, 9)
7. (8, 12), (-12, 7)
8. (6, 12), (-12, 5)
9. (4, 12), (-12, 3)
10. (2, 12), (-12, 1)
11. (0, 12), (-12, -1)
12. (-2, 12), (-12, -3)
13. (-4, 12), (-12, -5)
14. (-6, 12), (-12, -7)
15. (-8, 12), (-12, -9)
16. (-10, 12), (-12, -11)
17. (-12, 12), (-11, -12)
18. (-12, 8), (-7, -12)

19. (-12, 8), (-7, -12)
20. (-12, 6), (-5, -12)
21. (-12, 4), (-3, -12)
22. (-12, 2), (-1, -12)
23. (-12, 0), (1, -12)
24. (-12, -2), (3, -12)
25. (-12, -4), (5, -12)
26. (-12, -6), (7, -12)
27. (-12, -8), (9, -12)
28. (-12, -10), (11, -12)
29. (-12, -12), (12, -11)
30. (-10, -12), (12, -9)
31. (-8, -12), (12, -7)
32. (-6, -12), (12, -5)
33. (-4, -12), (12, -3)
34. (-2, -12), (12, -1)
35. (0, -12), (12, 1)
36. (2, -12), (12, 3)

37. (4, -12), (12, 5)
38. (6, -12), (12, 7)
39. (8, -12), (12, 9)
40. (10, -12), (12, 11)
41. (12, -12), (11, 12)
42. (12, -10), (9, 12)
43. (12, -8), (7, 12)
44. (12, -6), (5, 12)
45. (12, -4), (3, 12)
46. (12, -2), (1, 12)
47. (12, 0), (-1, 12)
48. (12, 2), (-3, 12)
49. (12, 4), (-5, 12)
50. (12, 6), (-7, 12)
51. (12,8), (-9, 12)
52. (12, 10), (-11, 12)

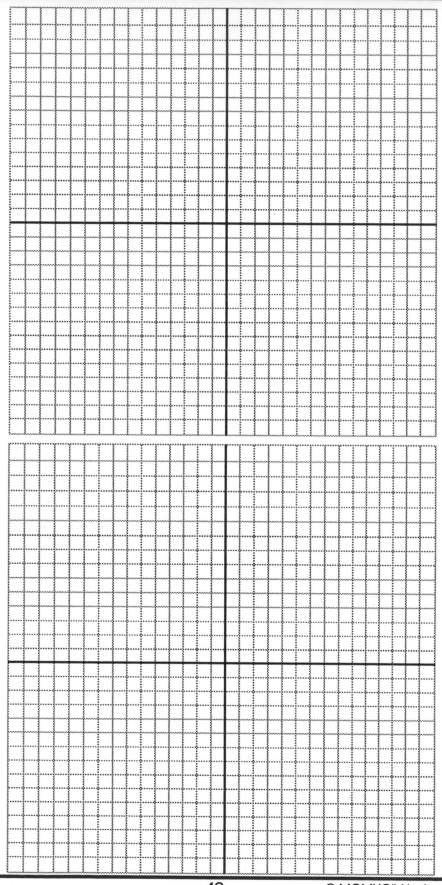

40

Keep in mind . . .
You only fail when you stop trying.

Congruent Segments

Given: $\overline{AB}$

A   B ℓ A'

Construct a segment congruent to $\overline{AB}$.
1. Use a straight edge to draw a working line, ℓ.
2. Choose a point on ℓ and label it A'.
3. Set your compass for radius $\overline{AB}$ by placing one end at point A and another at point B. Draw an arc.
4. Using AB as radius, place one end of compass on A' and draw an arc. Label the point of intersection B'.

$\overline{AB} \cong \overline{A'B'}$

1. Construct a segment congruent to $\overline{CD}$.

   C ●————————● D

2. Construct a segment congruent to $\overline{EF}$.

   E ●————————————● F

3. Construct a segment congruent to $\overline{XY}$.

   X ●————————● Y

4. Construct a segment whose length is $\overline{CD} + \overline{EF}$.

5. Construct a segment whose length is $\overline{EF} + \overline{XY}$.

6. Construct a segment whose length is $\overline{EF} - \overline{CD}$.

Perpendicular Bisectors

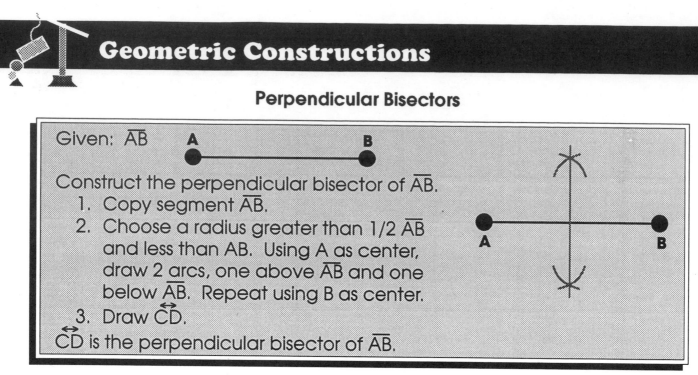

Given: $\overline{AB}$

Construct the perpendicular bisector of $\overline{AB}$.
1. Copy segment $\overline{AB}$.
2. Choose a radius greater than 1/2 $\overline{AB}$ and less than AB. Using A as center, draw 2 arcs, one above $\overline{AB}$ and one below $\overline{AB}$. Repeat using B as center.
3. Draw $\overleftrightarrow{CD}$.

$\overleftrightarrow{CD}$ is the perpendicular bisector of $\overline{AB}$.

I. Construct the perpendicular bisector of the following.

1.

2.

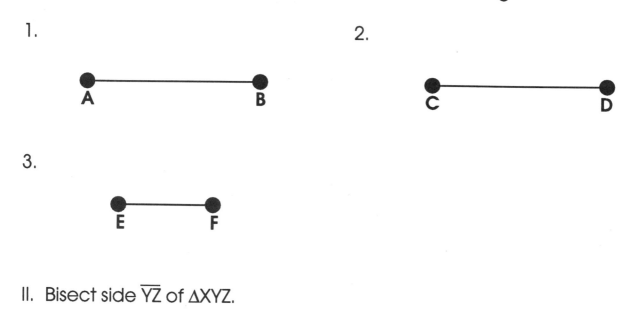

3.

II. Bisect side $\overline{YZ}$ of $\triangle XYZ$.

4.

5. Construct a segment whose length equals $\overline{XY} + \overline{YZ} + \overline{XZ}$.

Constructing Perpendiculars, Given a Point on the Line

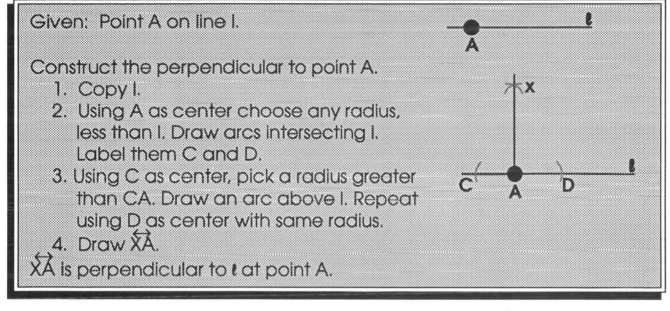

Given: Point A on line l.

Construct the perpendicular to point A.
1. Copy l.
2. Using A as center choose any radius, less than l. Draw arcs intersecting l. Label them C and D.
3. Using C as center, pick a radius greater than CA. Draw an arc above l. Repeat using D as center with same radius.
4. Draw $\overleftrightarrow{XA}$.

$\overleftrightarrow{XA}$ is perpendicular to l at point A.

I. Construct perpendicular lines to the given points.

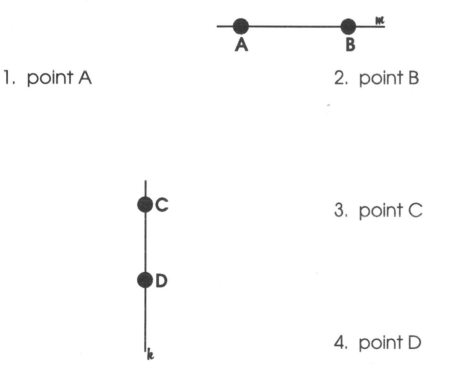

1. point A

2. point B

3. point C

4. point D

Constructing Perpendiculars, Given a Point Not on the Line

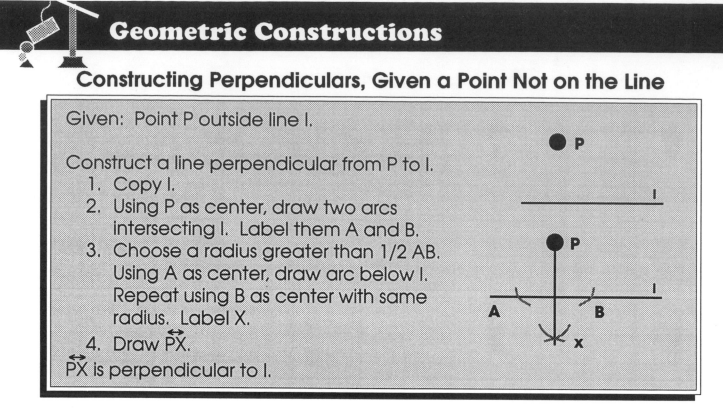

Given: Point P outside line l.

Construct a line perpendicular from P to l.
1. Copy l.
2. Using P as center, draw two arcs intersecting l. Label them A and B.
3. Choose a radius greater than 1/2 AB. Using A as center, draw arc below l. Repeat using B as center with same radius. Label X.
4. Draw $\overleftrightarrow{PX}$.

$\overleftrightarrow{PX}$ is perpendicular to l.

I. Construct perpendicular lines to l from:

1. point A

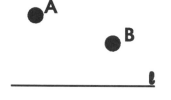

2. point B

II. Construct the perpendicular lines from each verticie to the opposite side in △ABC.

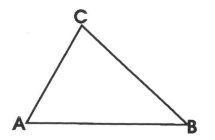

Congruent Angles

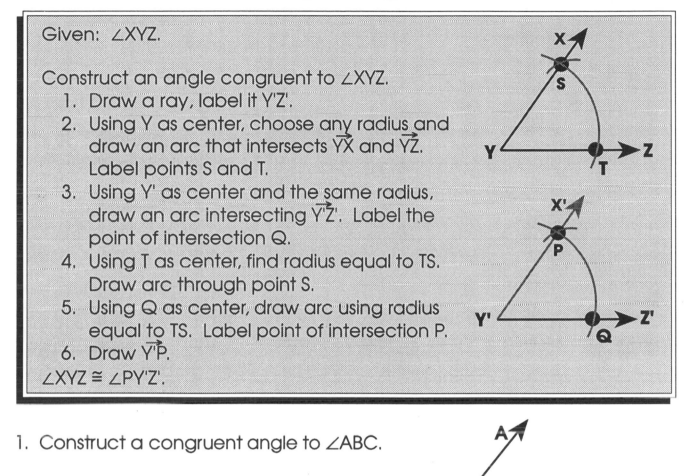

Given: ∠XYZ.

Construct an angle congruent to ∠XYZ.
1. Draw a ray, label it Y'Z'.
2. Using Y as center, choose any radius and draw an arc that intersects $\overrightarrow{YX}$ and $\overrightarrow{YZ}$. Label points S and T.
3. Using Y' as center and the same radius, draw an arc intersecting $\overrightarrow{Y'Z'}$. Label the point of intersection Q.
4. Using T as center, find radius equal to TS. Draw arc through point S.
5. Using Q as center, draw arc using radius equal to TS. Label point of intersection P.
6. Draw $\overrightarrow{Y'P}$.

∠XYZ ≅ ∠PY'Z'.

1. Construct a congruent angle to ∠ABC.

2. Construct a congruent angle to ∠XYZ.

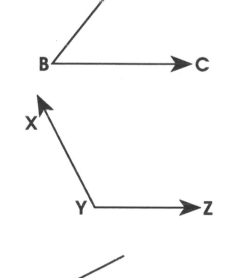

3. Construct △ABC using ∠A and ∠B.

Angle Bisectors

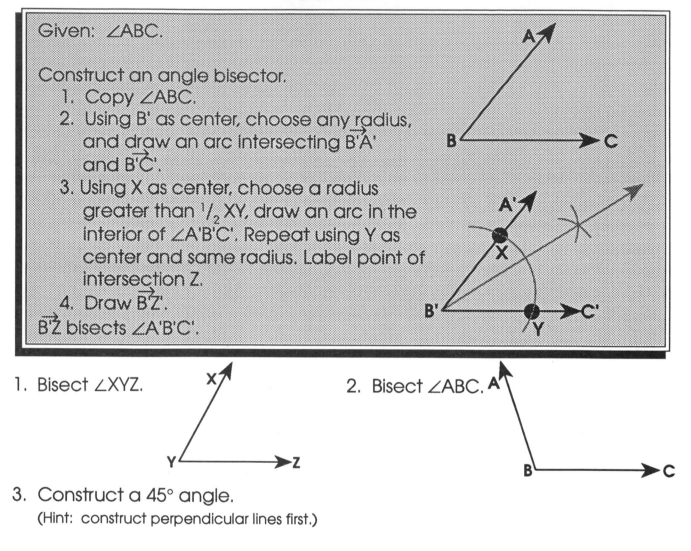

Given: ∠ABC.

Construct an angle bisector.
1. Copy ∠ABC.
2. Using B' as center, choose any radius, and draw an arc intersecting B'A' and B'C'.
3. Using X as center, choose a radius greater than ¹/₂ XY, draw an arc in the interior of ∠A'B'C'. Repeat using Y as center and same radius. Label point of intersection Z.
4. Draw B'Z.
B'Z bisects ∠A'B'C'.

1. Bisect ∠XYZ.

2. Bisect ∠ABC.

3. Construct a 45° angle.
   (Hint: construct perpendicular lines first.)

4. Construct an equilateral Δ. Use AB as the length of each side.

A●━━━━━━━●B

5. What is the measurement of each angle in #4? _____

6. Construct a 30° angle.
   (Hint: use your equilateral Δ.)

Geometric Constructions

Parallel Lines

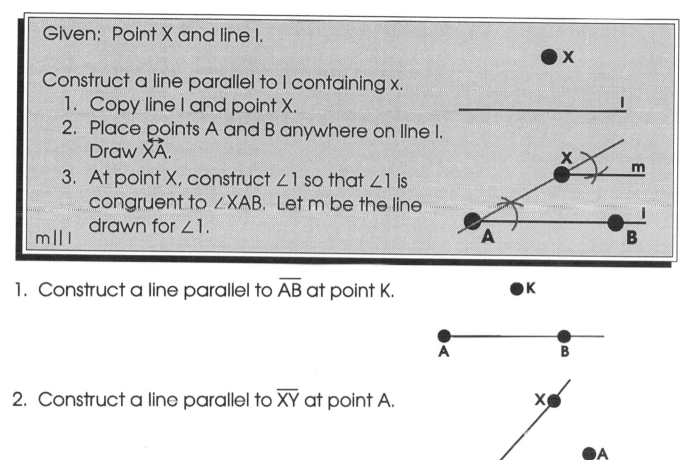

Given: Point X and line l.

Construct a line parallel to l containing x.
1. Copy line l and point X.
2. Place points A and B anywhere on line l. Draw $\overleftrightarrow{XA}$.
3. At point X, construct ∠1 so that ∠1 is congruent to ∠XAB. Let m be the line drawn for ∠1.

m||l

1. Construct a line parallel to $\overline{AB}$ at point K.

2. Construct a line parallel to $\overline{XY}$ at point A.

3. Construct a rectangle with length equal to $\overline{RT}$ and width equal to $\overline{RS}$.

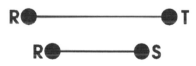

4. Construct a parallelogram with a 45° angle, length equal to $\overline{AB}$ and any width.

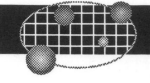

☞ **Keep in mind . . .**
Tackle all your problems by taking
them one at a time.

Nonlinear Equations—Parabolas

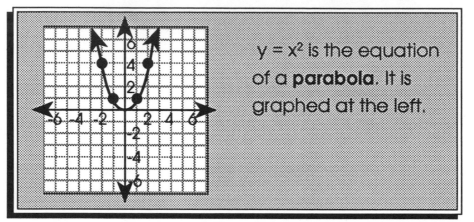

$y = x^2$ is the equation of a **parabola**. It is graphed at the left.

1. Looking at the curve $y = x^2$, what do you think the graph of $y = 2x^2$ would look like? _____
   Sketch the graph of $y = 2x^2$.

2. Sketch the graph of $y = \frac{1}{2}x^2$.

3. Sketch the graph of $y = x^2 + 2$.

4. Sketch the graph of $y = (x + 2)^2$.

5. Sketch the graph of $y = -x^2$.

6. What do you expect $y = (x - 3)^2 + 1$ to look like? _____
   Check your answer by graphing the equation.

7. What do you expect $y = (x + 1)^2 - 2$ to look like? _____
   Check your answer by graphing the equation.

8. What do you expect $y = 3x^2 - 2$ to look like? _____
   Check your answer by graphing the equation.

Nonlinear Equations—Circles

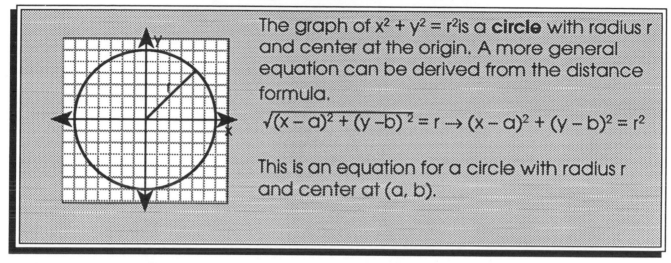

The graph of $x^2 + y^2 = r^2$ is a **circle** with radius r and center at the origin. A more general equation can be derived from the distance formula.

$$\sqrt{(x-a)^2 + (y-b)^2} = r \rightarrow (x-a)^2 + (y-b)^2 = r^2$$

This is an equation for a circle with radius r and center at (a, b).

1. Graph the following equations by plotting points.
   a. $x^2 + y^2 = 4$
   b. $x^2 + y^2 = 25$
   c. $(x-1)^2 + (y+1)^2 = 16$
   d. $(x+2)^2 + (y-2)^2 = 9$

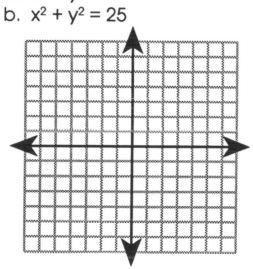
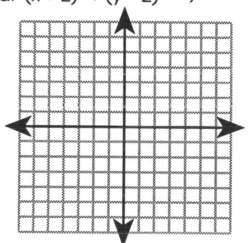

2. Give the center and radius for the circles below.
   a. $x^2 + y^2 = 9$
   b. $(x-3)^2 + (y-4)^2 = 16$
   c. $(x+2)^2 + (y-1)^2 = 4$
   d. $x^2 + (y+3)^2 = 25$
   e. $(x-1)^2 + (y+2)^2 = 4$
   f. $(x+5)^2 + (y-3)^2 = 81$
   g. $(x-7)^2 + (y+5)^2 = 24$
   h. $(x-3)^2 + (y-3)^2 = 18$

3. Write the equations of the following circles.
   a. r = 1   (2, -3)
   b. r = 2   (3, 4)
   c. r = 3   (2, 2)
   d. r = 6   (0, 0)
   e. r = 5   (-1, -3)
   f. r = 2   (-2, 4)
   g. r = 1   (3, -2)
   h. r = 4   (-2, -3)

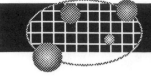

Nonlinear Equations

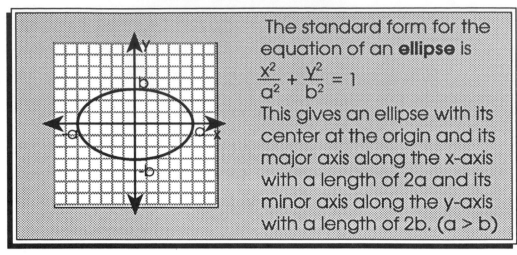

The standard form for the equation of an **ellipse** is

$$\frac{x^2}{a^2} + \frac{y^2}{b^2} = 1$$

This gives an ellipse with its center at the origin and its major axis along the x-axis with a length of 2a and its minor axis along the y-axis with a length of 2b. (a > b)

1. Graph the following equations.

   a. $\dfrac{x^2}{9} + \dfrac{y^2}{4} = 1$

   b. $\dfrac{x^2}{25} + \dfrac{y^2}{16} = 1$

   * c. $\dfrac{3x^2}{2} + \dfrac{3y^2}{1} = 6$

   * d. $4x^2 + 9y^2 = 36$

   (*Hiint: put these in standard form before graphing.)

2. The following are not in standard form.
   Identify major and minor axes and graph them.

   a. $4x^2 + y^2 = 16$

   b. $\dfrac{5x^2}{4} + \dfrac{4y^2}{5} = 20$

   * c. $\dfrac{(x-3)^2}{25} + \dfrac{(y-4)^2}{16} = 1$

   * d. $4(x+2)^2 + 9y^2 = 36$

   (Hint: you've seen something similar to this with circles.)

3. Write the equation for an ellipse with the following perimeters.

   a. a = 3, b = 2, center (0, 0)
   b. a = 4, b = 3, center (1, 2)
   c. a = b, b = 3, center (-3, 4)
   d. a = 12, b = 5, center (-2, -4)

Nonlinear Equations—Hyperbolas

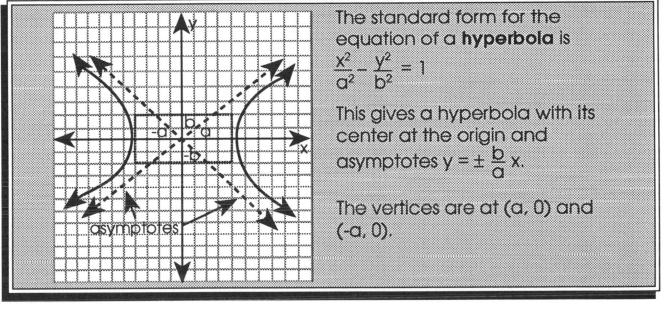

The standard form for the equation of a **hyperbola** is
$$\frac{x^2}{a^2} - \frac{y^2}{b^2} = 1$$

This gives a hyperbola with its center at the origin and asymptotes $y = \pm \frac{b}{a} x$.

The vertices are at $(a, 0)$ and $(-a, 0)$.

1. Graph the following equations.

   a. $\dfrac{x^2}{9} - \dfrac{y^2}{4} = 1$

   b. $\dfrac{x^2}{4} - \dfrac{y^2}{9} = 1$

   c. $\dfrac{y^2}{9} - \dfrac{x^2}{4} = 1$

   d. $\dfrac{y^2}{4} - \dfrac{x^2}{9} = 1$

2. The following are not in standard form.
   Identify asymptotes and graph them.

   a. $x^2 - 4y^2 = 4$

   b. $4x^2 - 9y^2 = 36$

   c. $(x + 1)^2 - 9(y - 1)^2 = 9$

   d. $(x - 1)^2 - (y - 2)^2 = 4$

3. Write the equation for a hyperbola with the following perimeters.*

   a. $a = 2$, $b = 4$, center $(2, -1)$

   b. $a = 3$, $b = 5$, center $(3, 2)$

   c. $a = 1$, $b = 3$, center $(-2, 4)$

   d. $a = 4$, $b = 2$, center $(-1, -3)$

   (* All open in the x direction.)

Ways To Prove Triangles Similar

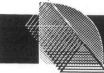 **Keep in mind . . .**
Every accomplishment great or small,
starts with the right decision, "I'll try."

AA (angle, angle) or **AAA(angle, angle, angle)** = 2 or 3 angles of one triangle congruent to the corresponding angles of another triangle ⇒ ~ Δs (corresponding sides are proportional).

SAS (side, angle, side) = two sides of one triangle are proportional to the corresponding sides of another triangle and the included angles are congruent ⇒ ~ Δs.

SSS (side, side, side) = three sides of one triangle are proportional to the corresponding sides of another triangle ⇒ ~ Δs.

Identify which property will prove these triangles similar.

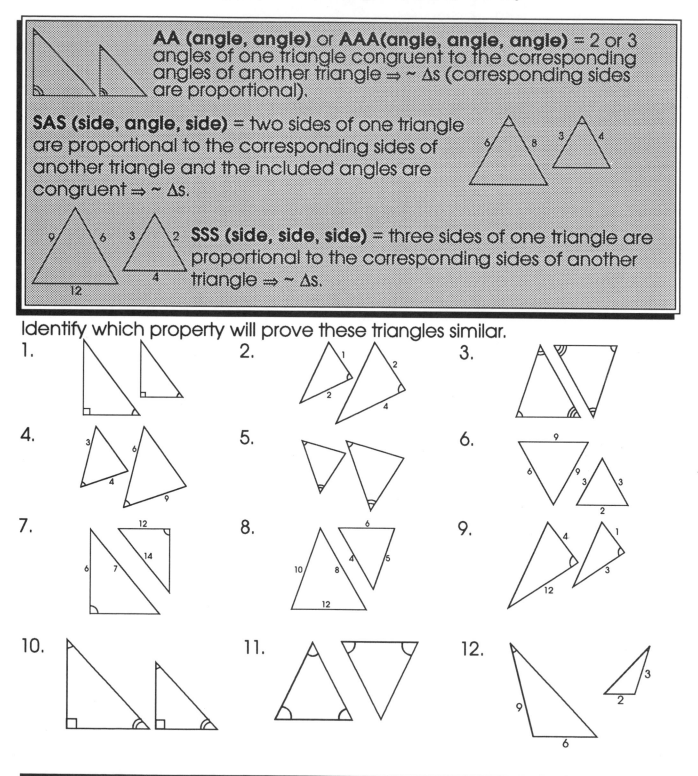

1.

2.

3.

4.

5.

6.

7.

8.

9.

10.

11.

12.

Working with Similar Triangles

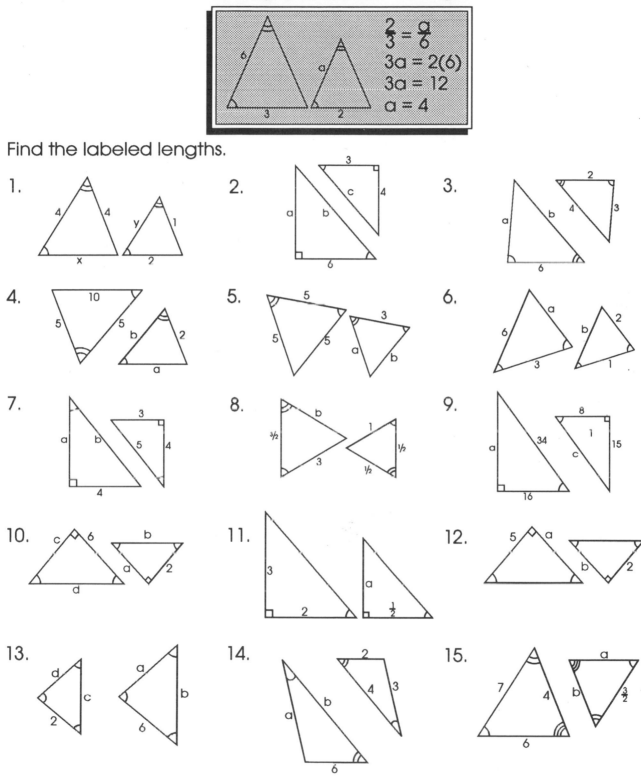

$$\frac{2}{3} = \frac{a}{6}$$
$$3a = 2(6)$$
$$3a = 12$$
$$a = 4$$

Find the labeled lengths.

Similar Triangles

More Similar Triangles

Find the area of the following triangles. (Hint: $A = \frac{1}{2}bh$)

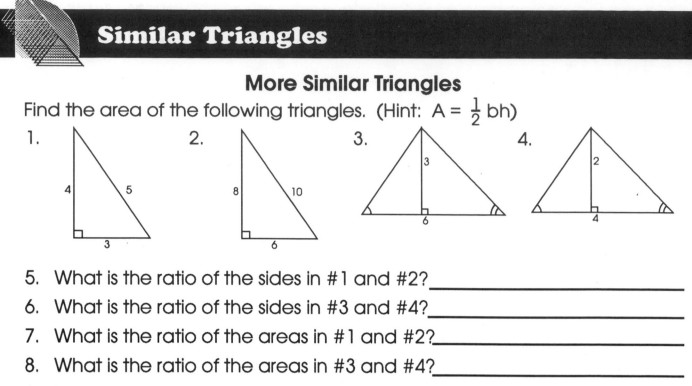

5. What is the ratio of the sides in #1 and #2? _____
6. What is the ratio of the sides in #3 and #4? _____
7. What is the ratio of the areas in #1 and #2? _____
8. What is the ratio of the areas in #3 and #4? _____
9. What can you conclude about this? _____

Find the ratio of the areas in the following sets of similar triangles with corresponding sides labeled.

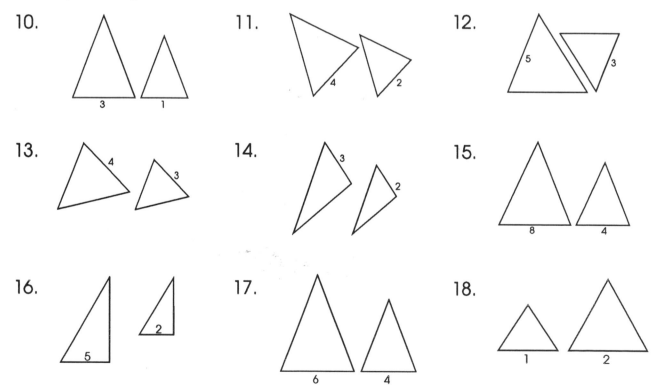

Two Column Proofs

Complete the following proofs.

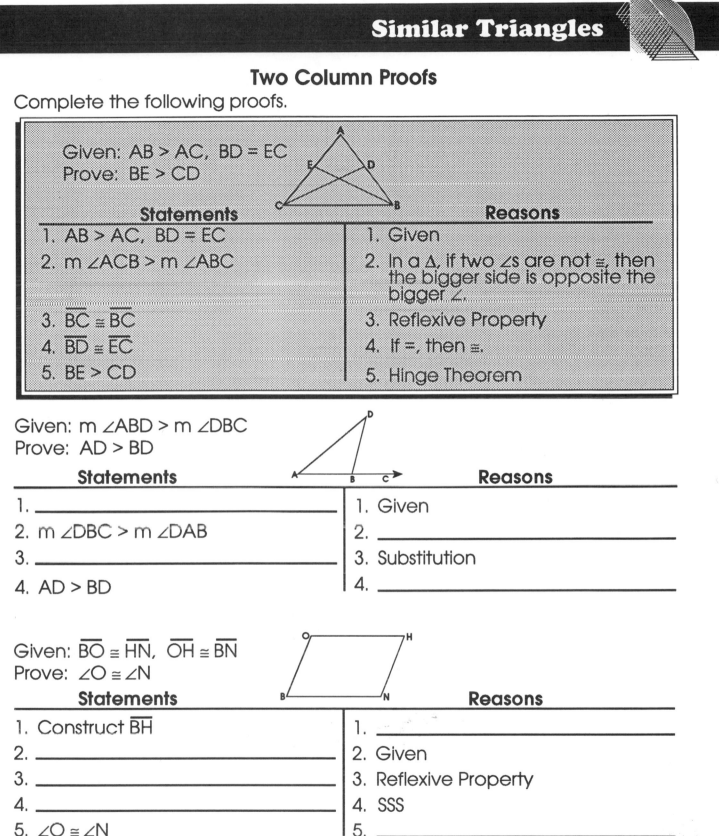

Given: AB > AC, BD = EC
Prove: BE > CD

Statements	Reasons
1. AB > AC, BD = EC	1. Given
2. m ∠ACB > m ∠ABC	2. In a Δ, if two ∠s are not ≅, then the bigger side is opposite the bigger ∠.
3. $\overline{BC} \cong \overline{BC}$	3. Reflexive Property
4. $\overline{BD} \cong \overline{EC}$	4. If =, then ≅.
5. BE > CD	5. Hinge Theorem

Given: m ∠ABD > m ∠DBC
Prove: AD > BD

Statements	Reasons
1. _____	1. Given
2. m ∠DBC > m ∠DAB	2. _____
3. _____	3. Substitution
4. AD > BD	4. _____

Given: $\overline{BO} \cong \overline{HN}$, $\overline{OH} \cong \overline{BN}$
Prove: ∠O ≅ ∠N

Statements	Reasons
1. Construct $\overline{BH}$	1. _____
2. _____	2. Given
3. _____	3. Reflexive Property
4. _____	4. SSS
5. ∠O ≅ ∠N	5. _____

Similar Triangles

More Two Column Proofs

Given: $\overline{CT} \parallel \overline{BG}$
Prove: $\triangle CAT \sim \triangle BAG$

Statements	Reasons
1. _____	1. Given
2. _____	2. If ‖ lines, then corresponding ∠s are ≅.
3. _____	3. Reflexive Property
4. $\triangle CAT \sim \triangle BAG$	4. _____

Given: $\overline{AC} \cong \overline{AT}$, $\overline{OD} \cong \overline{OG}$, $\overline{AC} \parallel \overline{OD}$
Prove: $\triangle CAT \sim \triangle DOG$

Statements	Reasons
1. _____	1. Given
2. ∠ACT ≅ ∠ODG	2. _____
3. ∠ACT ≅ ∠ATC, ∠ODG ≅ ∠OGD	3. _____
4. _____	4. Substitution
5. $\triangle CAT \sim \triangle DOG$	5. _____

Given: ∠BAD ≅ ∠CDA, ∠1 ≅ ∠4
Prove: ∠2 ≅ ∠3

Statements	Reasons
1. _____	1. Given
2. _____	2. AAP
3. m∠BAD = m∠CDA, m∠1 = m∠4	3. _____
4. _____	4. Substitution
5. _____	5. APOE
6. ∠2 ≅ ∠3	6. _____

Right Triangles

☞ **Keep in mind . . .**
You must believe to achieve.

The area of a right triangle is half the product of the legs.

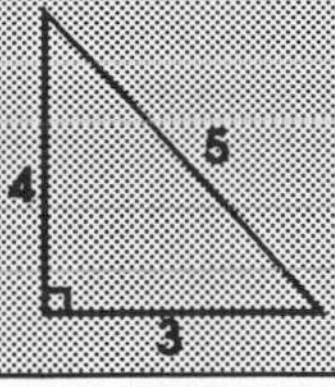

$A = \frac{1}{2}$ (3)(4)
$A = 6$ square units

Find the areas of the right triangles below.

1.

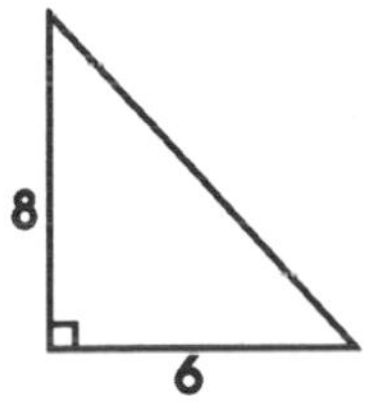

8

6

2.

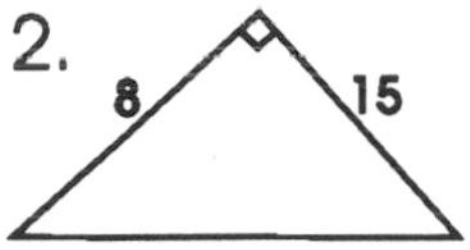

8   15

3.

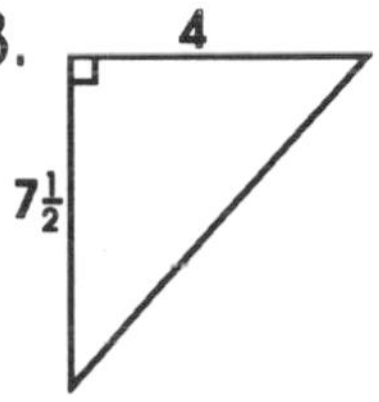

4

$7\frac{1}{2}$

4.

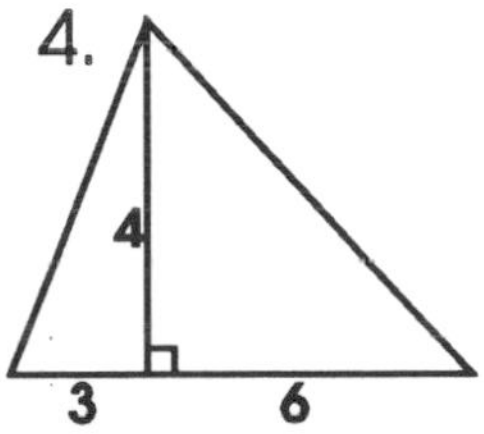

4

3   6

Pythagorean Theorem
$a^2 + b^2 = c^2$

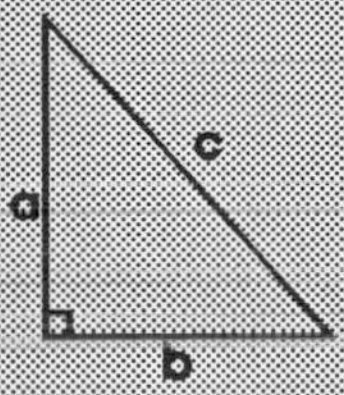

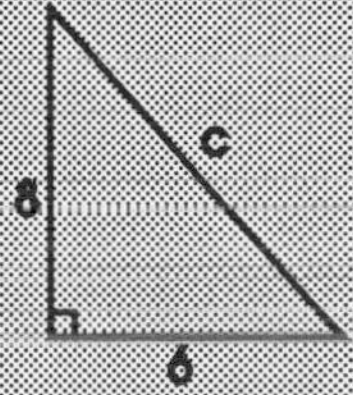

c

a

b

c

8

6

$6^2 + 8^2 = c^2$
$36 + 64 = c^2$
$100 = c^2$
$10 = c$

Find the missing side.

5.

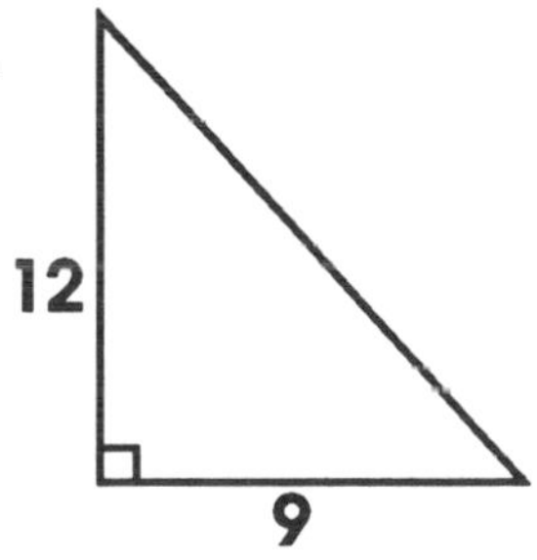

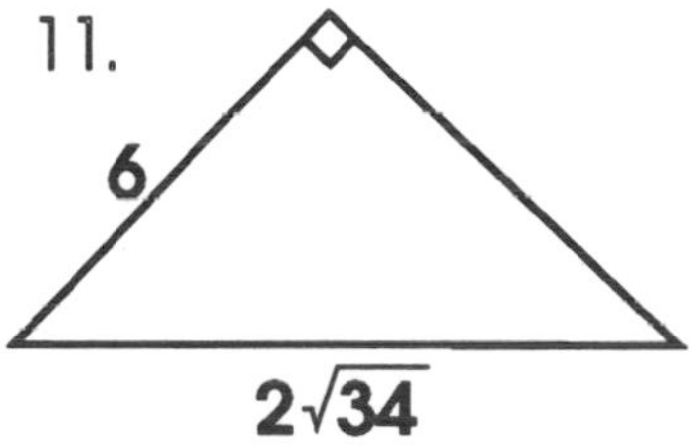

12

9

6.

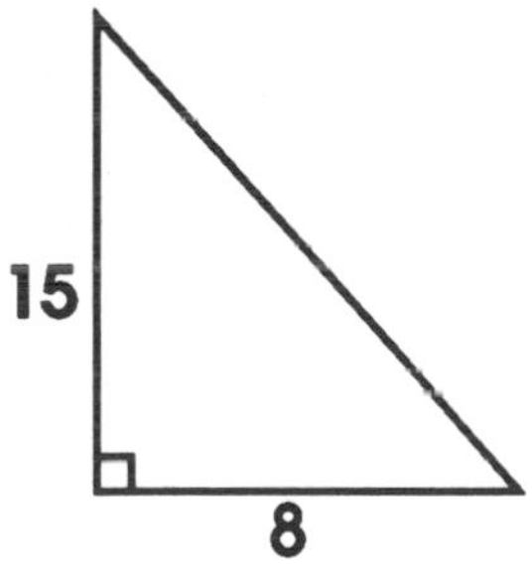

15

8

7.

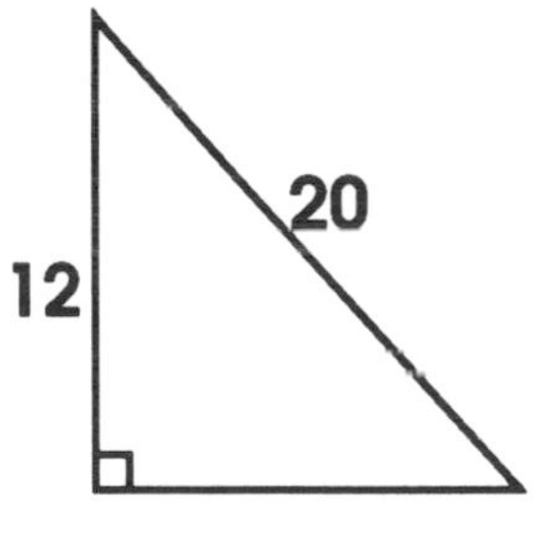

12   20

8.

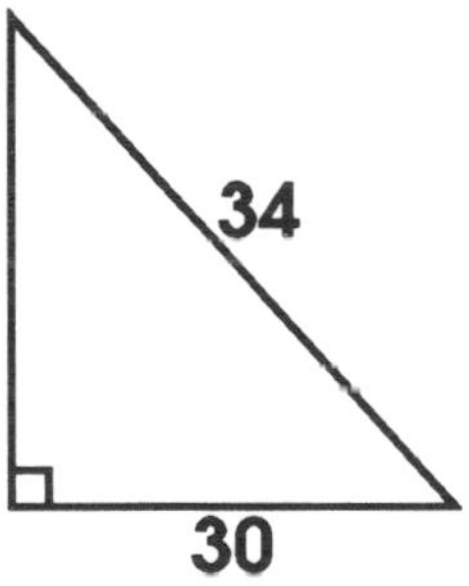

34

30

9.

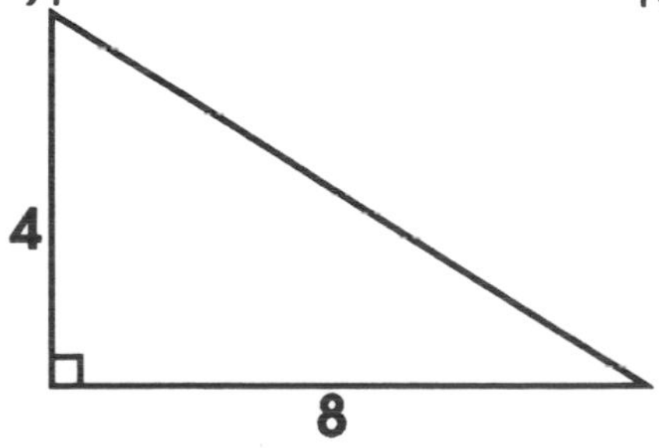

4

8

10.

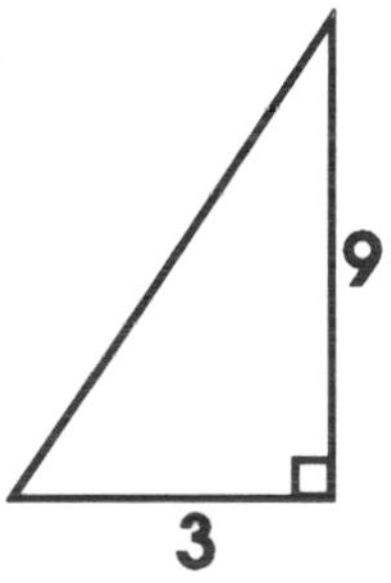

9

3

11.

6

$2\sqrt{34}$

12.

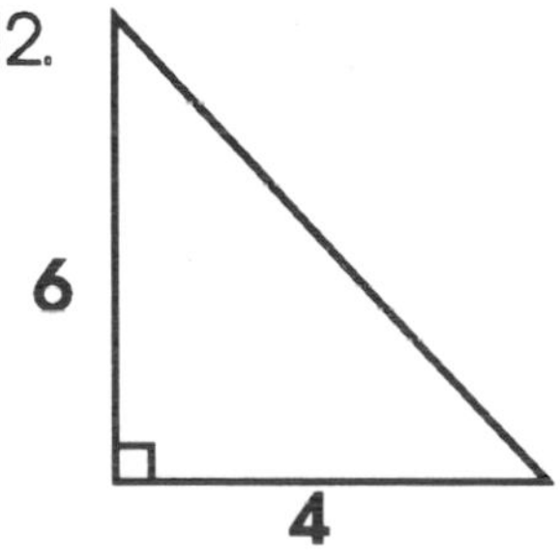

6

4

Special Right Triangles

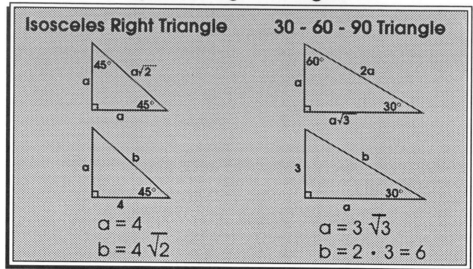

Isosceles Right Triangle

30 - 60 - 90 Triangle

$a = 4$
$b = 4\sqrt{2}$

$a = 3\sqrt{3}$
$b = 2 \cdot 3 = 6$

Find the missing sides.

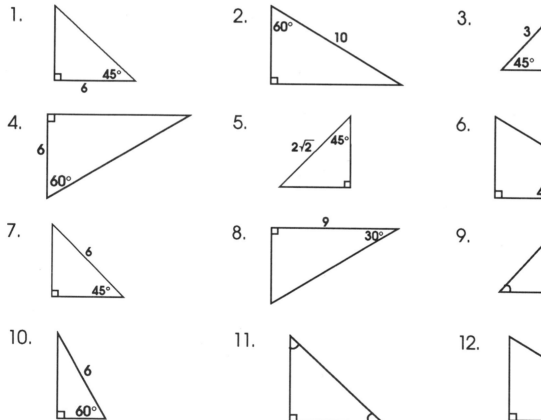

1.

2.

3.

4.

5.

6.

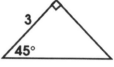

7.

8.

9.

10.

11.

12.

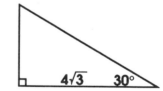

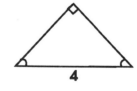

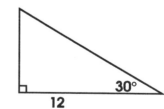

Right Triangle Trigonometry

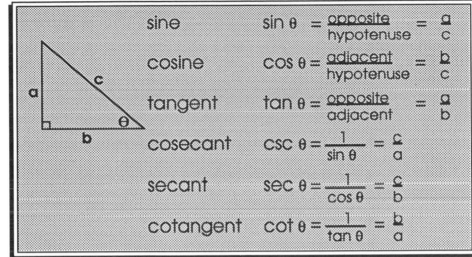

sine	$\sin \theta = \dfrac{\text{opposite}}{\text{hypotenuse}}$	$= \dfrac{a}{c}$
cosine	$\cos \theta = \dfrac{\text{adjacent}}{\text{hypotenuse}}$	$= \dfrac{b}{c}$
tangent	$\tan \theta = \dfrac{\text{opposite}}{\text{adjacent}}$	$= \dfrac{a}{b}$
cosecant	$\csc \theta = \dfrac{1}{\sin \theta}$	$= \dfrac{c}{a}$
secant	$\sec \theta = \dfrac{1}{\cos \theta}$	$= \dfrac{c}{b}$
cotangent	$\cot \theta = \dfrac{1}{\tan \theta}$	$= \dfrac{b}{a}$

Find the six trigonometric functions for the angles below.

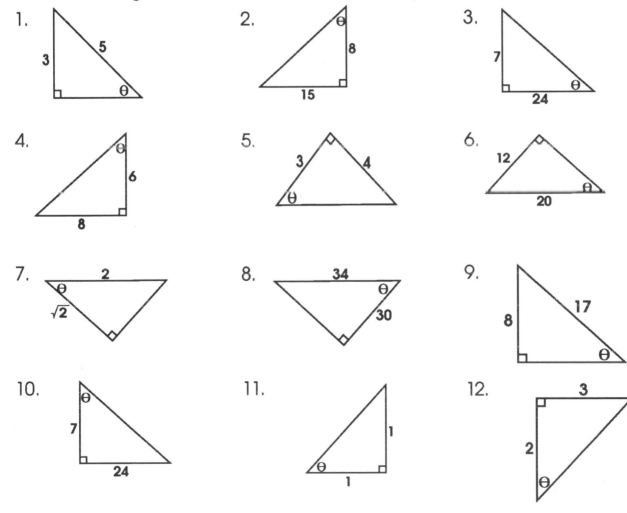

1.

2.

3.

4.

5.

6.

7.

8.

9.

10.

11.

12.

Trigonometric Identities

$\tan \theta = \dfrac{\sin \theta}{\cos \theta}$

$\sin (-\theta) = - \sin \theta \qquad \cos (-\theta) = \cos \theta$

$\cos (\theta + \beta) = \cos \theta \cos \beta - \sin \theta \sin \beta$

$\sin (\theta + \beta) = \sin \theta \cos \beta + \cos \theta \sin \beta$

$\cos \dfrac{\pi}{2} = 0 \quad \sin \dfrac{\pi}{2} = 1 \quad \tan \dfrac{\pi}{2}$ is undefined

$\cos \pi = -1 \quad \sin \pi = 0 \quad \tan \pi = 0$

$\cos (\theta - \beta) = \cos (\theta + (-\beta))$
$\qquad\qquad = \cos (\theta) \cos (-\beta) - \sin (\theta) \sin (-\beta)$
$\qquad\qquad = \cos \theta \cos \beta - \sin \theta (-\sin \beta)$
$\cos (\theta - \beta) = \cos \theta \cos \beta + \sin \theta \sin \beta$

Evaluate the following using the above identities.

1. $\sin (\theta - \beta)$

2. $\tan (\theta + \beta)$

3. $\tan (\theta - \beta)$

4. $\cos (\theta + \frac{\pi}{2})$

5. $\cos (\theta + \pi)$

6. $\sin (\theta + \frac{\pi}{2})$

7. $\sin (\theta + \pi)$

8. $\sin (2\theta)$

9. $\cos (2\theta)$

10. $\tan (2\theta)$

$\sin \theta = \sin\theta \cos^2\theta + \sin^3\theta$
$\qquad = \sin\theta (\cos^2\theta) + \sin\theta (\sin^2\theta)$
$\qquad = \sin\theta (\cos^2\theta + \sin^2\theta)$
$\qquad = \sin\theta (1)$
$\sin\theta = \sin\theta$

Verify the following identities.

1. $\csc^2\theta = 1 + \cot^2\theta$

2. $\sec^2\theta = 1 + \tan^2\theta$

3. $\cos\theta = \sec\theta - \tan\theta \sin\theta$

4. $\sin\theta = \csc\theta - \cot\theta \cos\theta$

Solving Other Triangles

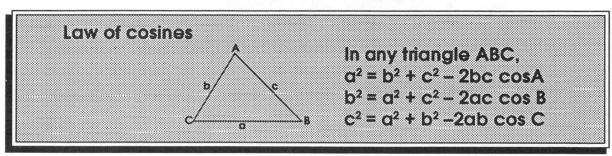

Law of cosines

In any triangle ABC,
$a^2 = b^2 + c^2 - 2bc \cos A$
$b^2 = a^2 + c^2 - 2ac \cos B$
$c^2 = a^2 + b^2 - 2ab \cos C$

Use the law of cosines to state an equation to find the missing part, x.

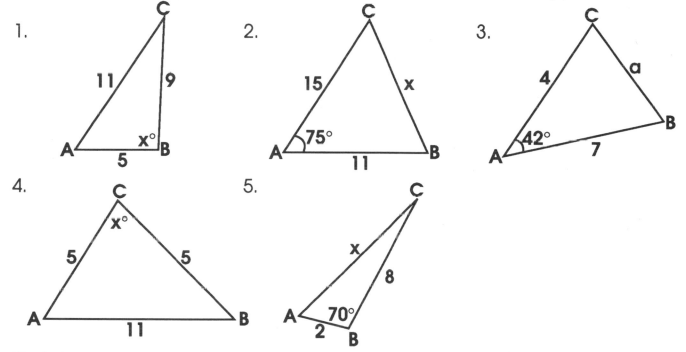

1.

2.

3.

4.

5.

Find the indicated part of △ABC. Round angles to the nearest tenth and lengths to three significant digits.

6. b = 12, c = 10, ∠A = 38°, a = _____

7. a = 14, b = 15, c = 18, ∠A = _____

8. a = 12, c = 11, ∠B = 81°, b = _____

9. a = 8, b = 9, c = 15, ∠C = _____

10. a = 5, b = 7, ∠C = 40°; c = _____

11. c = 20, b = 30, ∠A = 140°, a = _____

12. b = 2, a = 4, ∠C = 20°, c = _____

13. a = 5, b = 9, c = 11, ∠C = _____

14. a = 1.5, b = 3, c = 2, ∠B = _____

15. a = .6, b = .8, c = 1.2, ∠A = _____

Laws of Sines

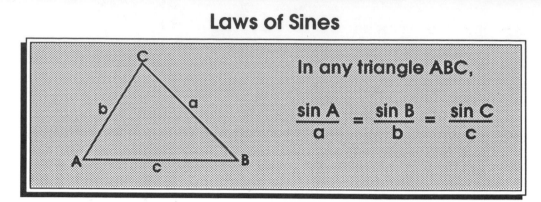

In any triangle ABC,

$$\frac{\sin A}{a} = \frac{\sin B}{b} = \frac{\sin C}{c}$$

Use the law of sines to state an equation to find the missing part, x.

1.
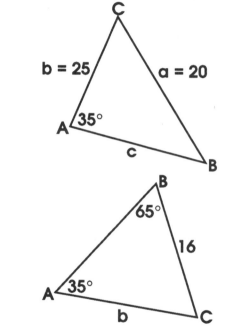

2.
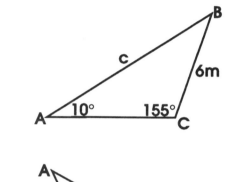

3.

4.
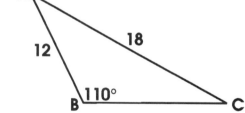

Find the indicated part of △ABC. Round angles to the nearest tenth and lengths to three significant digits.

5. $c = 10$, $\angle A = 48°$, $\angle C = 63°$, $a = $ _____

6. $a = 20$, $b = 15$, $\angle A = 40°$, $\angle B = $ _____

7. $a = 40$, $b = 50$, $\angle A = 37°$, $\angle B = $ _____

8. $a = 11$, $c = 15$, $\angle A = 40°$, $\angle C = $ _____

9. $c = 30$, $\angle A = 42°$, $\angle C = 98°$, $b = $ _____

10. $a = 1.5$, $b = 2.0$, $\angle B = 35°$, $\angle A = $ _____

11. $a = 16$, $\angle A = 35°$, $\angle C = 65°$, $c = $ _____

12. $b = 18$, $c = 32$, $\angle C = 100°$, $\angle B = $ _____

Quadrilaterals

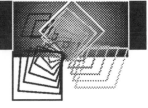

☞ **Keep in mind...**
If you put forth $^1/_2$ the effort, you only get a fraction of the results.

Properties of Parallelograms

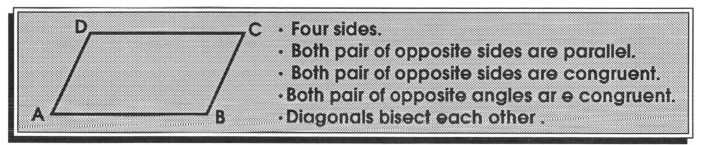

- Four sides.
- Both pair of opposite sides are parallel.
- Both pair of opposite sides are congruent.
- Both pair of opposite angles are congruent.
- Diagonals bisect each other.

Complete the following ▱ABCD.

1. $\overline{AB}$ ‖ _____

2. $\overline{AB} \cong$ _____

3. $\angle A \cong$ _____

4. $\overline{OA} \cong$ _____

5. $\overline{OB} \cong$ _____

6. $\overline{AD} \cong$ _____

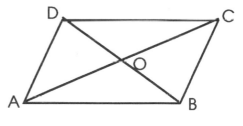

Find the missing values for each parallelogram.

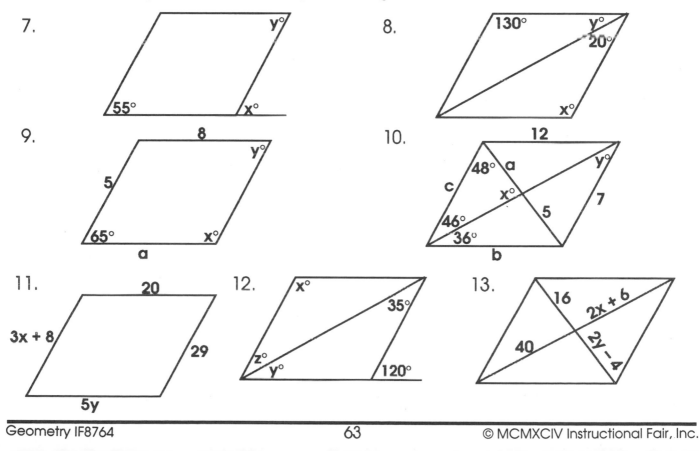

7. $y°$ $55°$ $x°$

8. $130°$ $y°$ $20°$ $x°$

9. 8 $y°$ 5 $65°$ $x°$ a

10. 12 $48°$ a c $x°$ $y°$ $46°$ 5 7 $36°$ b

11. 20 $3x + 8$ 29 $5y$

12. $x°$ $35°$ $z°$ $y°$ $120°$

13. 16 $2x + 6$ 40 $2y - 4$

Two Column Proofs

Five Ways to Prove that a Quadrilateral Is a Parallelogram
1. Show both pair of opposite sides are parallel.
2. Show both pair of opposite sides are congruent.
3. Show one pair of opposite sides are both congruent and parallel.
4. Show both pairs of opposite angles are congruent.
5. Show that diagonals bisect each other.

Given: ABCD is a ▱.
 ∠1 ≅ ∠2, $\overline{DF} ≅ \overline{EB}$
Prove: EBFD is a ▱.

Statements	Reasons
1. _____	1. Given
2. $\overline{AD} ≅ \overline{CB}$	2. _____
3. ∠A ≅ ∠C	3. _____
4. _____	4. AAS
5. $\overline{DE} ≅ \overline{FB}$	5. _____
6. EBFD is a ▱.	6. _____

Given: $\overline{AD} ∥ \overline{CB}$
 ∠DCA ≅ ∠BAC
Prove: ABCD is a ▱.

Statements	Reasons
1. _____	1. Given
2. $\overline{AC} ≅ \overline{AC}$	2. _____
3. ∠DAC ≅ ∠BCA	3. _____
4. ΔDAC ≅ ΔBCA	4. _____
5. $\overline{DA} ≅ \overline{BC}$	5. _____
6. ABCD is a ▱.	6. _____

More Two Column Proofs

Given: ABCE is a ▱.
FB ⊥ AD; DC ⊥ BC
Prove: FBCD is a ▱.

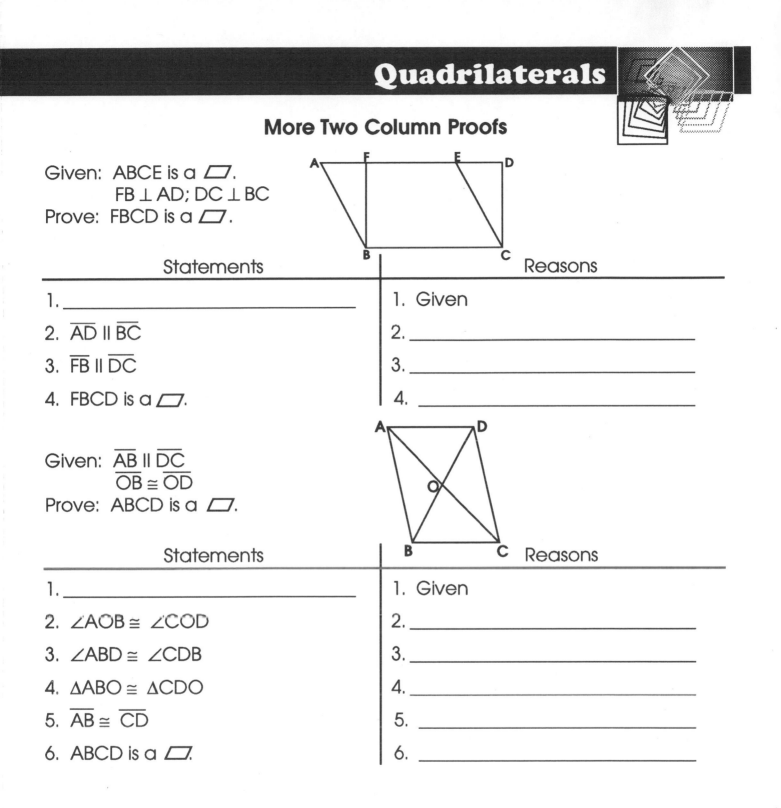

Statements	Reasons
1. _____	1. Given
2. $\overline{AD} \parallel \overline{BC}$	2. _____
3. $\overline{FB} \parallel \overline{DC}$	3. _____
4. FBCD is a ▱.	4. _____

Given: $\overline{AB} \parallel \overline{DC}$
$\overline{OB} \cong \overline{OD}$
Prove: ABCD is a ▱.

Statements	Reasons
1. _____	1. Given
2. ∠AOB ≅ ∠COD	2. _____
3. ∠ABD ≅ ∠CDB	3. _____
4. △ABO ≅ △CDO	4. _____
5. $\overline{AB} \cong \overline{CD}$	5. _____
6. ABCD is a ▱.	6. _____

On your own.

Given: $\overline{AD} \cong \overline{BC}$; ∠EBC ≅ ∠ECB
E is the midpoint of AD
∠1 ≅ ∠2
Prove: ABCD is a ▱.

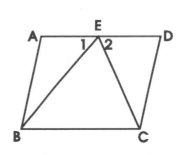

Quadrilaterals

Special Parallelograms

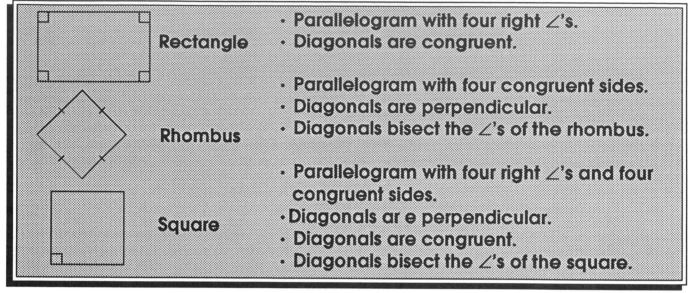

Rectangle
- Parallelogram with four right ∠'s.
- Diagonals are congruent.

Rhombus
- Parallelogram with four congruent sides.
- Diagonals are perpendicular.
- Diagonals bisect the ∠'s of the rhombus.

Square
- Parallelogram with four right ∠'s and four congruent sides.
- Diagonals ar e perpendicular.
- Diagonals are congruent.
- Diagonals bisect the ∠'s of the square.

In problems 1-8, list the letters of the quadrilaterals that the property holds true for: a) Parallelogram b) Rectangle c) Rhombus d) Square

1. Diagonals bisect each other.

2. All ∠'s are right ∠'s.

3. All sides are congruent.

4. Opposite sides are congruent.

5. Opposite angles are congruent.

6. Diagonals are congruent.

7. Diagonals are perpendicular.

8. Opposite sides are parallel.

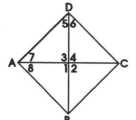
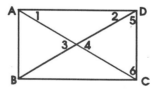

9. ABCD is a rhombus. If m ∠8 = 35, find the measures of ∠1, ∠2, ∠3, ∠4, ∠5, ∠6, ∠7.

10. ABCD is a rectangle. If m ∠1 = 20, find the measures of ∠2, ∠3, ∠4, ∠5, ∠6.

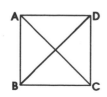
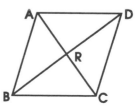

11. ABCD is a square. If $\overline{AC}$ = 16 and $\overline{BD}$ = 2x + 4, find x.

12. ABCD is a parallelogram. $\overline{AR}$ = 2x + 3, $\overline{RC}$ = 35, $\overline{BR}$ = 4y − 10, $\overline{DR}$ = 90. Find x and y.

Trapezoids

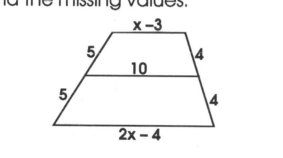

- Four sides.
- Exactly one pair of parallel sides.
- The median is parallel to the bases.
- Has a length equal to the average of the bases.

- A trapezoid with congruent legs.

isosceles trapezoid

Find the missing values.

1.

x – 3
5   4
10
5   4
2x – 4

2.

15
x
35

3.

x
30
5x

4.

2x
5x
6x + 12

5.

y°
4   4
x°
4   4
40°

6.

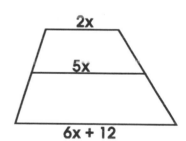

8
y°
8
60°
x

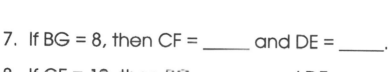

7. If BG = 8, then CF = _____ and DE = _____.

8. If CF = 10, then BG = _____ and DE = _____.

9. If DE = 15 and BG = 7, then CF = _____.

10. If CF = 2x + 4, BG = 2x + 1, and DE = 3x + 2, then x = _____.

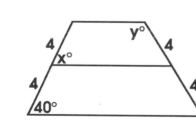

Circles

Circumference and Area

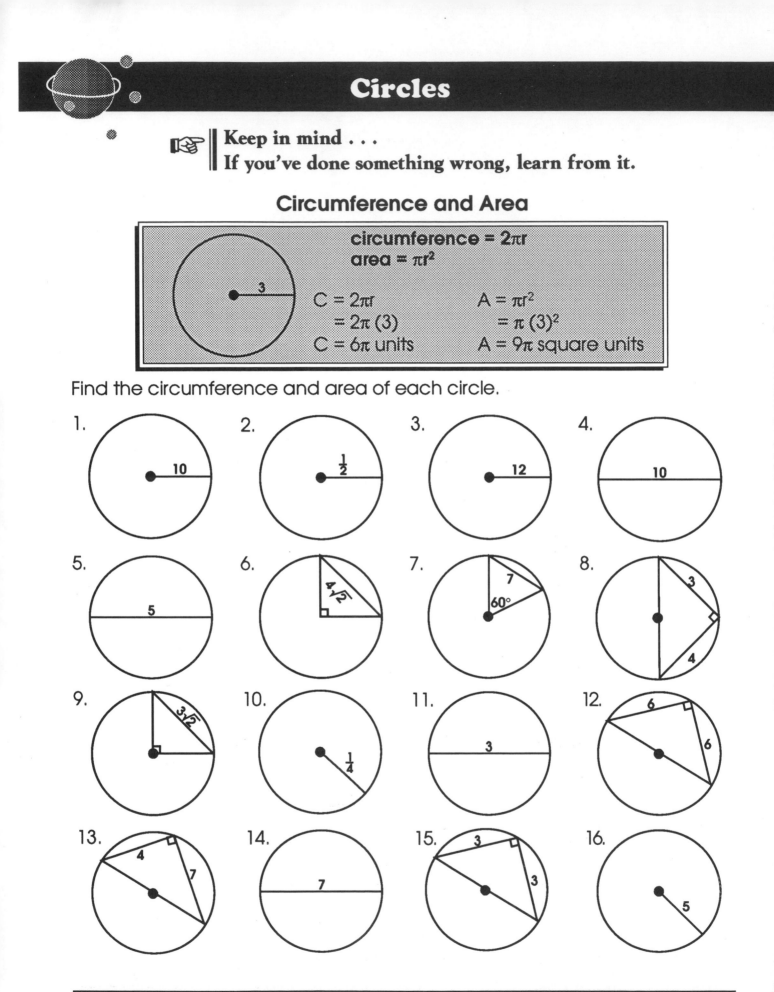

$$\text{circumference} = 2\pi r$$
$$\text{area} = \pi r^2$$

$$C = 2\pi r \qquad\qquad A = \pi r^2$$
$$= 2\pi (3) \qquad\qquad = \pi (3)^2$$
$$C = 6\pi \text{ units} \qquad A = 9\pi \text{ square units}$$

Find the circumference and area of each circle.

1. 10

2. ½

3. 12

4. 10

5. 5

6. $4\sqrt{2}$

7. 7, 60°

8. 3, 4

9. $3\sqrt{2}$

10. ¼

11. 3

12. 6, 6

13. 4, 7

14. 7

15. 3, 3

16. 5

Just for Fun

Draw the segments with the following endpoints.

1. (3, 81), (3, 1)
2. (5, 79), (5, 55)
3. (11, 75), (11, 68)
4. (47, 75), (47, 68)
5. (53, 79), (53, 55)
6. (55, 81), (55, 1)
7. (7, 49), (7, 45)
8. (7, 41), (7, 37)
9. (7, 33), (7, 29)
10. (7, 25), (7, 21)
11. (7, 17), (7, 13)
12. (7, 9), (7, 5)
13. (15, 49), (15, 45)
14. (15, 41), (15, 37)
15. (15, 33), (15, 29)
16. (15, 25), (15, 21)
17. (15, 17), (15, 13)
18. (15, 9), (15, 5)
19. (19, 49), (19, 45)
20. (19, 41), (19, 37)
21. (19, 33), (19, 29)
22. (19, 25), (19, 21)
23. (19, 17), (19, 13)
24. (19, 9), (19, 5)

25. (27, 49), (27, 45)
26. (27, 41), (27, 37)
27. (27, 33), (27, 29)
28. (27, 25), (27, 21)
29. (27, 17), (27, 13)
30. (27, 9), (27, 5)
31. (31, 49), (31, 45)
32. (31, 41), (31, 37)
33. (31, 33), (31, 29)
34. (31, 25), (31, 21)
35. (31, 17), (31, 13)
36. (31, 9), (31, 5)
37. (39, 49), (39, 45)
38. (39, 41), (39, 47)
39. (39, 33), (39, 29)
40. (39, 25), (39, 21)
41. (39, 17), (39, 13)
42. (39, 9), (39, 5)
43. (43, 49), (43, 45)
44. (43, 41), (43, 37)
45. (43, 33), (43, 29)
46. (43, 25), (43, 21)
47. (43, 17), (43, 13)
48. (43, 9), (43, 5)

49. (51, 49), (51, 45)
50. (51, 41), (51, 37)
51. (51, 33), (51, 29)
52. (51, 25), (51, 21)
53. (51, 17), (51, 13)
54. (51, 9), (51, 5)
55. (3, 81), (55, 81)
56. (5, 79), (53, 79)
57. (11, 75), (47, 75)
58. (11, 68), (47, 68)
59. (5, 55), (53, 55)
60. (3, 53), (55, 53)
61. (7, 49), (15, 49)
62. (19, 49), (25, 49)
63. (31, 49), (39, 49)
64. (43, 49), (51, 49)
65. (7, 45), (15, 45)
66. (19, 45), (25, 45)
67. (31, 45), (39, 45)
68. (43, 45), (51, 45)
69. (7, 41), (15, 41)
70. (19, 41), (25, 41)
71. (31, 41), (39, 41)
72. (43, 41), (51, 41)

Just for Fun

Continue drawing these segments and points.

73. (7, 37), (15, 37)
74. (19, 37), (25, 37)
75. (31, 37), (39, 37)
76. (43, 37), (51, 37)
77. (7, 33), (15, 33)
78. (19, 33), (25, 33)
79. (31, 33), (39, 33)
80. (43, 33), (51, 33)
81. (7, 29), (15, 29)
82. (19, 29), (25, 29)
83. (31, 29), (39, 29)
84. (43, 29), (51, 29)
85. (7, 25), (15, 25)
86. (19, 25), (25, 25)
87. (31, 25), (39, 25)
88. (43, 25), (51, 25)
89. (7, 21), (15, 21)
90. (19, 21), (25, 21)
91. (31, 21), (39, 21)
92. (43, 21), (51, 21)
93. (7, 17), (15, 17)
94. (19, 17), (25, 17)
95. (31, 17), (39, 17)
96. (43, 17), (51, 17)

97. (7, 13), (15, 13)
98. (19, 13), (25, 13)
99. (31, 13), (39, 13)
100. (43, 13), (51, 13)
101. (7, 9), (15, 9)
102. (19, 9), (25, 9)
103. (31, 9), (39, 9)
104. (43, 9), (51, 9)
105. (7, 5), (15, 5)
106. (19, 5), (25, 5)
107. (31, 5), (39, 5)
108. (43, 5), (51, 5)
109. (3, 1), (55, 1)
110. (9, 47), (10, 46)
111. (10, 46), (11, 48)
112. (11, 48), (13, 48)
113. (8, 40), (8, 38)
114. (8, 40), (9, 40)
115. (9, 40), (9, 39)
116. (9, 39), (8, 39)
117. (8, 39), (9, 38)
118. (10, 39)
119. (24, 39), (25, 39)
120. $(10\frac{1}{2}, 40)$, $(10\frac{1}{2}, 38)$

121. $(10\frac{1}{2}, 40)$, $(11\frac{1}{2}, 40)$
122. $(10\frac{1}{2}, 38)$, $(11\frac{1}{2}, 38)$
123. (12, 40), (12, 38)
124. (12, 40), (13, 39)
125. (13, 39), (14, 40)
126. (14, 40), (14, 38)
127. (10, 32), (12, 32)
128. (12, 32), (10, 30)
129. (10, 24), (10, 23)
130. (10, 23), (12, 23)
131. (12, 24), (12, 22)
132. (11, 16), (11, 14)
133. (10, 8), (12, 8)
134. (12, 8), (12, 6)
135. (12, 6), (10, 6)
136. (10, 6), (10, 8)
137. (21, 48), (22, 48)
138. (22, 48), (22, 47)
139. (22, 47), (21, 47)
140. (21, 47), (22, 47)
141. (24, 48), (22, 46)
142. (24, 47), (25, 47)
143. (25, 47), (25, 46)
144. (25, 46), (24, 46)

Just for Fun

145. $(24, 46), (24, 47)$

146. $(21, 40), (21, 38)$

147. $(21, 40), (22, 39)$

148. $(22, 39), (23, 40)$

149. $(23, 40), (23, 38)$

150. $(22, 32), (22, 30)$

151. $(22, 30), (24, 30)$

152. $(24, 30), (24, 32)$

153. $(24, 32), (22, 32)$

154. $(22, 31), (24, 31)$

155. $(24, 24), (22, 24)$

156. $(22, 24), (22, 23)$

157. $(22, 23), (24, 23)$

158. $(24, 23), (24, 22)$

159. $(24, 22), (22, 22)$

160. $(22, 16), (24, 16)$

161. $(24, 16), (24, 15)$

162. $(24, 15), (22, 15)$

163. $(22, 15), (22, 14)$

164. $(22, 14), (24, 14)$

165. $(23, 7)$

166. $(34, 7\frac{1}{2}), (36, 7\frac{1}{2})$

167. $(34, 6\frac{1}{2}), (36, 6\frac{1}{2})$

168. $(46, 7), (48, 7)$

169. $(47, 8), (47, 6)$

170. $(34, 14), (36, 14)$

171. $(36, 14), (36, 16)$

172. $(34, 16), (36, 16)$

173. $(35, 15), (36, 15)$

174. $(46, 15), (48, 15)$

175. $(34, 24), (36, 34)$

176. $(34, 24), (34, 22)$

177. $(34, 23), (36, 23)$

178. $(34, 22), (36, 22)$

179. $(36, 23), (36, 22)$

180. $(46, 24), (48, 22)$

181. $(46, 22), (48, 24)$

182. $(34, 32), (36, 32)$

183. $(34, 32), (34, 31)$

184. $(34, 31), (36, 31)$

185. $(36, 32), (36, 30)$

186. $(36, 30), (34, 30)$

187. $(46, 31), (48, 31)$

188. $(47, 32)$

189. $(47, 30)$

190. $(33, 40), (33, 38)$

191. $(33, 40), (34, 39)$

192. $(34, 39), (35, 40)$

193. $(35, 40), (35, 38)$

194. $(36, 39), (37, 39)$

195. $(36\frac{1}{2}, 39\frac{1}{2}), (36\frac{1}{2}, 38\frac{1}{2})$

196. $(45, 40), (47, 40)$

197. $(45, 40), (45, 38)$

198. $(45, 38), (47, 38)$

199. $(47\frac{1}{2}, 40), (49, 40)$

200. $(47\frac{1}{2}, 40), (47\frac{1}{2}, 38)$

201. $(47\frac{1}{2}, 38), (49, 38)$

202. $(47\frac{1}{2}, 39), (48\frac{1}{2}, 39)$

203. $(32, 48), (34, 48)$

204. $(34, 48), (34, 46)$

205. $(34, 46), (32, 46)$

206. $(32, 46), (32, 48)$

207. $(35, 48), (35, 46)$

208. $(35, 48), (36, 48)$

209. $(35, 47), (36, 47)$

210. $(37, 48), (38, 48)$

211. $(37, 48), (37, 46)$

212. $(37, 47), (38, 47)$

213. $(45, 48), (47, 48)$

214. $(47, 48), (47, 46)$

215. $(47, 46), (45, 46)$

216. $(45, 46), (45, 48)$

217. $(47\frac{1}{2}, 48), (47\frac{1}{2}, 46)$

218. $(47\frac{1}{2}, 48), (49, 46)$

219. $(49, 46), (49, 48)$

72

Sectors and Arcs

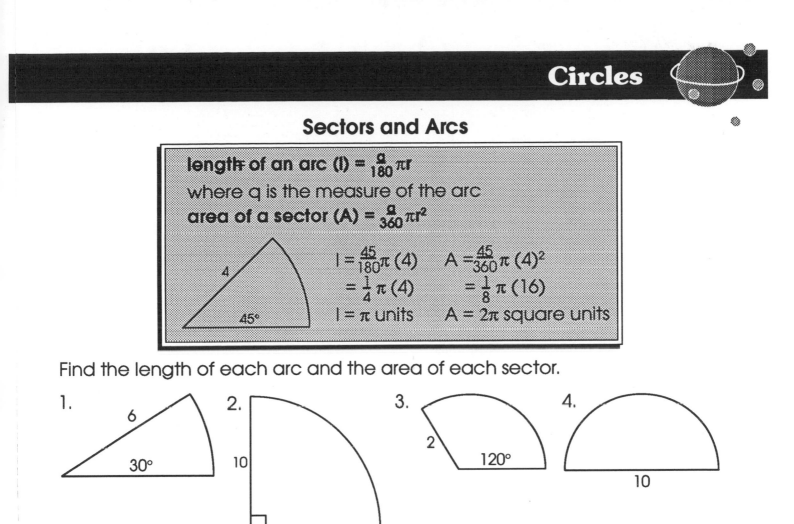

length of an arc $(l) = \frac{a}{180}\pi r$

where q is the measure of the arc

area of a sector $(A) = \frac{a}{360}\pi r^2$

$l = \frac{45}{180}\pi(4)$ $A = \frac{45}{360}\pi(4)^2$

   $= \frac{1}{4}\pi(4)$ $= \frac{1}{8}\pi(16)$

$l = \pi$ units $A = 2\pi$ square units

Find the length of each arc and the area of each sector.

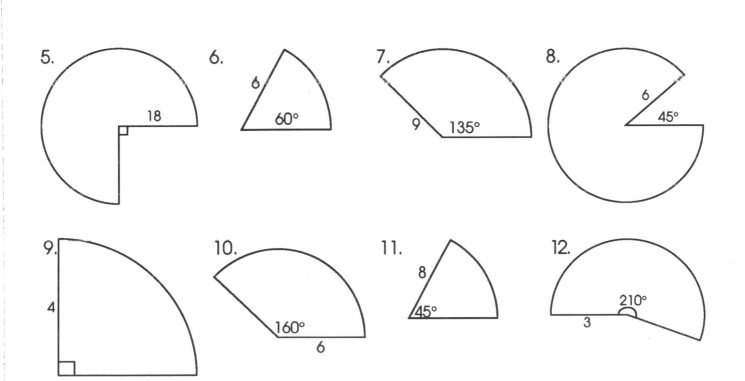

1. 6, 30°
2. 10
3. 2, 120°
4. 10

5. 18
6. 6, 60°
7. 9, 135°
8. 6, 45°

9. 4
10. 160°, 6
11. 8, 45°
12. 210°, 3

Just for Fun

Draw each figure without lifting your pencil from the paper and without tracing any line more than once.

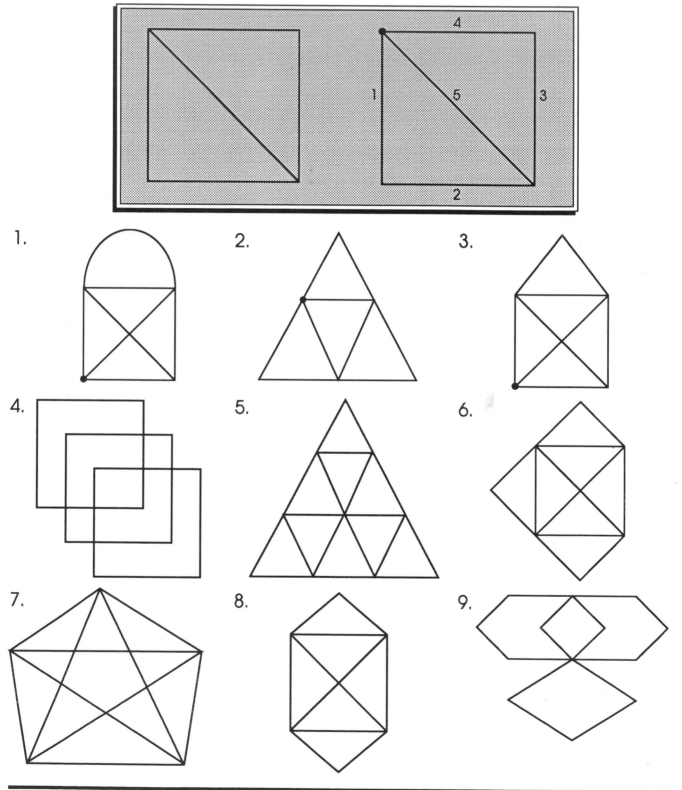

1.

2.

3.

4.

5.

6.

7.

8.

9.

Tangents, Secants and Chords

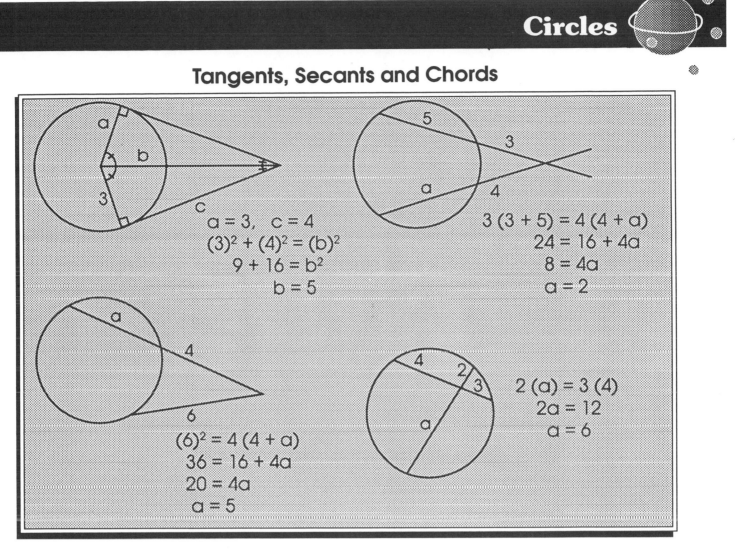

$a = 3, \quad c = 4$
$(3)^2 + (4)^2 = (b)^2$
$9 + 16 = b^2$
$b = 5$

$3(3 + 5) = 4(4 + a)$
$24 = 16 + 4a$
$8 = 4a$
$a = 2$

$(6)^2 = 4(4 + a)$
$36 = 16 + 4a$
$20 = 4a$
$a = 5$

$2(a) = 3(4)$
$2a = 12$
$a = 6$

Find the labeled lengths.

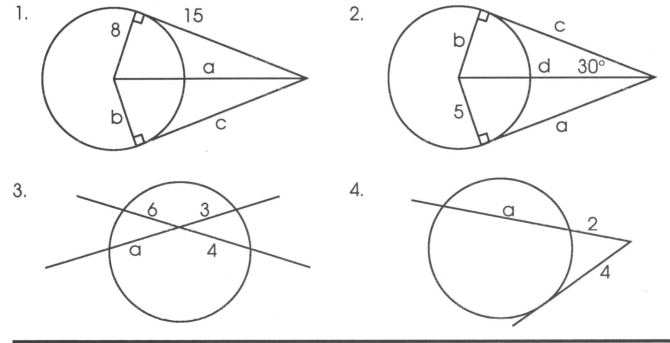

1.

2.

3.

4.

5.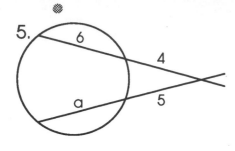

6.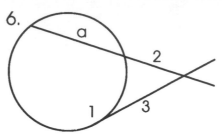

7.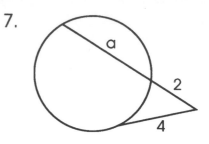

8.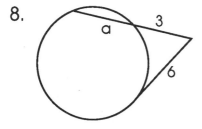

9.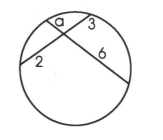

10.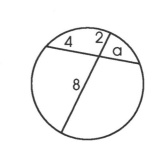

11.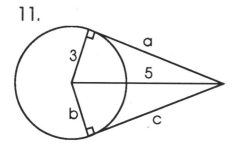

12.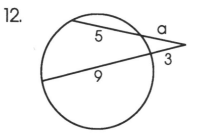

13.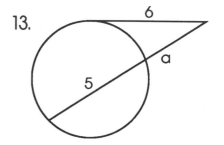

14.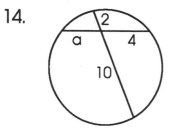

15.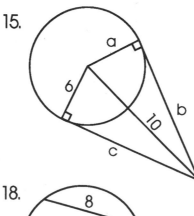

16.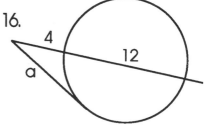

17.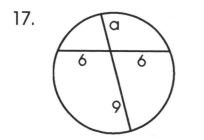

18.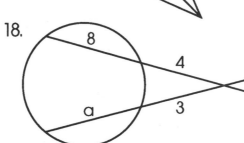

More Two Column Proofs

Complete the following proofs.

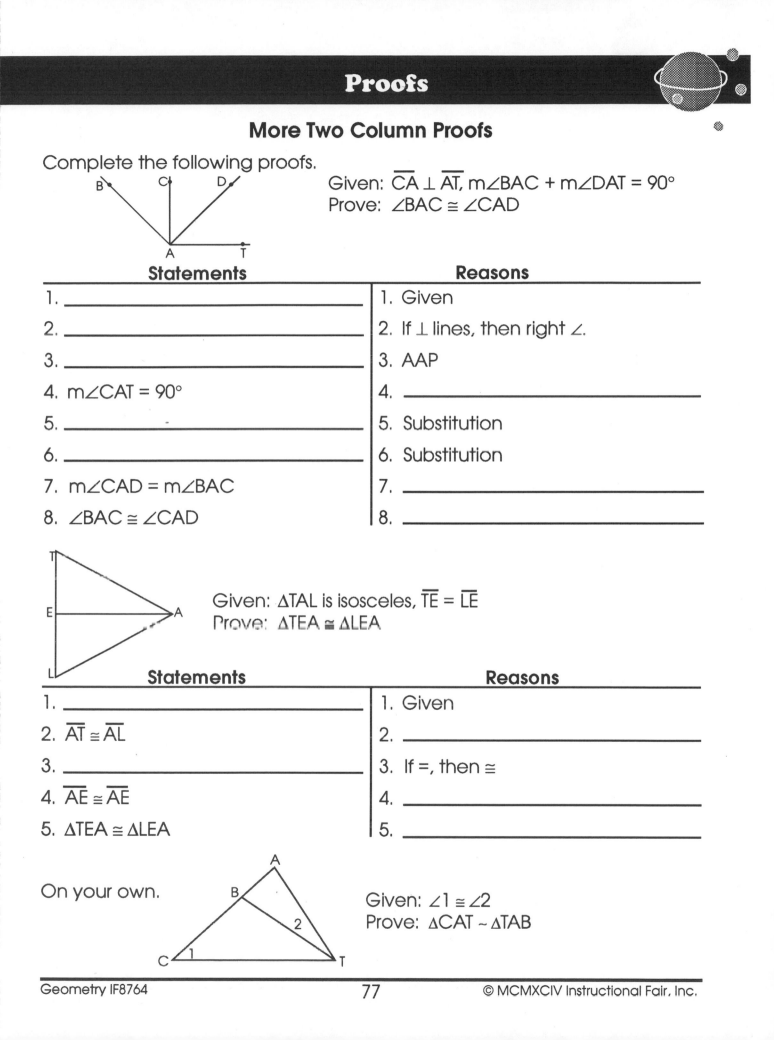

Given: $\overline{CA} \perp \overline{AT}$, m∠BAC + m∠DAT = 90°
Prove: ∠BAC ≅ ∠CAD

Statements	Reasons
1. _____	1. Given
2. _____	2. If ⊥ lines, then right ∠.
3. _____	3. AAP
4. m∠CAT = 90°	4. _____
5. _____	5. Substitution
6. _____	6. Substitution
7. m∠CAD = m∠BAC	7. _____
8. ∠BAC ≅ ∠CAD	8. _____

Given: ΔTAL is isosceles, $\overline{TE} = \overline{LE}$
Prove: ΔTEA ≅ ΔLEA

Statements	Reasons
1. _____	1. Given
2. $\overline{AT} \cong \overline{AL}$	2. _____
3. _____	3. If =, then ≅
4. $\overline{AE} \cong \overline{AE}$	4. _____
5. ΔTEA ≅ ΔLEA	5. _____

On your own.

Given: ∠1 ≅ ∠2
Prove: ΔCAT ~ ΔTAB

More Practice with Proofs

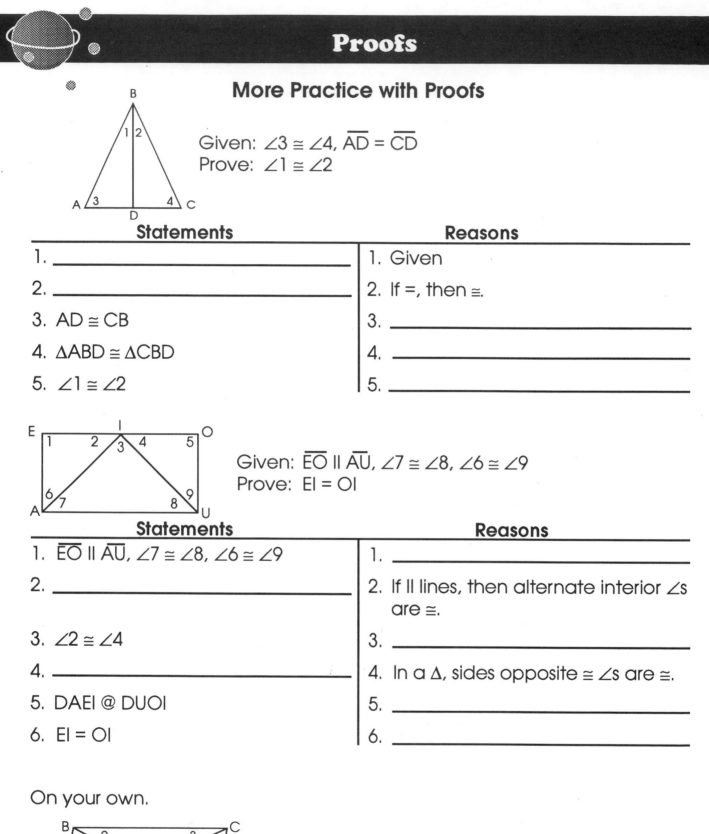

Given: $\angle 3 \cong \angle 4$, $\overline{AD} = \overline{CD}$
Prove: $\angle 1 \cong \angle 2$

Statements	Reasons
1. _____	1. Given
2. _____	2. If =, then ≅.
3. $AD \cong CB$	3. _____
4. $\triangle ABD \cong \triangle CBD$	4. _____
5. $\angle 1 \cong \angle 2$	5. _____

Given: $\overline{EO} \parallel \overline{AU}$, $\angle 7 \cong \angle 8$, $\angle 6 \cong \angle 9$
Prove: $EI = OI$

Statements	Reasons
1. $\overline{EO} \parallel \overline{AU}$, $\angle 7 \cong \angle 8$, $\angle 6 \cong \angle 9$	1. _____
2. _____	2. If ‖ lines, then alternate interior ∠s are ≅.
3. $\angle 2 \cong \angle 4$	3. _____
4. _____	4. In a $\triangle$, sides opposite ≅ ∠s are ≅.
5. DAEI @ DUOI	5. _____
6. $EI = OI$	6. _____

On your own.

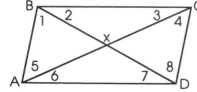

Given: ABCD is a parallelogram
Prove: x is the midpoint of $\overline{AC}$ and $\overline{BD}$
  (the diagonals bisect each other)

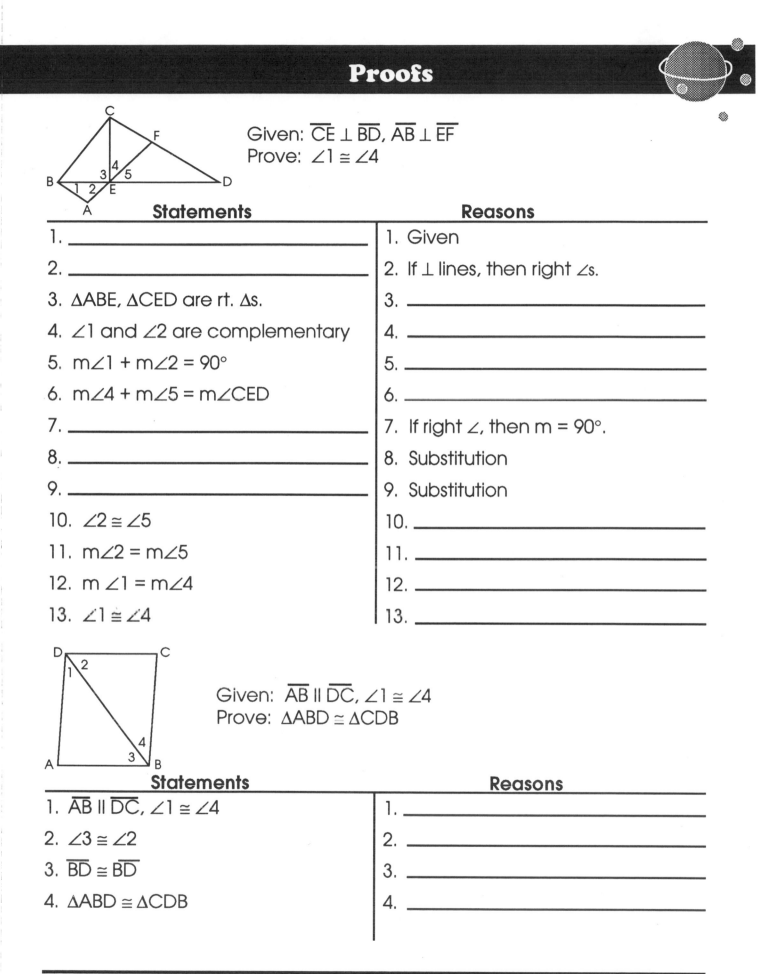

Given: $\overline{CE} \perp \overline{BD}$, $\overline{AB} \perp \overline{EF}$
Prove: $\angle 1 \cong \angle 4$

Statements	Reasons
1. _____	1. Given
2. _____	2. If $\perp$ lines, then right $\angle$s.
3. $\triangle ABE$, $\triangle CED$ are rt. $\triangle$s.	3. _____
4. $\angle 1$ and $\angle 2$ are complementary	4. _____
5. $m\angle 1 + m\angle 2 = 90°$	5. _____
6. $m\angle 4 + m\angle 5 = m\angle CED$	6. _____
7. _____	7. If right $\angle$, then m = 90°.
8. _____	8. Substitution
9. _____	9. Substitution
10. $\angle 2 \cong \angle 5$	10. _____
11. $m\angle 2 = m\angle 5$	11. _____
12. $m\angle 1 = m\angle 4$	12. _____
13. $\angle 1 \cong \angle 4$	13. _____

Given: $\overline{AB} \parallel \overline{DC}$, $\angle 1 \cong \angle 4$
Prove: $\triangle ABD \cong \triangle CDB$

Statements	Reasons
1. $\overline{AB} \parallel \overline{DC}$, $\angle 1 \cong \angle 4$	1. _____
2. $\angle 3 \cong \angle 2$	2. _____
3. $\overline{BD} \cong \overline{BD}$	3. _____
4. $\triangle ABD \cong \triangle CDB$	4. _____

☞ **Keep in mind . . .**
Aim for the stars.

A **polygonal region** is defined to be the union of a finite number of triangular regions in a single plane. The intersection of any two or more triangular regions is either a point or a segment.

This is polygonal region.

Determine if each region below is polygonal by breaking it into triangular regions.

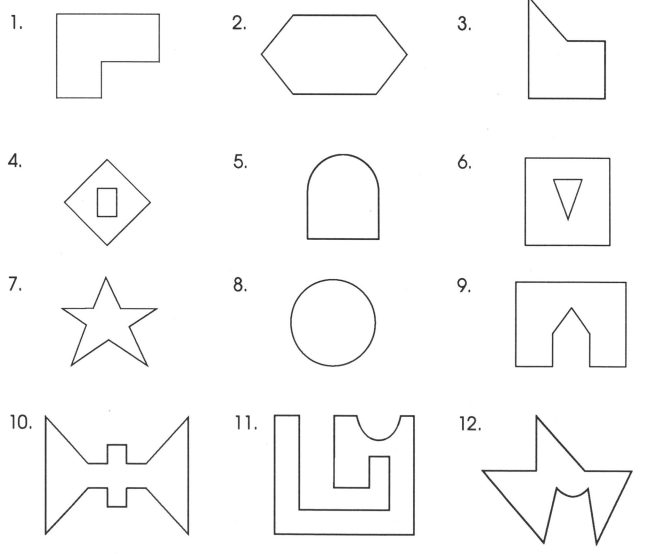

1.

2.

3.

4.

5.

6.

7.

8.

9.

10.

11.

12.

Polygons

Types of Polygons		
Number of Sides	*Name*	• A regular polygon has equal angles and equal sides.
3	triangle	
4	quadrilateral	• The sum of the measures of the angles of a convex polygon with n sides is $(n-2)180°$.
5	pentagon	
6	hexagon	
8	octagon	• The sum of the measures of the exterior angles of any convex polygon is 360°.
10	decagon	
n	n-gon	

Find the following for each polygon: a) The sum of the measures of the interior angles, b) The sum of the measures of the exterior angles.

1. A 32-sided polygon

2. A 12-sided polygon

3. A 6-sided polygon

4. An 8-sided polygon

5. A 3-sided polygon

6. A 5-sided polygon

Find the following for each regular polygon: a) The measure of each exterior angle, b) the measure of each interior angle.

7. A 6-sided polygon

8. A 5-sided polygon

9. A 3-sided polygon

10. An 8-sided polygon

11. A 4-sided polygon

12. A 10-sided polygon

13. A regular polygon has an exterior angle with a measure of 20°. Find the number of sides.

14. A regular polygon has an interior angle with a measure of 120°. Find the number of sides.

15. A regular polygon has 20 sides. Find the measure of each exterior angle.

16. A regular polygon has 10 sides. Find the measure of each interior angle.

Perimeter

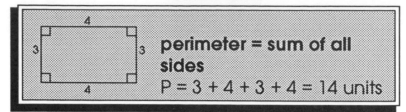

perimeter = sum of all sides
P = 3 + 4 + 3 + 4 = 14 units

Find the perimeters of the polygonal regions below.

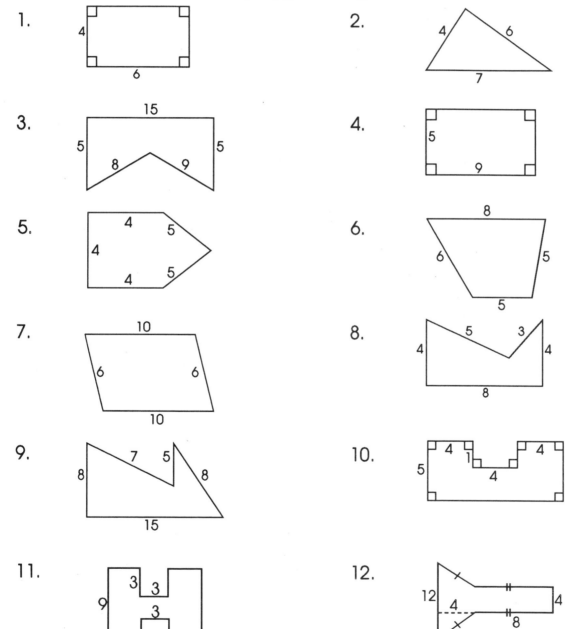

1.

2.

3.

4.

5.

6.

7.

8.

9.

10.

11.

12.

Area

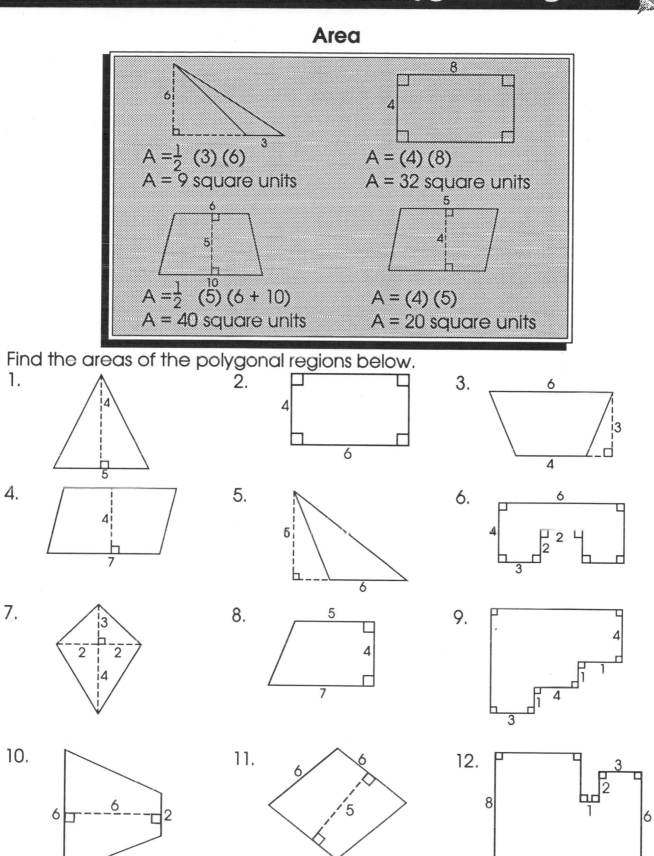

$A = \frac{1}{2}$ (3) (6)
A = 9 square units

A = (4) (8)
A = 32 square units

$A = \frac{1}{2}$ (5) (6 + 10)
A = 40 square units

A = (4) (5)
A = 20 square units

Find the areas of the polygonal regions below.

1.

2.

3.

4.

5.

6.

7.

8.

9.

10.

11.

12.

Regular Polygons

A **regular polygon** is a convex polygon with all sides congruent and all angles congruent.

apothem (a) = distance from the center of the polygon to a side

area = $\frac{1}{2}$ ap where p = perimeter

$A = \frac{1}{2} (\sqrt{3}) (6 + 6 + 6)$

$\quad = \frac{1}{2} (\sqrt{3}) (18)$

$A = 9\sqrt{3}$ square units

Find the areas of the regular polygonal regions below.

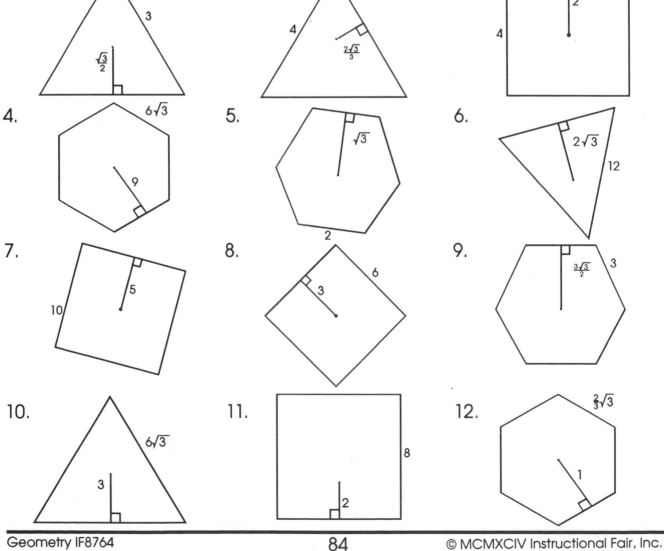

1.

2.

3.

4.

5.

6.

7.

8.

9.

10.

11.

12.

Solids

☞ **Keep in mind . . .**
When you start something, finish it.

Prisms

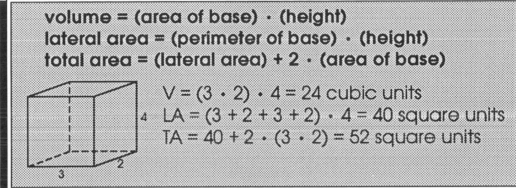

volume = (area of base) · (height)
lateral area = (perimeter of base) · (height)
total area = (lateral area) + 2 · (area of base)

V = (3 · 2) · 4 = 24 cubic units
LA = (3 + 2 + 3 + 2) · 4 = 40 square units
TA = 40 + 2 · (3 · 2) = 52 square units

Find the volume, lateral area and total area of the following prisms.

1.
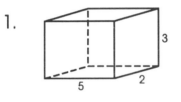

2.

3.
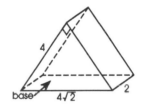

4.
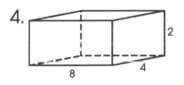

5.
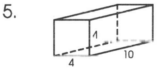

6.
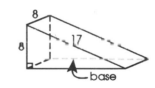

7.
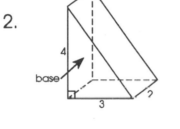

8.
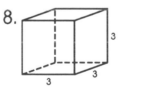

9.
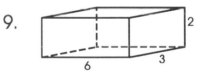

10.
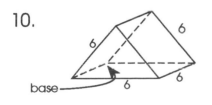

11.
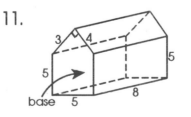

12.
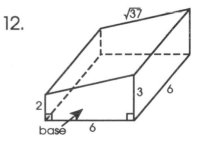

Right Circular Cylinders

volume = π · (radius)² · (height)
lateral area = 2 · π · (radius) · (height)
total area = (lateral area) + 2 · π · (radius)²

$V = π · (5)² · (6) = 150π$ cubic units
$LA = 2 · π · (5) · (6) = 60π$ square units
$TA = 60π + 2 · π · (5)² = 110π$ square units

Find the volume, lateral area and total area of the following right circular cylinders.

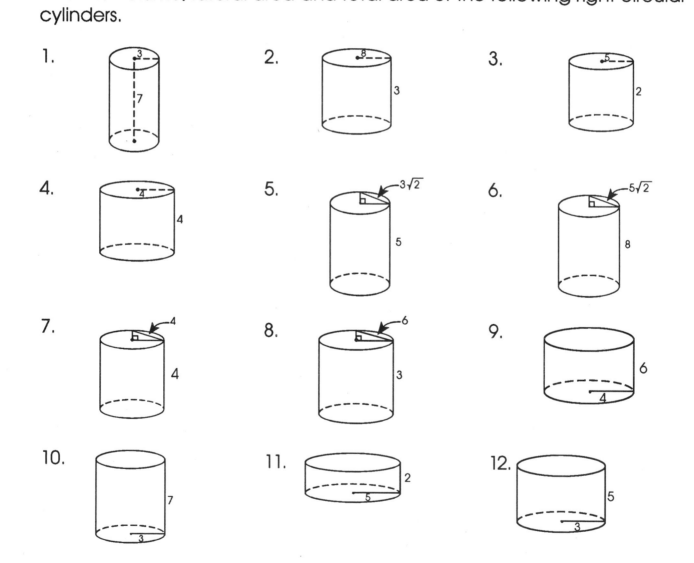

1. 3
    7

2. 8
    3

3. 5
    2

4. 4
    4

5. $3\sqrt{2}$
    5

6. $5\sqrt{2}$
    8

7. 4
    4

8. 6
    3

9. 6
    4

10. 7
    3

11. 2
    5

12. 5
    3

Pyramids

volume = $\frac{1}{3}$ · (area of base) · (height)

lateral area = $\frac{1}{2}$ · (perimeter) · (slant height)

total area = (lateral area) + (area of base)

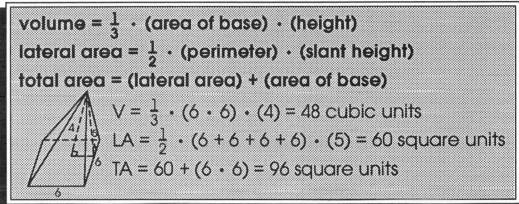

$V = \frac{1}{3} \cdot (6 \cdot 6) \cdot (4) = 48$ cubic units

$LA = \frac{1}{2} \cdot (6 + 6 + 6 + 6) \cdot (5) = 60$ square units

$TA = 60 + (6 \cdot 6) = 96$ square units

Find the volume, lateral area and total area of the following pyramids.

1.
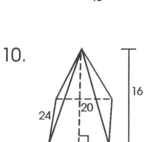

2.
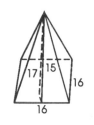

3.
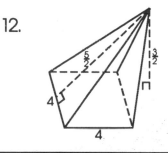

4.
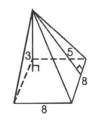

5.
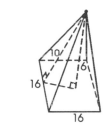

6.
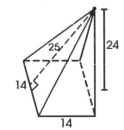

7.
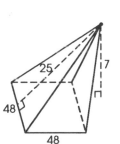

8.

9.
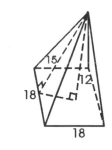

10.

11.

12.
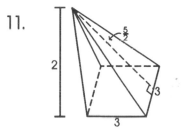

© MCMXCIV Instructional Fair, Inc.

Right Circular Cones

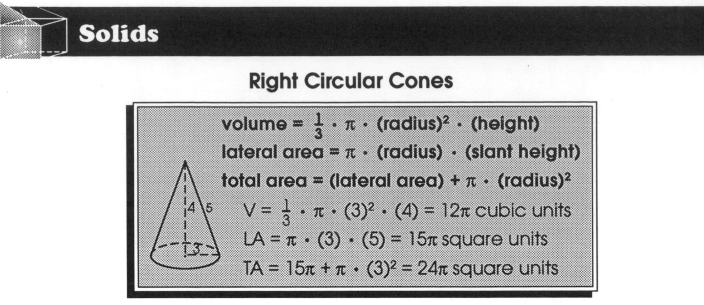

volume = $\frac{1}{3} \cdot \pi \cdot$ (radius)$^2 \cdot$ (height)

lateral area = $\pi \cdot$ (radius) $\cdot$ (slant height)

total area = (lateral area) + $\pi \cdot$ (radius)^2

$V = \frac{1}{3} \cdot \pi \cdot (3)^2 \cdot (4) = 12\pi$ cubic units

$LA = \pi \cdot (3) \cdot (5) = 15\pi$ square units

$TA = 15\pi + \pi \cdot (3)^2 = 24\pi$ square units

Find the volume, lateral area and total area of the following right circular cones.

1.

2.

3.

4.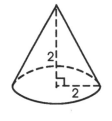

5.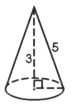

6.

7.

8.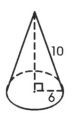

9.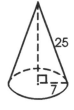

10.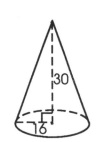

11.

12.

👉 **Keep in mind . . .**
If you work hard, then you begin to appreciate hard work.

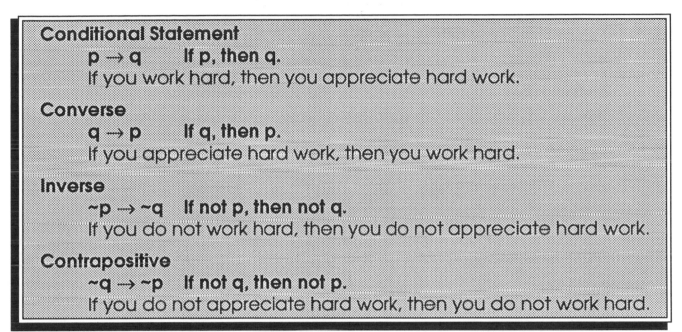

Conditional Statement
    p → q   If p, then q.
    If you work hard, then you appreciate hard work.

Converse
    q → p   If q, then p.
    If you appreciate hard work, then you work hard.

Inverse
    ~p → ~q   If not p, then not q.
    If you do not work hard, then you do not appreciate hard work.

Contrapositive
    ~q → ~p   If not q, then not p.
    If you do not appreciate hard work, then you do not work hard.

Write the converse, inverse and contrapositive of the given conditional statements.

1. If it is hot, then it is summer.

2. If I study, then I do well in school.

3. r → ~s

4. If it is Saturday, then I do not go to school.

5. ~r → s

6. If I do not go to sleep, then I will get tired.

7. ~r → ~s

8. If it is not raining, then the streets are not wet.

9. If Mike lives in Missouri, then he lives south of Canada.

10. r → s

11. If 5x = 20, then x = 4.

12. If AB + BC = AC, then B is between A and C.

Match the following geometrical terms and their "Just for Fun" definitions.

_____ 1. a broken angle

_____ 2. place where people are sent for committing crimes

_____ 3. a beast

_____ 4. a clever angle

_____ 5. an angle that is never wrong

_____ 6. used to tie up packages

_____ 7. what girls want to find at the beach

_____ 8. They voted "yes" on tractors for Cuba.

_____ 9. printer's dessert

_____ 10. a sharp weapon

_____ 11. what little acorns say when they grow up

_____ 12. the one in charge

_____ 13. what a person should do when it rains

_____ 14. a dead parrot

_____ 15. the way the poet wrote his love letters

a. line

b. pi

c. chord

d. prism

e. tangent

f. geometry

g. acute angle

h. polygon

i. rectangle

j. protractor

k. coincide

l. right angle

m. inverse

n. sphere

o. ruler

Logic Puzzle

Use the following statements to determine the names of the men playing each position on this baseball team.

1. Andy dislikes the catcher.
2. Ed's sister is engaged to the second baseman.
3. The center fielder is taller than the right fielder.
4. Harry and the third baseman live in the same building.
5. Paul and Allen each won $20.00 from the pitcher at pinochle.
6. Ed and the outfielders play poker during their free time.
7. The pitcher's wife is the third baseman's sister.
8. All the battery and infield, except Allen, Harry and Andy, are shorter than Sam. (battery = catcher and pitcher)
9. Paul, Andy and the shortstop lost $150.00 each at the racetrack.
10. Paul, Harry, Bill and the catcher took a trouncing from the second baseman at the pool.
11. Sam is undergoing a divorce suit.
12. The catcher and the third baseman each have two children.
13. Ed, Paul, Jerry, the right fielder and the center fielder are bachelors. The others are married.
14. The shortstop, the third baseman and Bill each cleaned up betting on the fight.
15. One of the outfielders is either Mike or Andy.
16. Jerry is taller than Bill. Mike is shorter then Bill. Each of them is heavier than the third baseman.

	C	P	SS	1st	2nd	3rd	LF	CF	RF
Mike									
Ed									
Harry									
Paul									
Allen									
Bill									
Jerry									
Sam									
Andy									

More Two Column Proofs

Complete the following proofs.

Given: $\overline{AB} \cong \overline{CB}$, $\overline{BD}$ bisects $\angle ABC$
Prove: $\overline{BD} \perp \overline{AC}$

Statements	Reasons
1. $\overline{AB} \cong \overline{CB}$, $\overline{BD}$ bisects $\angle ABC$	1. _____
2. $\angle ABE \cong \angle CBE$	2. _____
3. $\overline{BE} \cong \overline{BE}$	3. _____
4. $\triangle ABE \cong \triangle CBE$	4. _____
5. _____	5. CPCTC
6. _____	6. If 2 $\angle$s form a linear pair, they are supplementary.
7. $\angle BEA$ and $\angle BEC$ are right $\angle$s.	7. _____
8. $\overline{BD} \perp \overline{AC}$	8. _____

Given: $\overline{EI}$ bisects $\angle KEV$, $\overline{EI}$ bisects $\angle KIV$
Prove: $\overline{KE} \cong \overline{VE}$, $\overline{KI} \cong \overline{VI}$

Statements	Reasons
1. _____	1. Given
2. _____	2. If bisected, then two $\cong$ angles.
3. $\overline{EI} \cong \overline{EI}$	3. _____
4. $\triangle KEI \cong \triangle VEI$	4. _____
5. $\overline{KE} \cong \overline{VE}$, $\overline{KI} \cong \overline{VI}$	5. _____

Proofs

Given: B is the midpoint of $\overline{AC}$, D is the midpoint of $\overline{CE}$,
F is the midpoint of $\overline{AE}$

Prove: $\triangle CBD \cong \triangle BAF \cong \triangle DFE \cong \triangle FDB$

Statements	Reasons
1. _____	1. Given
2. $BF = \frac{1}{2}CE$, $BD = \frac{1}{2}AE$, $FD = \frac{1}{2}AC$	2. _____
3. _____	3. If midpoint, then two $\cong$ segments.
4. $AB = BC$, $AF = FE$, $CD = DE$	4. _____
5. _____	5. Definition of Between
6. $AB + AB = AC$, $CD + CD = CE$, $AF + AF = AE$	6. _____
7. _____	7. Combining Similar Terms
8. $AB = \frac{1}{2}AC$, $CD = \frac{1}{2}CE$, $AF = \frac{1}{2}AE$	8. _____
9. _____	9. Substitution
10. $\overline{AB} \cong \overline{FD}$, $\overline{CD} \cong \overline{BF}$, $\overline{AF} \cong \overline{BD}$	10. _____
11. _____	11. Substitution
12. $\triangle CBD \cong \triangle BAF \cong \triangle DFE \cong \triangle FDB$	12. _____

How are the four small triangles and the one large triangle related?

Given: MNOP is a rectangle; $\overline{MO}$ and $\overline{PN}$ are diagonals
Prove: $\triangle MQN \cong \triangle PQO$

Statements	Reasons
1. MNOP is a rectangle; $\overline{MO}$ and $\overline{PN}$ are diagonals	1. _____
2. $\overline{MN} \parallel \overline{PO}$, $\overline{MP} \parallel \overline{NO}$	2. _____
3. $\angle NMO \cong \angle POM$, $\angle MNP \cong \angle OPN$	3. _____
4. _____	4. In a rectangle, opposite sides are $\cong$.
5. $\triangle MQN \cong \triangle PQO$	5. _____

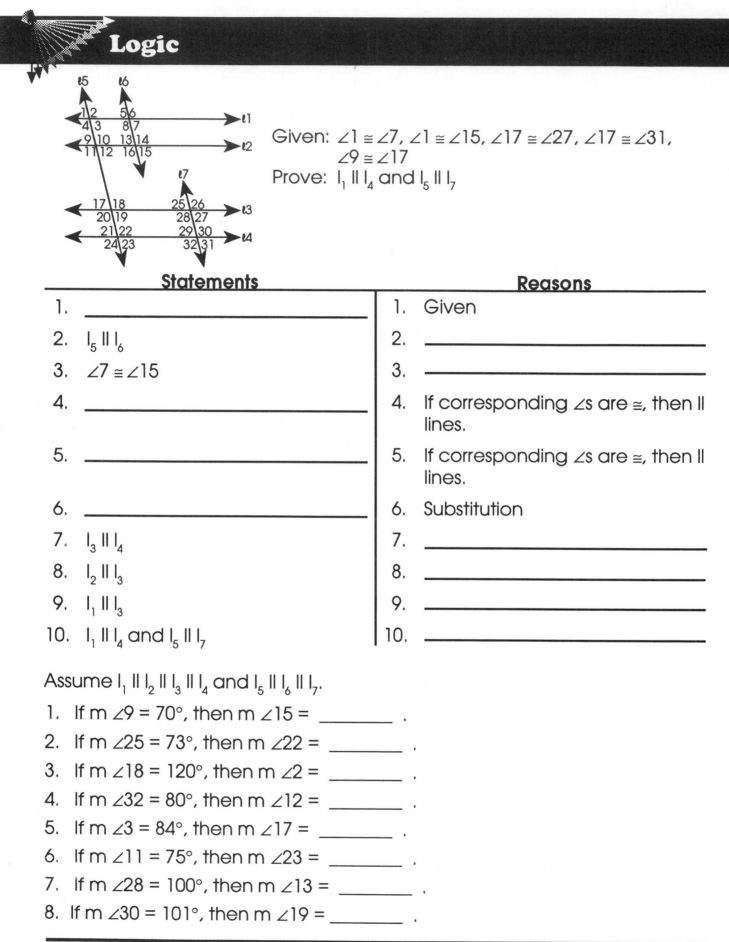

Given: $\angle 1 \cong \angle 7$, $\angle 1 \cong \angle 15$, $\angle 17 \cong \angle 27$, $\angle 17 \cong \angle 31$, $\angle 9 \cong \angle 17$

Prove: $l_1 \parallel l_4$ and $l_5 \parallel l_7$

Statements	Reasons
1. _____	1. Given
2. $l_5 \parallel l_6$	2. _____
3. $\angle 7 \cong \angle 15$	3. _____
4. _____	4. If corresponding $\angle$s are $\cong$, then $\parallel$ lines.
5. _____	5. If corresponding $\angle$s are $\cong$, then $\parallel$ lines.
6. _____	6. Substitution
7. $l_3 \parallel l_4$	7. _____
8. $l_2 \parallel l_3$	8. _____
9. $l_1 \parallel l_3$	9. _____
10. $l_1 \parallel l_4$ and $l_5 \parallel l_7$	10. _____

Assume $l_1 \parallel l_2 \parallel l_3 \parallel l_4$ and $l_5 \parallel l_6 \parallel l_7$.

1. If m $\angle 9 = 70°$, then m $\angle 15 =$ _____ .

2. If m $\angle 25 = 73°$, then m $\angle 22 =$ _____ .

3. If m $\angle 18 = 120°$, then m $\angle 2 =$ _____ .

4. If m $\angle 32 = 80°$, then m $\angle 12 =$ _____ .

5. If m $\angle 3 = 84°$, then m $\angle 17 =$ _____ .

6. If m $\angle 11 = 75°$, then m $\angle 23 =$ _____ .

7. If m $\angle 28 = 100°$, then m $\angle 13 =$ _____ .

8. If m $\angle 30 = 101°$, then m $\angle 19 =$ _____ .

☞ **Keep in mind . . .**
Challenges make you discover things about
yourself that you never really knew.

— Cicely Tyson

Radians

A radian is defined to be the measure of an angle which has its vertex at the center of a circle and which intercepts an arc whose length is equal to the radius.

The circumference and the radius are related by the equation $C = 2\pi r$. Thus, there are 2π radians in the complete circle. From this, we can obtain the following:

$$2\pi \text{ radians} = 360°$$

$$1 \text{ radian} = \frac{180°}{\pi} \doteq 57.3°$$

$$1° = \frac{\pi}{180°} \text{ radians} \doteq 0.01745 \text{ radians}$$

Convert the following angle measures from degrees to radians or from radians to degrees.

(degrees $\times \frac{\pi}{180}$ = radians, radians $\times \frac{180}{\pi}$ = degrees).

1. 180°

2. $\frac{\pi}{2}$ radians

3. 27°

4. 45°

5. 6.2832 radians

6. 4.7 radians

7. 2 radians

8. 90°

9. .05235 radians

10. $\frac{\pi}{3}$ radians

11. 1.0472 radians

12. 36°

Application of Radians

The length of an arc is directly proportional to the size of the central angle. In other words, the greater the angle, the greater the arc. Since there are 2π radians in the complete circle, then the length of the arc can be expressed as $S = \theta r$, where θ is the measure of the central angle and S is the length of the arc.

$$\theta = \frac{\pi}{2} \text{ rad., } r = 2 \qquad \theta = 45°, r = 8$$

$$S = \theta r \qquad\qquad \theta = 45° \times \frac{\pi}{180°} = \frac{\pi}{4} \text{ radians}$$

$$= \left(\frac{\pi}{2}\right)(2) \qquad\qquad S = \left(\frac{\pi}{4}\right)(8)$$

$$S = \pi \text{ units} \qquad\qquad S = 2\pi \text{ units}$$

Complete the following table.

	θ	r	S
1.	180°	1	
2.		1	3π
3.	$\frac{\pi}{4}$ rad.	5	
4.		2	4π
5.	2 rad.	3	
6.	$\frac{\pi}{2}$ rad.		2π
7.	45°	4	
8.	3 rad.		4
9.	1°	1	
10.	270°	6	

Special Graphing

Keep in mind . . .
Friends x Laughter = Lots of Joy

Polar Coordinates

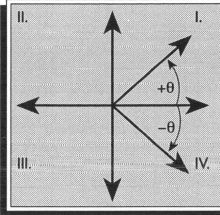

II.   I.

III.   IV.

A point in a plane can also be given a unique representation by using polar coordinates. A positive angle is generated by the counterclockwise rotation of the positive x-axis about the origin. Similarly, a negative angle is generated by the clockwise rotation of the positive x-axis about the origin. A point can be named by giving the distance from the origin and the measure of the angle in the form (r, θ).

Graph the following polar coordinates.

1. $(2, \frac{\pi}{2})$

2. $(3, \pi)$

3. $(1, 45°)$

4. $(5, -\frac{\pi}{2})$

5. $(4, 270°)$

6. $(2, -\frac{3}{2}\pi)$

7. $(2, 540°)$

8. $(2, 2\pi)$

In which quadrant would you expect to find the following points?

9. $(2, \frac{\pi}{4})$

10. $(4, \frac{3}{4}\pi)$

11. $(3, -\frac{\pi}{3})$

12. $(1, \pi)$

13. $(2, \frac{15}{3}\pi)$

14. $(4, -\frac{4\pi}{3})$

15. $(3, -700°)$

16. $(-1, 45°)$

Special Graphing

Converting Polar and Rectangular Coordinates

The equations below can be used to convert between polar coordinates and rectangular coordinates.

$$x = r \cdot \cos \theta \qquad \tan \theta = \frac{y}{x}$$

$$y = r \cdot \sin \theta \qquad r = \sqrt{x^2 + y^2}$$

Find the polar coordinates corresponding to the following rectangular coordinates.

1. $(2, 0)$ 3. $(0, 5)$ 5. $(-2, -2)$

2. $(3, 4)$ 4. $(4, 4)$ 6. $(-6, 8)$

Find the rectangular coordinates corresponding to the following polar coordinates.

7. $(2, \frac{\pi}{2})$ 9. $(4, \pi)$ 11. $(5, \frac{\pi}{3})$

8. $(3, -\frac{\pi}{4})$ 10. $(2, 0)$ 12. $(\sqrt{2}, \frac{\pi}{4})$

Express the following equations in polar notation.

13. $x = 2$ 14. $x^2 + y^2 = 4$ 15. $y = 2x + 1$

16. $y = 4$ 17. $x^2 + y^2 - 3 = 13$ 18. $y = 3x$

Express the following equations in rectangular notation.

19. $r = 5$ 20. $r = 3 \csc \theta$ 21. $\tan \theta = 3$

22. $r = 2 \sec \theta$ 23. $r = 7$ 24. $\tan \theta = 2$

Graphs of Sine and Cosine Functions

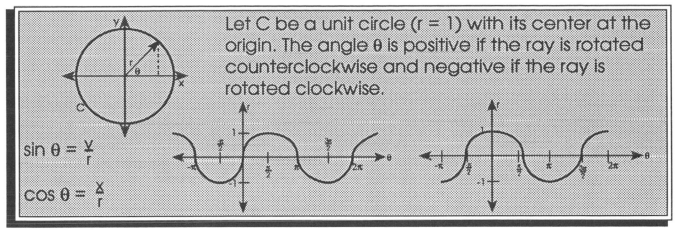

Let C be a unit circle (r = 1) with its center at the origin. The angle θ is positive if the ray is rotated counterclockwise and negative if the ray is rotated clockwise.

$\sin \theta = \dfrac{y}{r}$

$\cos \theta = \dfrac{x}{r}$

Complete the following table of values.

y = sin x

	x	y
1.	0	____
2.	$\frac{\pi}{2}$	____
3.	π	____
4.	$\frac{3\pi}{2}$	____
5.	2π	____
6.	$-\frac{\pi}{2}$	____

y = cos x

	x	y
7.	0	____
8.	$\frac{\pi}{2}$	____
9.	π	____
10.	$\frac{3\pi}{2}$	____
11.	2π	____
12.	$-\frac{\pi}{2}$	____

13. What is the value of y when $\sin \theta = 0$?

14. At what values of θ is $\sin \theta = 0$?

15. What is the greatest value $\sin \theta$ may assume?

16. Name two values of θ that make $\sin \theta$ a maximum.

17. When Is $\cos \theta = 0$?

18. What range of values may $\cos \theta$ assume?

19. What is the value of $\sin \theta$ when θ = 90°?

20. θ = π radian. What is $\sin \theta$? What is $\cos \theta$?

21. θ = -4π radian. What is $\sin \theta$? What is $\cos \theta$?

22. θ = $\frac{3\pi}{2}$ radian $\cos \theta = \frac{x}{r}$ What is the value of x?

Some Useful Postulates and Theorems

Angle Addition Postulate (AAP) If a point X lies in the interior of ∠ABC, then
m ∠ABC = m ∠ABX + m ∠XBC.

Supplement Postulate If two angles form a linear pair, then these two angles are supplementary.

Side-Angle-Side Postulate (SAS) If two sides and the included angle of one triangle are congruent to the corresponding parts of another triangle, then the two triangles are congruent.

Angle-Side-Angle Postulate (ASA) If two angles and the included side of one triangle are congruent to the corresponding parts of another triangle, then the two triangles are congruent.

Hypotenuse-Leg Postulate (HL) If the hypotenuse and one leg of a right triangle are congruent to the corresponding parts of another right triangle, then the two triangles are congruent.

Parallel Postulate Given a line l and a point p not on l there is exactly one line parallel to l through p.

Congruence Postulate Given two congruent triangles, the triangular regions they determine have the same area.

Angle-Angle Postulate (AA) If two angles of one triangle are congruent to the corresponding angles of another triangle, then the two angles are similar.

Area Addition Postulate If two or more polygonal regions intersect in only points, segments or not at all, then the area of their union is the sum of their individual areas.

Arc Addition Postulate If the arcs $\overarc{AB}$ and $\overarc{BC}$ of a circle intersect in the single point B, then m $\overarc{AB}$ + m $\overarc{BC}$ = m $\overarc{ABC}$

Addition Property of Equality (APOE) If two sides of an equation are equal, then if an equal quantity is added to both sides the equation will still be equal.

Area

triangle = $\frac{1}{2}$ · (base) · (height)

rectangle = (base) · (height)

square = (side)^2

parallelogram = (base) · (height)

trapezoid = $\frac{1}{2}$ · (height) · (sum of bases)

circle = π · (radius)^2

Volume

pyramid = $\frac{1}{3}$ · (area of base) · (height)

cone = $\frac{1}{3}$ · π · (radius)^2 · (height)

cylinder = π · (radius)^2 · (height)

prism = (area of base) · (height)

sphere = $\frac{4}{3}$ · π · (radius)^3

Some Useful Definitions and Theorems

Between   If A is on $\overleftrightarrow{BC}$, then A is between B and C if and only if BA + AC = BC.

Bisect   A bisects $\overline{BC}$ if A is the midpoint of $\overline{BC}$.

Complementary Angles   Two angles are complementary if the sum of their measures is 90°.

CPCTC   Corresponding parts of congruent triangles are congruent.

Midpoint   A is the midpoint of $\overline{BC}$ if $\overline{BA} \cong \overline{AC}$

Pythagorean Theorem $a^2 + b^2 = c^2$

Reflexive Property   Given a segment, angle, triangle, etc. it is congruent to itself.

Right Angle   A right angle is one that has a measure of 90°.

Right Triangle   A right triangle is one that contains a right angle.

Substitution   Given items a, b and c, if a = b and a = c, then b = c.

Supplementary Angles   Two angles are supplementary if the sum of their measures is 180°.

Vertical Angles   If the sides of two angles form opposite rays, then the angles are vertical angles.

- Vertical angles are congruent.
- If congruent, then equal.
- If equal, then congruent.
- Perpendicular lines form right angles.
- If parallel lines, then (corresponding, alternate interior, alternate exterior) angles are congruent.
- If parallel lines, then (same side interior, same side exterior) angles are supplementary.
- If (corresponding, alternate interior, alternate exterior) angles are congruent, then lines are parallel.
- If (same side interior, same side exterior) angles are supplementary, then lines are parallel.
- Two lines parallel to a third are parallel.
- In a triangle, angles opposite congruent sides are congruent.
- In a triangle, sides opposite congruent angles are congruent.
- Complements of congruent angles are congruent.
- Supplements of congruent angles are congruent.
- The two acute angles of a right triangle are complementary.
- The sum of the angles of a triangle is 180°.
- In a triangle, if two angles are not congruent, then the larger side is opposite the larger angle.
- In a triangle, an exterior angle is greater than either remote interior angle.

Hinge Theorem: Given that two sides of one triangle are congruent to two sides of a second triangle and the included angle of the first triangle is smaller than the included angle of the second triangle, then the third side of the first triangle is smaller than the third side of the second triangle.

Answer Key

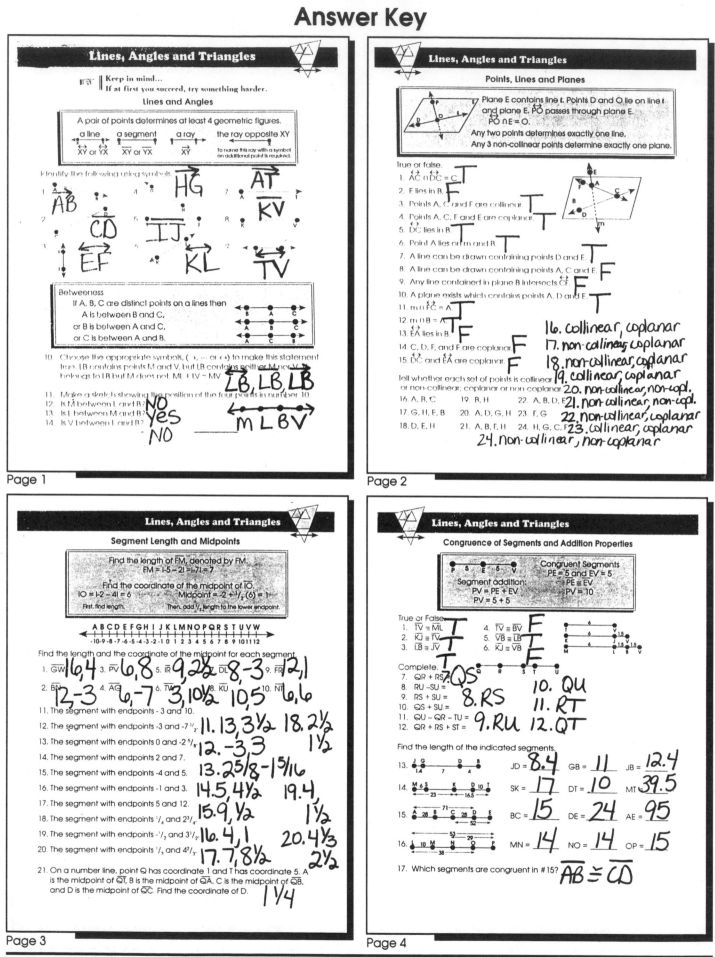

Page 1

Lines, Angles and Triangles

Keep in mind...
If at first you succeed, try something harder.

Lines and Angles

A pair of points determines at least 4 geometric figures.

a line	a segment	a ray	the ray opposite XY
$\overleftrightarrow{XY}$ or $\overleftrightarrow{YX}$	$\overline{XY}$ or $\overline{YX}$	$\overrightarrow{XY}$	To name this ray with a symbol an additional point is required.

Identify the following using symbols.

1. $\overrightarrow{AB}$ 4. $\overrightarrow{HG}$ 7. $\overrightarrow{AT}$, $\overline{KV}$
2. $\overline{CD}$ 5. $\overline{IJ}$ 8. $\overleftrightarrow{TV}$
3. $\updownarrow \overline{EF}$ 6. $\overrightarrow{KL}$

Betweenness
If A, B, C are distinct points on a lines then
A is between B and C,
or B is between A and C,
or C is between A and B.

10. Choose the appropriate symbols, (∈, ⊄ or ⊂) to make this statement true. LB contains points M and V, but LB contains neither M nor V ... belongs to LB but M does not. ML + LV = MV

$\angle B$, LB, LB

11. Make a sketch showing the position of the four points in number 10.
12. Is M between L and B? NO
13. Is L between M and B? YES
14. Is V between L and B? NO

M L B V

Page 2

Lines, Angles and Triangles

Points, Lines and Planes

Plane E contains line ℓ. Points D and O lie on line ℓ and plane E. $\overline{PO}$ passes through plane E.
$\overline{PO} \cap E = O$.
Any two points determines exactly one line.
Any 3 non-collinear points determine exactly one plane.

True or false.
1. $\overleftrightarrow{AC} \cap \overleftrightarrow{DC} = C$ T
2. E lies in B.   F
3. Points A, C and E are collinear   T
4. Points A, C, F and E are coplanar.   T
5. $\overleftrightarrow{DC}$ lies in B.   T
6. Point A lies on m and B.   T
7. A line can be drawn containing points D and E.   T
8. A line can be drawn containing points A, C and E.   F
9. Any line contained in plane B intersects $\overleftrightarrow{CF}$.   F
10. A plane exists which contains points A, D and E.   T
11. $m \cap \overrightarrow{PC} = A$.   T
12. $m \cap B = A$.   T
13. $\overleftrightarrow{EA}$ lies in B.   F
14. C, D, F and F are coplanar.   F
15. $\overleftrightarrow{DC}$ and $\overleftrightarrow{EA}$ are coplanar.   F

Tell whether each set of points is collinear or non-collinear; coplanar or non-coplanar.
16. A, B, C   19. B, H   22. A, B, D
17. G, H, E, B   20. A, D, G, H   23. F, G
18. D, E, H   21. A, B, F, H   24. H, G, C, F

16. collinear, coplanar
17. non-collinear, coplanar
18. non-collinear, coplanar
19. collinear, coplanar
20. non-collinear, non-copl.
21. non-collinear, non-copl.
22. non-collinear, coplanar
23. collinear, coplanar
24. non-collinear, non-coplanar

Page 3

Lines, Angles and Triangles

Segment Length and Midpoints

Find the length of $\overline{FM}$, denoted by FM.
FM = |-5 − 2| = |-7| = 7
Find the coordinate of the midpoint of $\overline{IO}$.
IO = |-2 − 4| = 6   Midpoint = −2 + ½(6) = 1
First, find length.   Then, add ½ length to the lower endpoint.

A B C D E F G H I J K L M N O P Q R S T U V W
-10-9-8-7-6-5-4-3-2-1 0 1 2 3 4 5 6 7 8 9 10 11 12

Find the length and the coordinate of the midpoint for each segment.
1. $\overline{GW}$ 16, 4   3. $\overline{PV}$ 6, 8   5. $\overline{IR}$ 9, 2½   7. $\overline{DL}$ 8, -3   9. $\overline{FR}$ 12, 1
2. $\overline{BN}$ 12, -3   4. $\overline{AG}$ 6, -7   6. $\overline{TW}$ 3, 10½   8. $\overline{KU}$ 10, 5   10. $\overline{NT}$ 6, 6

11. The segment with endpoints -3 and 10.   11. 13, 3½   18. 2½
12. The segment with endpoints -3 and -7½.   12. -3, 3   1½
13. The segment with endpoints 0 and -2⅝.   13. 2⅝, -1⁵⁄₁₆
14. The segment with endpoints 2 and 7.   14. 5, 4½   19. 4,
15. The segment with endpoints -4 and 5.
16. The segment with endpoints -1 and 3.   15. 9, ½   1½
17. The segment with endpoints 5 and 12.   16. 4, 1   20. 4⅓
18. The segment with endpoints ¼ and 2¾.   17. 7, 8½   2½
19. The segment with endpoints -½ and 3½.
20. The segment with endpoints ⅓ and 4⅔.

21. On a number line, point Q has coordinate 1 and T has coordinate 5. A is the midpoint of $\overline{QT}$, B is the midpoint of $\overline{QA}$, C is the midpoint of $\overline{QB}$, and D is the midpoint of $\overline{QC}$. Find the coordinate of D.   1¼

Page 4

Lines, Angles and Triangles

Congruence of Segments and Addition Properties

P 5 E 5 V	Congruent Segments
Segment addition:	PE = 5 and EV = 5
PV = PE + EV	PE ≅ EV
PV = 5 + 5	PV = 10

True or False.
1. $\overline{TV} \cong \overline{ML}$ T   4. $\overline{TV} \cong \overline{BV}$ F
2. $\overline{KJ} \cong \overline{TV}$ T   5. $\overline{VB} \cong \overline{LB}$ F
3. $\overline{LB} \cong \overline{JV}$ T   6. $\overline{KJ} \cong \overline{VB}$ F

Complete.
7. QR + RS =   7. QS
8. RU − SU =   8. RS
9. RS + SU =   9. RU
10. QS + SU =   10. QU
11. QU − QR − TU =   11. RT
12. QR + RS + ST =   12. QT

Find the length of the indicated segments.
13. JD = 8.4   GB = 11   JB = 12.4
14. SK = 17   DT = 10   MT = 39.5
15. BC = 15   DE = 24   AE = 95
16. MN = 14   NO = 14   OP = 15

17. Which segments are congruent in #15? $\overline{AB} \cong \overline{CD}$

Answer Key

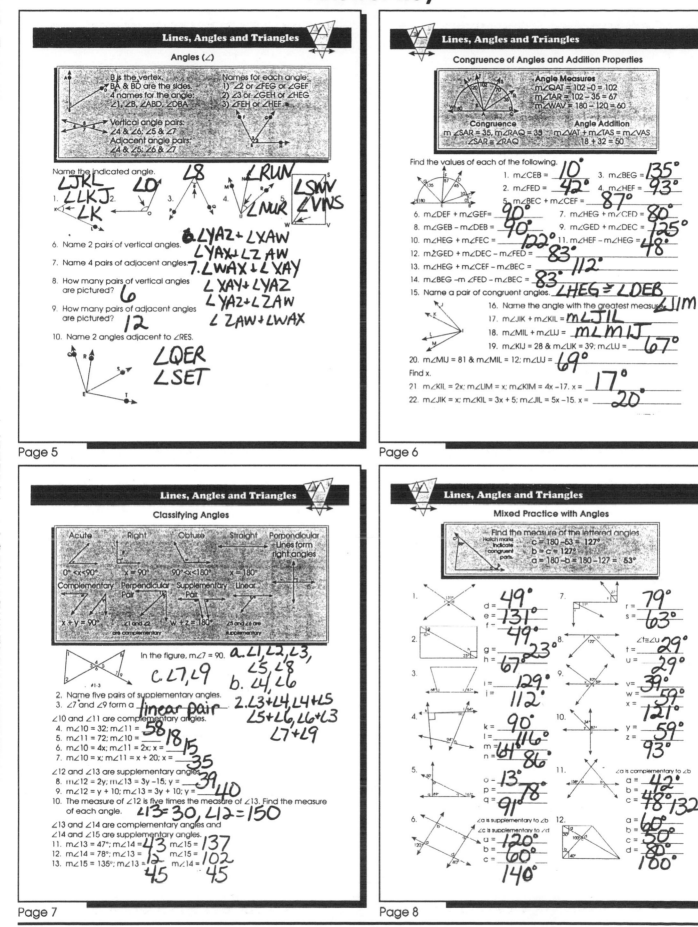

Lines, Angles and Triangles
Angles (∠)

B is the vertex,
BA & BD are the sides.
4 names for the angle:
∠1, ∠B, ∠ABD, ∠DBA

Names for each angle:
1) ∠2 or ∠FEG or ∠GEF
2) ∠3 or ∠GEH or ∠HEG
3) ∠FEH or ∠HEF

Vertical angle pairs:
∠4 & ∠6; ∠5 & ∠7
Adjacent angle pairs:
∠4 & ∠5; ∠6 & ∠7

Name the indicated angle.
1. ∠JKL ∠LKJ ∠K
2. ∠O
3. ∠8
4. ∠RUN ∠NUR ∠RUN ∠SWV ∠VNS

6. Name 2 pairs of vertical angles. ∠YAZ + ∠XAW ∠YAX ∠ZAW

7. Name 4 pairs of adjacent angles. 7. ∠WAX + ∠XAY ∠XAY + ∠YAZ ∠YAZ + ∠ZAW ∠ZAW + ∠WAX

8. How many pairs of vertical angles are pictured? 6

9. How many pairs of adjacent angles are pictured? 12

10. Name 2 angles adjacent to ∠RES. ∠QER ∠SET

Page 5

Lines, Angles and Triangles
Congruence of Angles and Addition Properties

Angle Measures
m∠QAT = 102 – 0 = 102
m∠TAR = 102 – 35 = 67
m∠WAV = 180 – 120 = 60

Congruence
m∠SAR = 35, m∠RAQ = 35
∠SAR ≅ ∠RAQ

Angle Addition
m∠VAT + m∠TAS = m∠VAS
18 + 32 = 50

Find the values of each of the following.
1. m∠CEB = 10°
2. m∠FED = 42°
3. m∠BEG = 135°
4. m∠HEF = 93°
5. m∠BEC + m∠CEF = 87°
6. m∠DEF + m∠GEF = 90°
7. m∠HEG + m∠CED = 80°
8. m∠GEB – m∠DEB = 90°
9. m∠GED + m∠DEC = 125°
10. m∠HEG + m∠FEC = 122°
11. m∠HEF – m∠HEG = 48°
12. m∠GED + m∠DEC – m∠FED = 83°
13. m∠HEG + m∠CEF – m∠BEC = 112°
14. m∠BEG – m∠FED – m∠BEC = 83°
15. Name a pair of congruent angles. ∠HEG ≅ ∠DEB
16. Name the angle with the greatest measure. ∠JIM
17. m∠JIK + m∠KIL = m∠JIL
18. m∠MIL + m∠LIJ = m∠MIJ
19. m∠KIJ = 28 & m∠LIK = 39; m∠LIJ = 67°
20. m∠MIJ = 81 & m∠MIL = 12; m∠LIJ = 69°

Find x.
21. m∠KIL = 2x; m∠LIM = x; m∠KIM = 4x – 17. x = 17°
22. m∠JIK = x; m∠KIL = 3x + 5; m∠JIL = 5x – 15. x = 20

Page 6

Lines, Angles and Triangles
Classifying Angles

Acute
0° < x < 90°

Right
x = 90°

Obtuse
90° < x < 180°

Straight
x = 180°

Perpendicular
Lines form right angles

Complementary
x + y = 90°

Perpendicular Pair
∠1 and ∠2 are complementary

Supplementary Pair
w + z = 180°

Linear
∠5 and ∠6 are supplementary

In the figure, m∠7 = 90. a. ∠1, ∠2, ∠3, ∠5, ∠8 c. ∠7, ∠9 b. ∠4, ∠6

2. Name five pairs of supplementary angles. 2. ∠3 + ∠4, ∠4 + ∠5, ∠5 + ∠6, ∠6 + ∠3, ∠7 + ∠9
3. ∠7 and ∠9 form a linear pair
∠10 and ∠11 are complementary angles.
4. m∠10 = 32; m∠11 = 58
5. m∠11 = 72; m∠10 = 18
6. m∠10 = 4x; m∠11 = 2x; x = 15
7. m∠10 = x; m∠11 = x + 20; x = 35
∠12 and ∠13 are supplementary angles.
8. m∠12 = 2y; m∠13 = 3y –15; y = 39
9. m∠12 = y + 10; m∠13 = 3y + 10; y = 40
10. The measure of ∠12 is five times the measure of ∠13. Find the measure of each angle. ∠13 = 30, ∠12 = 150
∠13 and ∠14 are complementary angles and
∠14 and ∠15 are supplementary angles.
11. m∠13 = 47°; m∠14 = 43 m∠15 = 137
12. m∠14 = 78°; m∠13 = 12 m∠15 = 102
13. m∠15 = 135°; m∠13 = 45 m∠14 = 45

Page 7

Lines, Angles and Triangles
Mixed Practice with Angles

Find the measure of the lettered angles.
Hatch marks indicate congruent parts.
c = 180 – 53 = 127°
b = c = 127°
a = 180 – b = 180 – 127 = 53°

1. d = 49° e = 131° f =
2. g = 23° h = 67° (49°)
3. i = 129° j = 112°
4. k = 90° l = 116° m = 64° n = 86°
5. o = 13° p = 78° q = 91°
6. ∠a is supplementary to ∠b ∠c is supplementary to ∠d a = 120° b = 60° c = 140°
7. r = 79° s = 63°
8. ∠t ≅ ∠u t = 29° u = 29°
9. v = 39° w = 59° x = 121°
10. y = 59° z = 93°
11. ∠a is complementary to ∠b a = 42° b = 48° c = 132°
12. a = 60° b = 50° c = 80° d = 100°

Page 8

Answer Key

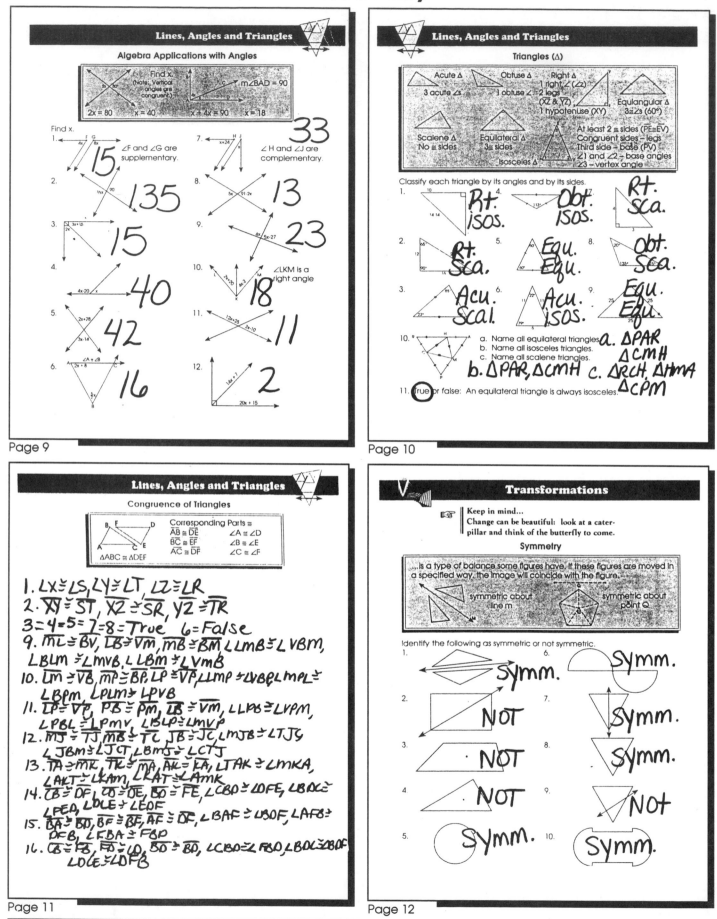

Answer Key

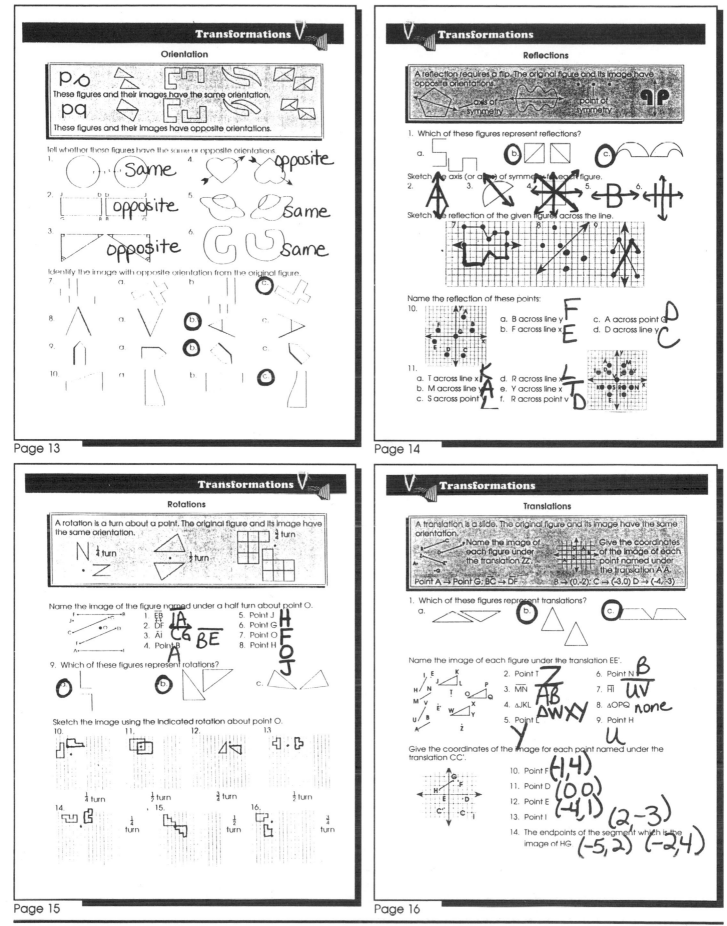

Page 13

Transformations
Orientation

These figures and their images have the same orientation.

These figures and their images have opposite orientations.

Tell whether these figures have the same or opposite orientations.

1. same
2. opposite
3. opposite
4. opposite
5. same
6. same

Identify the image with opposite orientation from the original figure.

7. c
8. b
9. b
10. c

Page 14

Transformations
Reflections

A reflection requires a flip. The original figure and its image have opposite orientations.

axis of symmetry   point of symmetry

1. Which of these figures represent reflections?
   b. c.

2. Sketch the axis (or axes) of symmetry for each figure.

Sketch the reflection of the given figures across the line.

Name the reflection of these points:
10.
   a. B across line y   F
   b. F across line x   E
   c. A across point G   D
   d. D across line y   C

11.
   a. T across line x   K
   b. M across line y   A
   c. S across point p   L
   d. R across line x   L
   e. Y across line x   T
   f. R across point v   D

Page 15

Transformations
Rotations

A rotation is a turn about a point. The original figure and its image have the same orientation.

N 1/4 turn   Z   1/2 turn   3/4 turn

Name the image of the figure named under a half turn about point O.

1. EB   IA
2. DF   CG
3. AI   A   BE
4. Point B
5. Point J   H
6. Point G   F
7. Point O   O
8. Point H   J

9. Which of these figures represent rotations?
   b.

Sketch the image using the indicated rotation about point O.

10. 1/4 turn
11. 1/2 turn
12. 3/4 turn
13. 1/2 turn
14. 1/4 turn
15. 1/2 turn
16. 3/4 turn

Page 16

Transformations
Translations

A translation is a slide. The original figure and its image have the same orientation.

Name the image of each figure under the translation ZZ'.

Give the coordinates of the image of each point named under the translation A'A.

Point A → Point G; BC → DF   B → (0,-2); C → (-3,0) D → (-4,-3)

1. Which of these figures represent translations?
   a.   b.   c.

Name the image of each figure under the translation EE'.
2. Point T   Z
3. MN   AB
4. ΔJKL   ΔWXY
5. Point L   Y
6. Point N   B
7. FI   UV
8. ΔOPQ   none
9. Point H   U

Give the coordinates of the image for each point named under the translation CC'.

10. Point F   (-1,4)
11. Point D   (0,0)
12. Point E   (-4,1)
13. Point I   (2,-3)
14. The endpoints of the segment which is the image of HG   (-5,2) (-2,4)

Page 17

Mixed Practice with Transformations

A C E H O R S T W X Z

1-5. Sketch each letter which is point symmetric and mark the point of symmetry.

H · O S X Z

6-13. Sketch each letter that is line symmetric and draw all lines of symmetry.

A C E H O S W X

Each of these figures have been moved in a series of basic motions. Name the motion indicated by the lettered arrow.

14.
a. rot.
b. ref.
c. trans.

15.
a. rot.
b. trans.
c. rot.

16.
a. ref.
b. ref.
c. rot.
d. trans.

Tell which single basic motion will make these figures coincide?

17. rot.

18. ref.

19. ref.

20. trans.

21. ref.

22. rot.

Page 18

Transformations with Dots & Graphs

1. Draw the reflection of △MSD around line t and label it M'S'D'; draw one half turn rotation around point P and label it M'S'D''.

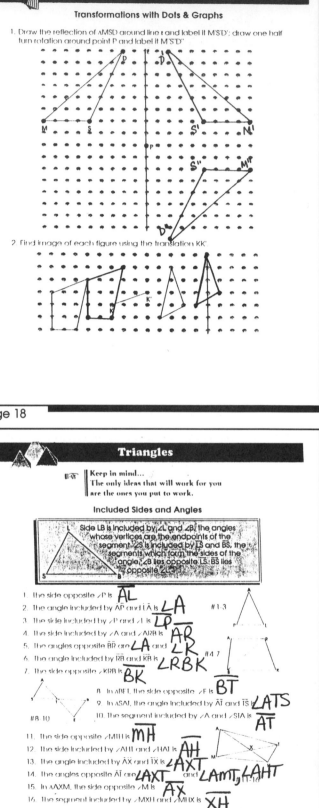

2. Find image of each figure using the translation KK'.

Page 19

More Transformations with Dots & Graphs

For each point named, give its reflection across the
a. x-axis   b. origin   c. y-axis

1. (2,-3)   (2, 3) (-3, 2) (-2, -3)
2. (-4,-1)   (-4, 1) (1, 4) (4, -1)
3. (5,5)   (5, -5) (-5, -5) (-5, 5)
4. (-1,2)   (-1, -2) (2, -1) (1, 2)

5. Find the image of △TDV:
a. for the rotation of a $\frac{1}{4}$ turn counterclockwise.
b. for the translation AA'.
c. for the reflection across O.

6. Find the image of QRST:
a. for the reflection across the x-axis.
b. for the rotation about 0 of a $\frac{1}{2}$ turn clockwise.
c. for the translation of BB'.

7. Find the image of △CAT:
a. for the reflection across the y-axis.
b. for the translation XX'.
c. for the rotation about O of a $\frac{3}{4}$ turn clockwise.

Page 20

Keep in mind...
The only ideas that will work for you are the ones you put to work.

Included Sides and Angles

Side LB is included by ∠L and ∠B; the angles whose vertices are the endpoints of the segment. ∠S is included by LS and BS, the segments which form the sides of the angle. ∠B lies opposite LS; BS lies opposite ∠L.

1. The side opposite ∠P is $\overline{AL}$
2. The angle included by AP and LA is ∠A
3. The side included by ∠P and ∠L is $\overline{LP}$
4. The side included by ∠A and ∠ARB is $\overline{AR}$
5. The angles opposite $\overline{BR}$ are ∠A and ∠R
6. The angle included by $\overline{RB}$ and $\overline{KB}$ is ∠RBK
7. The side opposite ∠KRB is $\overline{BK}$
8. In △BET, the side opposite ∠E is $\overline{BT}$
9. In △SAT, the angle included by $\overline{AT}$ and $\overline{TS}$ is ∠ATS
10. The segment included by ∠A and ∠SIA is $\overline{AT}$
11. The side opposite ∠MHI is $\overline{MH}$
12. The side included by ∠AHI and ∠HAI is $\overline{AH}$
13. The angle included by $\overline{AX}$ and $\overline{TX}$ is ∠AXT
14. The angles opposite $\overline{AT}$ are ∠AXT and ∠AMT, ∠AHT
15. In △AXM, the side opposite ∠M is $\overline{AX}$
16. The segment included by ∠MXH and ∠MHX is $\overline{XH}$

Answer Key

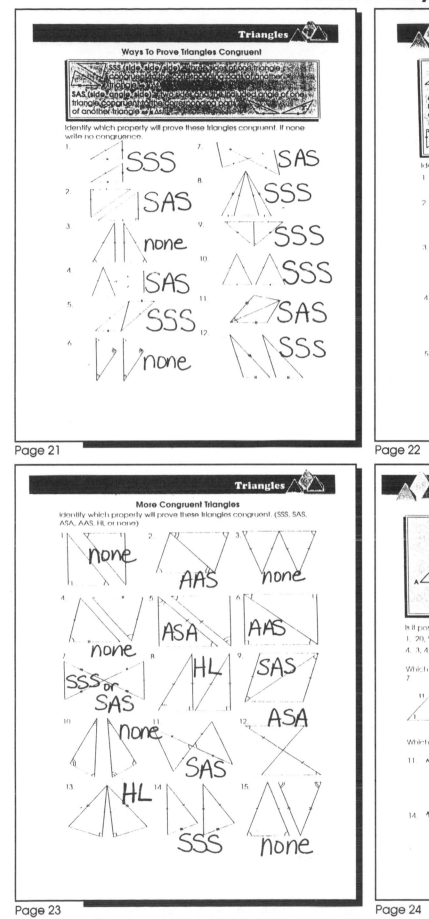

Page 21

Triangles
Ways To Prove Triangles Congruent

SSS (side, side, side) = three sides of one triangle congruent to the corresponding parts of another triangle ≅ ≅ Δs.

SAS (side, angle, side) = two sides and the included angle of one triangle congruent to the corresponding parts of another triangle ≅ ≅ Δs.

Identify which property will prove these triangles congruent. If none write no congruence.

1. SSS
2. SAS
3. none
4. SAS
5. SSS
6. none
7. SAS
8. SSS
9. SSS
10. SSS
11. SAS
12. SSS

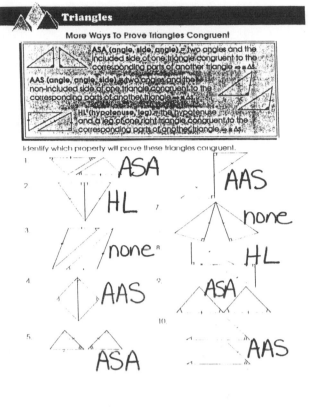

Page 22

Triangles
More Ways To Prove Triangles Congruent

ASA (angle, side, angle) = two angles and the included side of one triangle congruent to the corresponding parts of another triangle ≅ ≅ Δs.

AAS (angle, angle, side) = two angles and the non-included side of one triangle congruent to the corresponding parts of another triangle ≅ ≅ Δs.

HL (hypotenuse, leg) = the hypotenuse and a leg of one right triangle congruent to the corresponding parts of another triangle ≅ ≅ Δs.

Identify which property will prove these triangles congruent.

1. ASA
2. HL
3. none
4. AAS
5. ASA
6. AAS
7. none
8. HL
9. ASA
10. AAS

Page 23

Triangles
More Congruent Triangles

Identify which property will prove these triangles congruent. (SSS, SAS, ASA, AAS, HL or none)

1. none
2. AAS
3. none
4. none
5. ASA
6. AAS
7. SSS or SAS
8. HL
9. SAS
10. none
11. SAS
12. ASA
13. HL
14. SSS
15. none

Page 24

Triangles
Triangle Inequality Properties

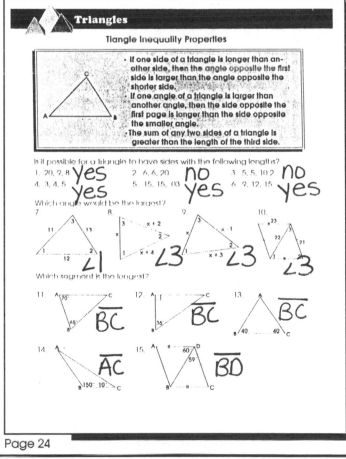

- If one side of a triangle is longer than another side, then the angle opposite the first side is larger than the angle opposite the shorter side.
- If one angle of a triangle is larger than another angle, then the side opposite the first page is longer than the side opposite the smaller angle.
- The sum of any two sides of a triangle is greater than the length of the third side.

Is it possible for a triangle to have sides with the following lengths?

1. 20, 9, 8   yes
2. 6, 6, 20   no
3. 5, 5, 10.2   no
4. 3, 4, 5   yes
5. 15, 15, .03   yes
6. 9, 12, 15   yes

Which angle would be the largest?

7. ∠1
8. ∠3
9. ∠3
10. ∠3

Which segment is the longest?

11. $\overline{BC}$
12. $\overline{BC}$
13. $\overline{BC}$
14. $\overline{AC}$
15. $\overline{BD}$

Answer Key

Proofs in Two Column Form

Given: D is the midpoint of $\overline{AC}$ and $\overline{AB} \cong \overline{BC}$.
Prove: $\triangle ABD \cong \triangle CBD$

Statements	Reasons
1. D is the midpoint of $\overline{AC}$	1. Given
2. $\overline{AD} \cong \overline{CD}$	2. Definition of Midpoint
3. $\overline{AB} \cong \overline{CB}$	3. Given
4. $\overline{BD} \cong \overline{BD}$	4. Reflexive Property
5. $\triangle ABD \cong \triangle CBD$	5. SSS

Complete the following proofs.

Given: $\overline{GH}$ and $\overline{IJ}$ bisect each other.
Prove: $\triangle FGI \cong \triangle JHI$

Statements	Reasons
1. $\overline{GH}$ and $\overline{IJ}$ bisect each other	1. **Given**
2. $\overline{GI} \cong \overline{HI}$, $\overline{FI} \cong \overline{JI}$	2. Definition of Bisect
3. $\angle GIF \cong \angle HIJ$	3. Vertical angles are congruent
4. $\triangle FGI \cong \triangle JHI$	4. **SAS**

Given: $\overline{KL} \cong \overline{PO}$; $\overline{LN} \cong \overline{OM}$; $\overline{KM} \cong \overline{PN}$
Prove: $\triangle KLM \cong \triangle PON$

Statements	Reasons
1. $\overline{LN} \cong \overline{OM}$	1. **Given**
2. $LN + NM = NM + MO$	2. Addition Prop. of Equality
3. $LN + NM = LM$; $NM + MO = NO$	3. Definition of Between
4. $LM \cong NO$	4. Substitution Property
5. $\overline{KL} \cong \overline{PO}$, $\overline{KM} \cong \overline{PN}$	5. **given**
6. $\triangle KLM \cong \triangle PON$	6. **SSS**

More Practice with Proofs

Complete the following proofs.
Given: $m \angle 1 = 40°$; $m \angle 3 = 40°$; $\angle 2 \cong \angle 4$
Prove: $\triangle RIQ \cong \triangle IRS$

Statements	Reasons
1. $m \angle 1 = 40°$; $m \angle 3 = 40°$; $\angle 2 \cong \angle 4$	1. **given**
2. $\angle 1 \cong \angle 3$	2. **Definition of $\cong$ $\angle$'s.**
3. $\overline{RI} \cong \overline{IR}$	3. **reflexive**
4. $\triangle RIQ \cong \triangle IRS$	4. **ASA**

Given: $\overline{WY} \cong \overline{XV}$; $\overline{VW} \perp \overline{WX}$; $\overline{YX} \perp \overline{WX}$
Prove: $\triangle XWV \cong \triangle WXY$

Statements	Reasons
1. $\overline{VW} \perp \overline{WX}$, $\overline{YX} \perp \overline{WX}$	1. **given**
2. $\angle VWX$, $\angle YXW$ are rt. $\angle$'s.	2. **Definition Perpendicular Lines**
3. $\triangle XWV$, $\triangle WXY$ are right $\triangle$s.	3. **Definition of rt. $\triangle$'s.**
4. $\overline{WY} \cong \overline{XV}$	4. Given
5. $\overline{WX} \cong \overline{WX}$	5. **Reflexive**
6. $\triangle XWV \cong \triangle WXY$	6. **HL**

Given: $\angle 1 \cong \angle 6$; $\angle 3 \cong \angle 4$; B is the midpoint of $\overline{AC}$
Prove: $\triangle ABE \cong \triangle CBD$

Statements	Reasons
1. $\angle 1 \cong \angle 6$ $\angle 3 \cong \angle 4$, B is midpoint to $\overline{AC}$.	1. Given
2. $\overline{AB} \cong \overline{BC}$	2. **Definition of mid-point.**
3. $\angle 1$ is supplement. to $\angle 2$	3. **Definition of Supplementary**
4. $\angle 5$ is supplementary to $\angle 6$	4. **Def. of supplementary.**
5. $\angle 2 \cong \angle 5$	5. **Supplements of $\cong$ $\angle$'s are $\cong$.**
6. $\triangle ABE \cong \triangle CBD$	6. **ASA**

Just for Fun

Try to decode these words and phrases.

```
wear ..........long,underwear
long
```

1. mind / mind / matter / over / matter = **mind over matter**	2. big man / to MAN wn / in town = **big man in town**	3. LU CKY = **lucky break**	4. D N A T S / Stand up = **Stand up**
5. life / death life / after / death = **life after death**	6. Swimming / water / swimming / under / water = **swimming under water**	7. man on / MOmanON / the moon = **man on the moon**	8. sit / s i t / down = **sit down**
9. do you / stand / do you = **do you understand**	10. myself I'm	11. E N M / A P / M I / O R / R E = **I'm beside myself**	12. Jack in / b JA o CK x / the box = **Jack in the box**
13. mixed / DKI / up kid = **mixed up kid**	14. ı ı ı / . . .	15. T M / A U / H S / W T = **What goes up must come down**	16. d / don't / Stand by / the / edge

10. I'm beside myself
11. Rise and fall of the Roman Empire
14. Dark circles under the eyes
15. What goes up must come down

Coordinate Geometry

Keep in mind . . .
You learn by doing.

The Coordinate Plane

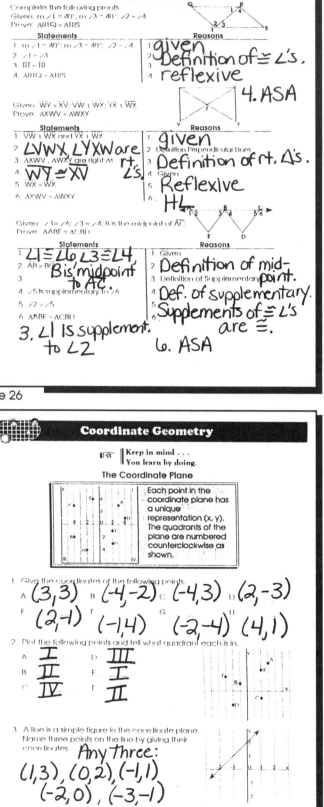

Each point in the coordinate plane has a unique representation (x, y). The quadrants of the plane are numbered counterclockwise as shown.

1. Give the coordinates of the following points.

A **(3,3)** B **(-4,-2)** C **(-4,3)** D **(2,-3)**
F **(2,-1)** **(-1,4)** **(-2,-4)** H **(4,1)**

2. Plot the following points and tell what quadrant each is in.

A **I** D **III**
B **II** E **II**
C **IV** F **II**

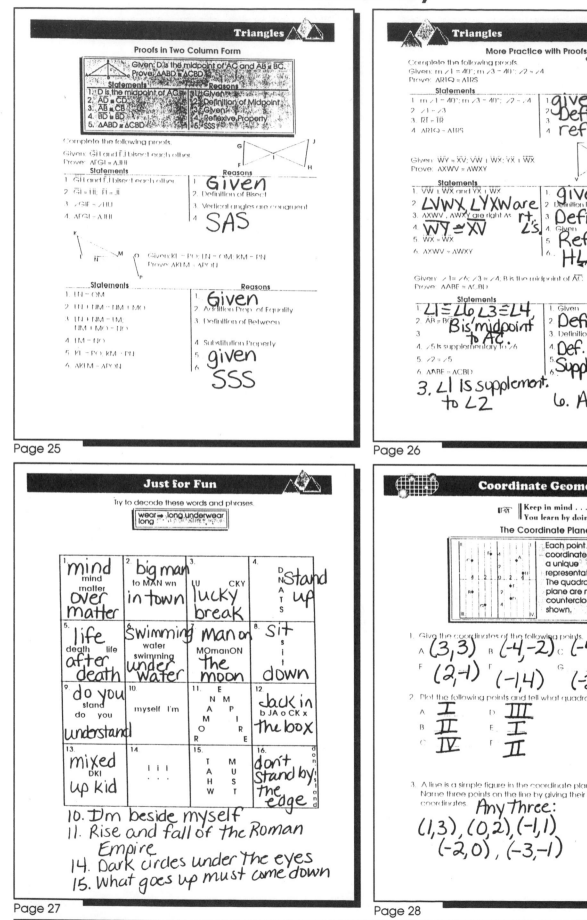

3. A line is a simple figure in the coordinate plane. Name three points on the line by giving their coordinates.

Any three:
(1,3), (0,2), (-1,1)
(-2,0), (-3,-1)

Answer Key

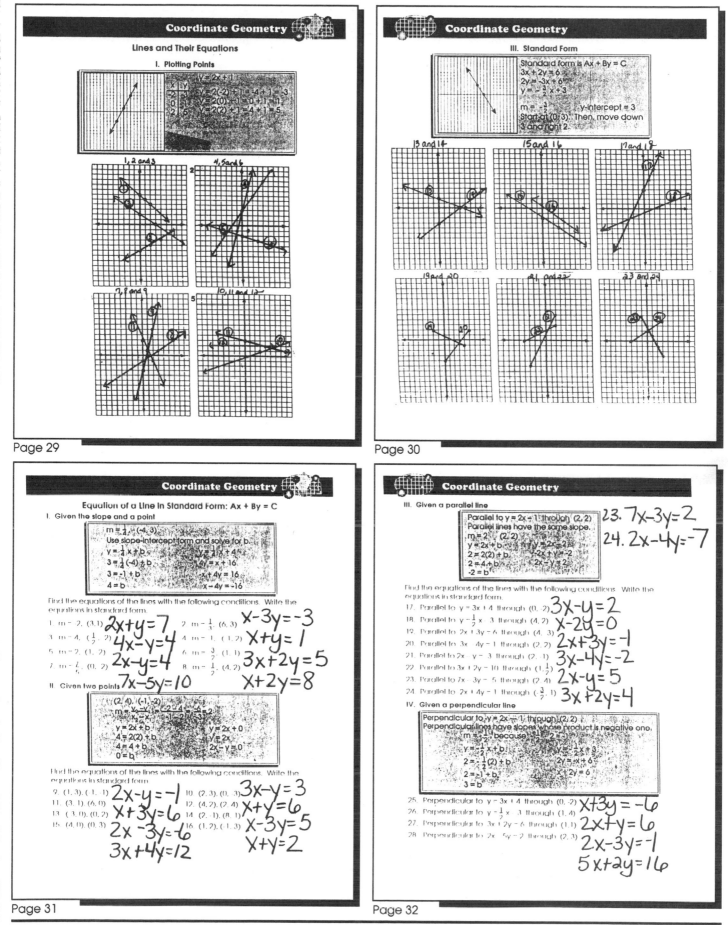

Coordinate Geometry
Lines and Their Equations
I. Plotting Points

$y = 2x + 1$

x	y
-2	-3	$y = 2(-2) + 1 = -4 + 1 = -3$
0	1	$y = 2(0) + 1 = 0 + 1 = 1$
2	5	$y = 2(2) + 1 = 4 + 1 = 5$

1, 2 and 3

4, 5 and 6

7, 8 and 9

10, 11 and 12

Coordinate Geometry
III. Standard Form

Standard form is $Ax + By = C$
$3x + 2y = 6$
$2y = -3x + 6$
$y = -\frac{3}{2}x + 3$

$m = -\frac{3}{2}$ y-intercept = 3
Start at (0, 3). Then, move down
3 and right 2.

13 and 14

15 and 16

17 and 18

19 and 20

21 and 22

23 and 24

Coordinate Geometry
Equation of a Line in Standard Form: Ax + By = C
I. Given the slope and a point

$m = 2, (-4, 3)$
Use slope-intercept form and solve for b.
$y = \frac{1}{2}x + b$ $y = \frac{1}{2}x + 4$
$3 = \frac{1}{2}(-4) + b$ $4y = x + 16$
$3 = -1 + b$ $2x + 4y = 16$
$4 = b$ $x - 4y = -16$

Find the equations of the lines with the following conditions. Write the equations in standard form.

1. $m = 2, (3, 1)$ $2x + y = 7$
2. $m = \frac{1}{3}, (6, 3)$ $x - 3y = -3$
3. $m = 4, (\frac{1}{2}, 2)$ $4x - y = 4$
4. $m = -1, (1, 2)$ $x + y = 1$
5. $m = 2, (1, 2)$ $2x - y = 4$
6. $m = -\frac{3}{2}, (1, 1)$ $3x + 2y = 5$
7. $m = \frac{2}{5}, (0, 2)$ $7x - 5y = 10$
8. $m = -\frac{1}{2}, (4, 2)$ $x + 2y = 8$

II. Given two points

$(2, 4), (-1, 2)$
$m = \frac{y_2 - y_1}{x_2 - x_1} = \frac{2-4}{-1-2} = \frac{-2}{-3} = \frac{2}{3}$
$y = 2x + b$ $y = 2x + 0$
$4 = 2(2) + b$ $y = 2x$
$4 = 4 + b$ $2x - y = 0$
$0 = b$

Find the equations of the lines with the following conditions. Write the equations in standard form.

9. $(1, 3), (-1, -1)$ $2x - y = -1$
10. $(2, 3), (0, 3)$ $3x - y = 3$
11. $(3, 1), (6, 0)$
12. $(4, 2), (2, 4)$ $x + y = 6$
13. $(3, 0), (0, 2)$ $x + 3y = 6$
14. $(2, -1), (8, 1)$ $x + y = 6$
15. $(4, 0), (0, 3)$ $2x - 3y = 6$
16. $(1, 2), (-1, 3)$ $x - 3y = 5$
                         $3x + 4y = 12$ $x + y = 2$

Coordinate Geometry
III. Given a parallel line

Parallel to $y = 2x - 1$ through $(2, 2)$
Parallel lines have the same slope.
$m = 2$ $(2, 2)$
$y = 2x + b$ $y = 2x - 2$
$2 = 2(2) + b$ $-2x + y = -2$
$2 = 4 + b$ $2x - y = 2$
$-2 = b$

Find the equations of the lines with the following conditions. Write the equations in standard form.

17. Parallel to $y = 3x + 4$ through $(0, 2)$ $3x - y = 2$
18. Parallel to $y = \frac{1}{2}x - 3$ through $(4, 2)$ $x - 2y = 0$
19. Parallel to $2x + 3y = 6$ through $(4, 3)$ $2x + 3y = -1$
20. Parallel to $3x - 4y = 1$ through $(2, 2)$
21. Parallel to $2x - y = 3$ through $(2, 1)$ $3x - 4y = -2$
22. Parallel to $3x + 2y = 10$ through $(1, \frac{1}{2})$ $2x - y = 5$
23. Parallel to $7x - 3y = 5$ through $(2, 4)$ $3x + 2y = 4$
24. Parallel to $2x + 4y = 1$ through $(\frac{3}{2}, 1)$

23. $7x - 3y = 2$
24. $2x - 4y = -7$

IV. Given a perpendicular line

Perpendicular to $y = 2x - 1$ through $(2, 2)$
Perpendicular lines have slopes whose product is negative one.
$m = -\frac{1}{2}$ because $-\frac{1}{2} \cdot 2 = -1$
$y = -\frac{1}{2}x + b$ $y = -\frac{1}{2}x + 3$
$2 = -\frac{1}{2}(2) + b$ $2y = -x + 6$
$2 = -1 + b$ $x + 2y = 6$
$3 = b$

25. Perpendicular to $y = 3x + 4$ through $(0, 2)$ $x + 3y = -6$
26. Perpendicular to $y = \frac{1}{2}x - 3$ through $(1, 4)$
27. Perpendicular to $3x + 2y = 6$ through $(1, 1)$ $2x + y = 6$
28. Perpendicular to $2x - 5y = 2$ through $(2, 3)$ $2x - 3y = -1$
                                                       $5x + 2y = 16$

Answer Key

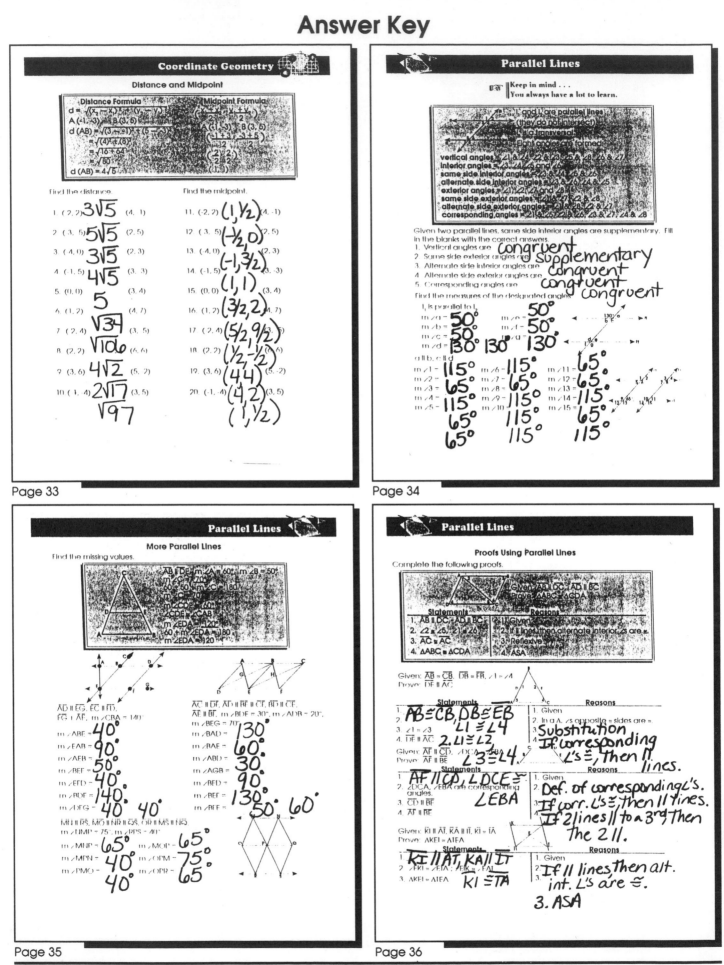

Coordinate Geometry
Distance and Midpoint

Distance Formula: $d = \sqrt{(x_2-x_1)^2 + (y_2-y_1)^2}$
Midpoint Formula: $\left(\frac{x_1+x_2}{2}, \frac{y_1+y_2}{2}\right)$

A $(-1,-3)$, B $(3,5)$
$d(AB) = \sqrt{(3+1)^2 + (5+3)^2}$
$= \sqrt{(4)^2 + (8)^2}$
$= \sqrt{16+64}$
$= \sqrt{80}$
$d(AB) = 4\sqrt{5}$

Find the distance.

1. $(-2,2)$ $3\sqrt{5}$ $(4,-1)$
2. $(3,5)$ $5\sqrt{5}$ $(2,5)$
3. $(-4,0)$ $3\sqrt{5}$ $(2,3)$
4. $(-1,5)$ $4\sqrt{5}$ $(3,-3)$
5. $(0,0)$ 5 $(3,4)$
6. $(1,2)$ $\sqrt{34}$ $(4,7)$
7. $(2,4)$ $\sqrt{106}$ $(3,5)$
8. $(2,2)$ $\sqrt{106}$ $(6,6)$
9. $(3,6)$ $4\sqrt{2}$ $(5,2)$
10. $(-1,-4)$ $2\sqrt{17}$ $(3,5)$ $\sqrt{97}$

Find the midpoint.

11. $(-2,2)$ $(1,\frac{1}{2})$ $(4,-1)$
12. $(3,5)$ $(-\frac{1}{2},0)$ $(2,5)$
13. $(-4,0)$ $(-1,\frac{3}{2})$ $(2,3)$
14. $(-1,5)$ $(-1,\frac{3}{2})$ $(3,-3)$
15. $(0,0)$ $(1,1)$ $(3,4)$
16. $(1,2)$ $(\frac{3}{2},2)$ $(4,7)$
17. $(2,4)$ $(\frac{5}{2},\frac{9}{2})$ $(3,5)$
18. $(2,2)$ $(\frac{1}{2},-\frac{1}{2})$ $(6,6)$
19. $(3,6)$ $(4,4)$ $(5,-2)$
20. $(-1,-4)$ $(4,2)$ $(3,5)$ $(1,\frac{1}{2})$

Page 33

Parallel Lines

☞ Keep in mind . . .
You always have a lot to learn.

Given two parallel lines, same side interior angles are supplementary. Fill in the blanks with the correct answers.

1. Vertical angles are **congruent**
2. Same side exterior angles are **supplementary**
3. Alternate side interior angles are **congruent**
4. Alternate side exterior angles are **congruent**
5. Corresponding angles are **congruent**

Find the measures of the designated angles.

l_1 is parallel to l_2
$m\angle a = 50°$ $m\angle e = 50°$
$m\angle b = 50°$ $m\angle f = 50°$
$m\angle c = 130°$ $m\angle g = 130°$
$m\angle d = 130°$

$a \parallel b$, $c \parallel d$
$m\angle 1 = 115°$ $m\angle 6 = 115°$ $m\angle 11 = 65°$
$m\angle 2 = 65°$ $m\angle 7 = 65°$ $m\angle 12 = 65°$
$m\angle 3 = 65°$ $m\angle 8 = 65°$ $m\angle 13 = 65°$
$m\angle 4 = 115°$ $m\angle 9 = 115°$ $m\angle 14 = 115°$
$m\angle 5 = 115°$ $m\angle 10 = 115°$ $m\angle 15 = 65°$
$65°$ $65°$ $65°$
$65°$ $115°$ $115°$

Page 34

Parallel Lines
More Parallel Lines

Find the missing values.

$AB \parallel DE$, $m\angle A = 60°$, $m\angle B = 50°$
$m\angle C = 70°$
$m\angle D = 50°$ $m\angle C = 180°$
$m\angle C = 70°$
$m\angle CDE = 60°$
$m\angle CDE = \angle AB$
$m\angle EDA = 120°$
$60 + m\angle EDA = 180$
$m\angle EDA = 120$

$AD \parallel EG$, $EC \parallel FD$,
$FG \parallel AF$, $m\angle CBA = 140°$
$m\angle ABE = 40°$
$m\angle EAB = 90°$
$m\angle AEB = 50°$
$m\angle BEF = 40°$
$m\angle EFD = 40°$
$m\angle BDF = 140°$
$m\angle DFG = 40°$ $40°$

$MN \parallel RS$, $MO \parallel NR \parallel QS$, $OR \parallel MS \parallel NQ$,
$m\angle NMP = 75°$, $m\angle RPS = 40°$
$m\angle MNP = 65°$ $m\angle MOP = 65°$
$m\angle MPN = 40°$ $m\angle OPM = 75°$
$m\angle PMQ = 40°$ $m\angle OPR = 65°$
$40°$

$AC \parallel DF$, $AD \parallel BE \parallel CF$, $BD \parallel CE$,
$AE \parallel BF$, $m\angle BDE = 30°$, $m\angle ADB = 20°$
$m\angle BEG = 70°$
$m\angle BAD = 130°$
$m\angle BAE = 60°$
$m\angle ABD = 30°$
$m\angle AGB = 90°$
$m\angle BFD = 130°$
$m\angle BEF = 50°$ $60°$

Page 35

Parallel Lines
Proofs Using Parallel Lines

Complete the following proofs.

Given: $AB \parallel DC$, $AD \parallel BC$
Prove: $\triangle ABC \cong \triangle CDA$

Statements	Reasons
1. $AB \parallel DC$, $AD \parallel BC$	1. Given
2. $\angle 1 \cong \angle 5$, $\angle 1 \cong \angle 6$	2. If lines, then alternate interior $\angle$s are $\cong$
3. $AC \cong AC$	3. Reflexive
4. $\triangle ABC \cong \triangle CDA$	4. ASA

Given: $AB \cong CB$, $DB \cong EB$, $\angle 1 \cong \angle 4$
Prove: $DE \parallel AC$

Statements	Reasons
1. $AB \cong CB$, $DB \cong EB$	1. Given
2. $\angle 1 \cong \angle 4$	2. In a $\triangle$, $\angle$s opposite $\cong$ sides are $\cong$
3. $\angle 1 \cong \angle 2$	3. Substitution
4. $DE \parallel AC$ $\angle 1 \cong \angle 2$	4. If corresponding $\angle$'s $\cong$, then $\parallel$ lines.

Given: $AF \parallel CD$, $\angle DCA \cong \angle BA$
Prove: $AF \parallel BE$ $\angle 3 \cong \angle 4$

Statements	Reasons
1. $AF \parallel CD$, $\angle DCE \cong \angle EBA$	1. Given
2. $\angle DCA$, $\angle EBA$ are corresponding angles	2. Def. of corresponding $\angle$'s.
3. $CD \parallel BE$	3. If corr. $\angle$'s $\cong$, then $\parallel$ lines.
4. $AF \parallel BE$	4. If 2 lines $\parallel$ to a 3rd, then the 2 $\parallel$.

Given: $KI \parallel AT$, $KA \parallel IT$, $KI \cong IA$
Prove: $\triangle AKEI \cong \triangle TEA$ $KI \cong TA$

Statements	Reasons
1. $KI \parallel AT$, $KA \parallel IT$	1. Given
2. $\angle FKI \cong \angle EIA$, $\angle FIK \cong \angle EAI$	2. If $\parallel$ lines, then alt. int. $\angle$'s are $\cong$.
3. $\triangle AKEI \cong \triangle TEA$ $KI \cong TA$	3. ASA

Page 36

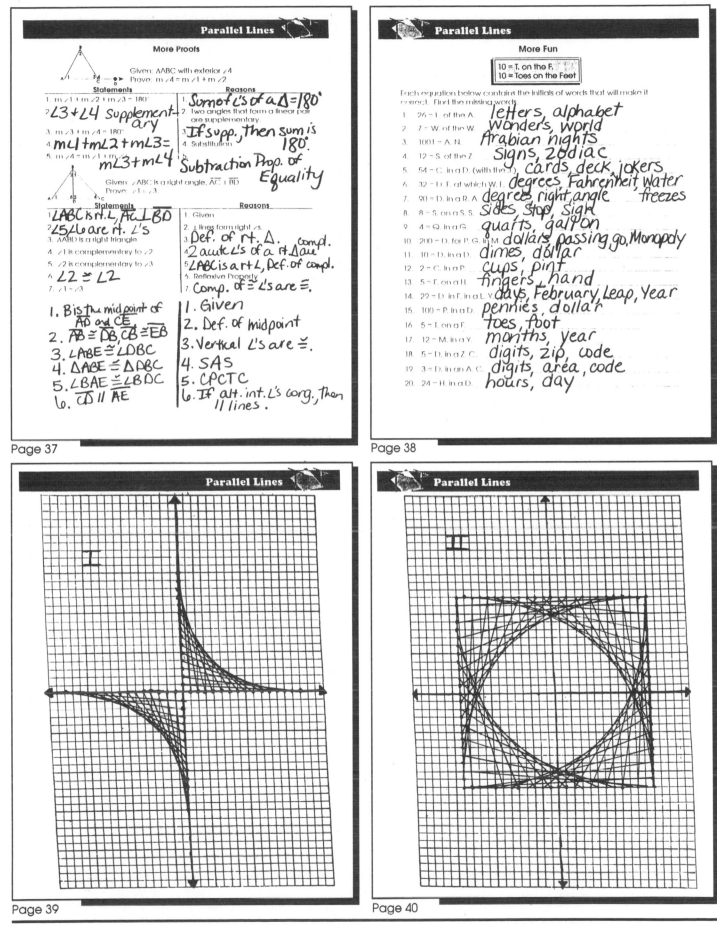

Parallel Lines

More Proofs

Given: △ABC with exterior ∠4
Prove: m∠4 = m∠1 + m∠2

Statements	Reasons
1. m∠1 + m∠2 + m∠3 = 180°	1. Sum of ∠'s of a △ = 180°
2. ∠3 + ∠4 supplementary	2. Two angles that form a linear pair are supplementary.
3. m∠3 + m∠4 = 180°	3. If supp., then sum is 180°.
4. m∠1 + m∠2 + m∠3 = m∠3 + m∠4	4. Substitution
5. m∠4 = m∠1 + m∠2	5. Subtraction Prop. of Equality

Given: ∠ABC is a right angle, $\overline{AC} \perp \overline{BD}$
Prove: ∠1 ≅ ∠3

Statements	Reasons
1. ∠ABC is rt. ∠, $\overline{AC} \perp \overline{BD}$	1. Given
2. ∠5 & ∠6 are rt. ∠'s	2. ⊥ lines form right ∠s.
3. △ABD is a right triangle	3. Def. of rt. △.
4. ∠1 is complementary to ∠2	4. 2 acute ∠'s of a rt △ are compl.
5. ∠2 is complementary to ∠3	5. ∠ABC is a rt ∠, Def. of compl.
6. ∠2 ≅ ∠2	6. Reflexive Property
7. ∠1 ≅ ∠3	7. Comp. of ≅ ∠'s are ≅.

1. B is the midpoint of $\overline{AD}$ and $\overline{CE}$	1. Given
2. $\overline{AB} ≅ \overline{DB}, \overline{CB} ≅ \overline{EB}$	2. Def. of midpoint
3. ∠ABE ≅ ∠DBC	3. Vertical ∠'s are ≅.
4. △ABE ≅ △DBC	4. SAS
5. ∠BAE ≅ ∠BDC	5. CPCTC
6. $\overline{CD} \parallel \overline{AE}$	6. If alt. int. ∠'s cong., then ∥ lines.

Page 37

Parallel Lines

More Fun

10 = T. on the F.
10 = Toes on the Feet

Each equation below contains the initials of words that will make it correct. Find the missing words.

1. 26 = L. of the A. — letters, alphabet
2. 7 = W. of the W. — wonders, world
3. 1001 = A. N. — Arabian nights
4. 12 = S. of the Z. — signs, zodiac
5. 54 = C. in a D. (with the J.) — cards, deck, jokers
6. 32 = D. F. at which W. F. — degrees, Fahrenheit, water freezes
7. 90 = D. in a R. A. — degrees, right angle
8. 8 = S. on a S. S. — sides, stop, sign
9. 4 = Q. in a G. — quarts, gallon
10. 200 = D. for P. G. in M. — dollars, passing go, Monopoly
11. 10 = D. in a D. — dimes, dollar
12. 2 = C. in a P. — cups, pint
13. 5 = F. on a H. — fingers, hand
14. 29 = D. in F. in a L. Y. — days, February, Leap, Year
15. 100 = P. in a D. — pennies, dollar
16. 5 = T. on a F. — toes, foot
17. 12 = M. in a Y. — months, year
18. 5 = D. in a Z. C. — digits, zip, code
19. 3 = D. in an A. C. — digits, area, code
20. 24 = H. in a D. — hours, day

Page 38

Parallel Lines

I

Page 39

Parallel Lines

II

Page 40

Answer Key

Geometric Constructions

U.5 Keep in mind . . .
You only fail when you stop trying.

Congruent Segments

Given: $\overline{AB}$

Construct a segment congruent to $\overline{AB}$.
1. Use a straight edge to draw a working line, l.
2. Choose a point on l and label it A'.
3. Set your compass for radius AB by placing one end at point A and another at point B. Draw an arc.
4. Using AB as radius, place one end of compass on A' and draw an arc. Label the point of intersection B'.
$\overline{AB} \cong \overline{A'B'}$

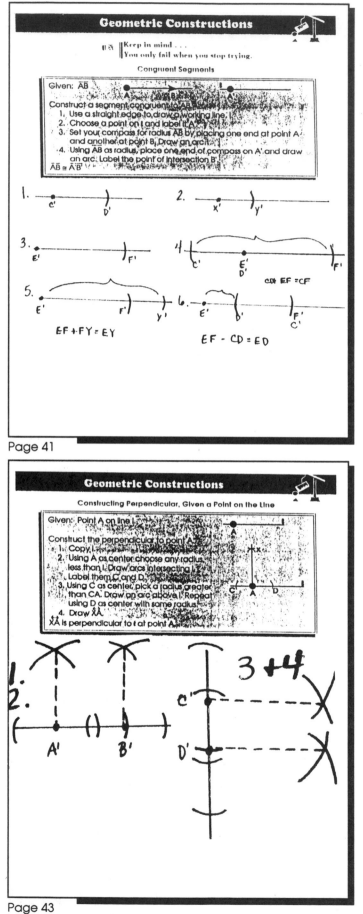

1. C' D'
2. X' Y'
3. E' F'
4. C' D' E' F'   CD+ EF =CF
5. E' F' Y'   EF + FY = EY
6. E' D' F' C'   EF - CD = ED

Geometric Constructions

Perpendicular Bisectors

Given: $\overline{AB}$

Construct the perpendicular bisector of $\overline{AB}$.
1. Copy segment $\overline{AB}$.
2. Choose a radius greater than $\frac{1}{2}\overline{AB}$ and less than AB. Using A as the center, draw 2 arcs, one above AB and one below $\overline{AB}$. Repeat using B as center.
3. Draw $\overleftrightarrow{CD}$.
$\overleftrightarrow{CD}$ is the perpendicular bisector of $\overline{AB}$.

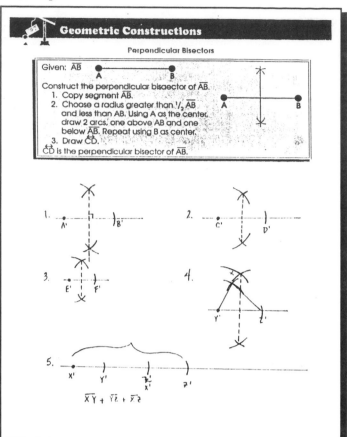

1. A' B'
2. C' D'
3. E' F'
4. Y' Z'
5. X' Y' X' Z' $\overline{XY} + \overline{YZ} + \overline{XZ}$

Geometric Constructions

Constructing Perpendicular, Given a Point on the Line

Given: Point A on line l

Construct the perpendicular to point A.
1. Copy l.
2. Using A as center choose any radius less than l. Draw arcs intersecting l. Label them C and D.
3. Using C as center, pick a radius greater than CA. Draw an arc above l. Repeat using D as center with same radius.
4. Draw $\overleftrightarrow{XA}$.
$\overleftrightarrow{XA}$ is perpendicular to l at point A.

1.
2.
3 + 4

A' B' C' D'

Geometric Constructions

Constructing Perpendiculars, Given a Point Not on the Line

Given: Point P outside line l.

Construct a line perpendicular from P to l.
1. Copy l.
2. Using P as center, draw two arcs intersecting l. Label them A and B.
3. Choose a radius greater than $\frac{1}{2}$ AB. Use A as center, draw arc below l. Repeat using B as center with same radius. Label X.
4. Draw $\overleftrightarrow{PX}$.
$\overleftrightarrow{PX}$ is perpendicular to l.

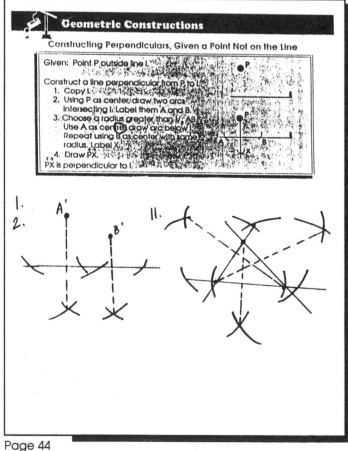

1.
2. A' B'
II.

Answer Key

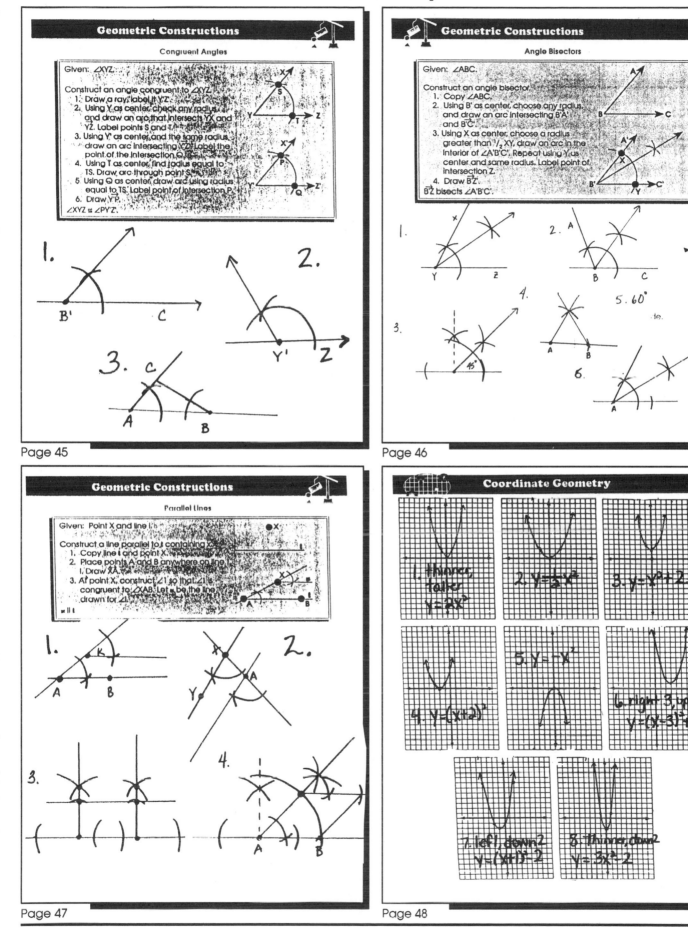

Page 45

Page 46

Page 47

Page 48

Geometry IF8764

115

© MCMXCIV Instructional Fair, Inc.

Answer Key

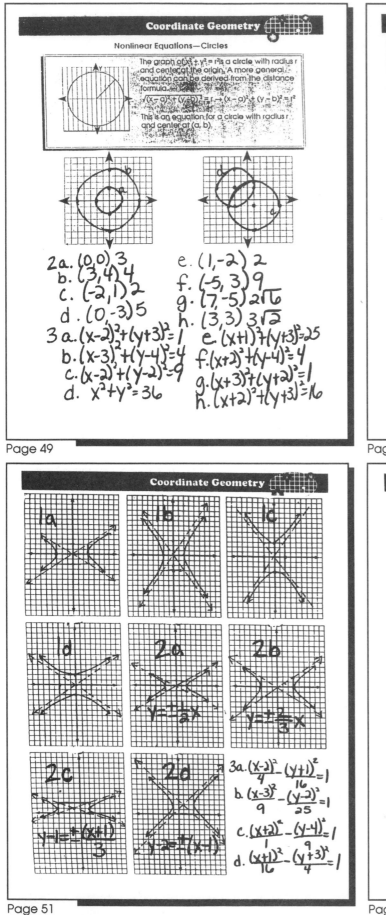

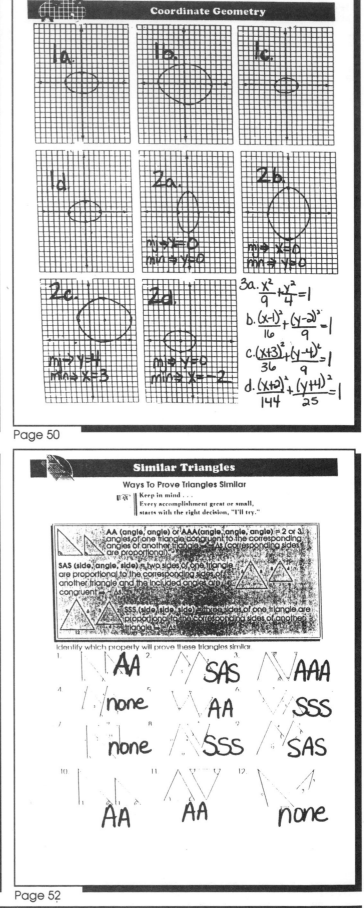

Page 49

Coordinate Geometry

Nonlinear Equations—Circles

The graph of $x^2 + y^2 = r^2$ is a circle with radius r and center at the origin. A more general equation can be derived from the distance formula.

$\sqrt{(x-a)^2 + (y-b)^2} = r \rightarrow (x-a)^2 + (y-b)^2 = r^2$

This is an equation for a circle with radius r and center at (a, b).

2a. $(0,0)$, 3
 b. $(3,4)$ 4
 c. $(-2,1)$ 2
 d. $(0,-3)$ 5
 e. $(1,-2)$ 2
 f. $(-5, 3)$ 9
 g. $(7,-5)$ $2\sqrt{6}$
 h. $(3,3)$ $3\sqrt{2}$

3 a. $(x-2)^2 + (y+3)^2 = 1$
 b. $(x-3)^2 + (y-4)^2 = 4$
 c. $(x-2)^2 + (y-2)^2 = 9$
 d. $x^2 + y^2 = 36$
 e. $(x+1)^2 + (y+3)^2 = 25$
 f. $(x+2)^2 + (y-4)^2 = 4$
 g. $(x+3)^2 + (y+2)^2 = 1$
 h. $(x+2)^2 + (y+3)^2 = 16$

Page 50

Coordinate Geometry

2a. maj $\Rightarrow$ y=0, min $\Rightarrow$ y=0
2b. maj $\Rightarrow$ x=0, min $\Rightarrow$ y=0
2c. maj $\Rightarrow$ y=4, min $\Rightarrow$ x=3
2d. maj $\Rightarrow$ y=0, min $\Rightarrow$ x=-2

3a. $\frac{x^2}{9} + \frac{y^2}{4} = 1$
 b. $\frac{(x-1)^2}{16} + \frac{(y-2)^2}{9} = 1$
 c. $\frac{(x+3)^2}{36} + \frac{(y-4)^2}{9} = 1$
 d. $\frac{(x+2)^2}{144} + \frac{(y+1)^2}{25} = 1$

Page 51

Coordinate Geometry

2a. $y = \pm\frac{1}{2}x$
2b. $y = \pm\frac{2}{3}x$
2c. $y-1 = \pm\frac{1}{3}(x+1)$
2d. $y-2 = \pm(x-1)$

3a. $\frac{(x-2)^2}{4} - \frac{(y+1)^2}{16} = 1$
 b. $\frac{(x-3)^2}{9} - \frac{(y-2)^2}{25} = 1$
 c. $\frac{(x+2)^2}{1} - \frac{(y-4)^2}{9} = 1$
 d. $\frac{(x+1)^2}{16} - \frac{(y+3)^2}{4} = 1$

Page 52

Similar Triangles

Ways To Prove Triangles Similar

Keep in mind . . .
Every accomplishment great or small, starts with the right decision, "I'll try."

AA (angle, angle) or AAA (angle, angle, angle) = 2 or 3 angles of one triangle congruent to the corresponding angles of another triangle. ~ As (corresponding sides are proportional).

SAS (side, angle, side) = two sides of one triangle are proportional to the corresponding sides of another triangle and the included angles are congruent. ~ Δs

SSS (side, side, side) = three sides of one triangle are proportional to the corresponding sides of another triangle. ~ Δs

Identify which property will prove these triangles similar

1. AA
2. SAS
3. AAA
4. none
5. AA
6. SSS
7. none
8. SSS
9. SAS
10. AA
11. AA
12. none

Answer Key

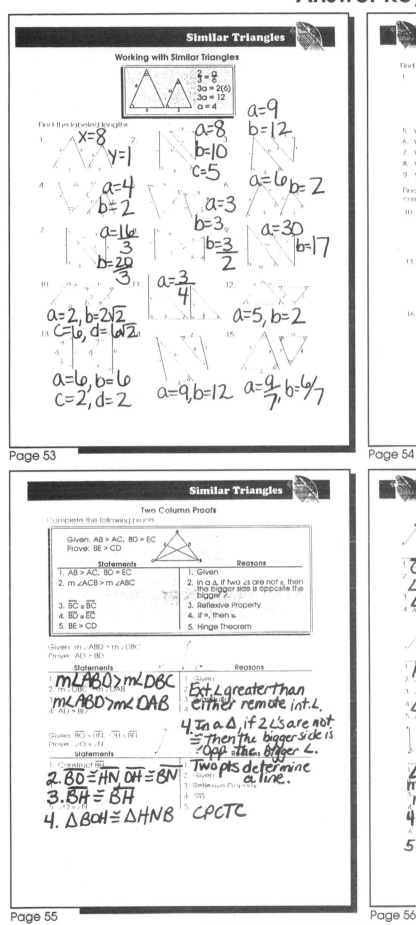

Working with Similar Triangles

$$\frac{2}{3} = \frac{a}{6}$$
$$3a = 2(6)$$
$$3a = 12$$
$$a = 4$$

Find the labeled lengths

1. $x = 8$, $y = 1$

2. $a = 8$, $b = 10$, $c = 5$

3. $a = 9$, $b = 12$

4. $a = 4$, $b = 2$

5. $a = 3$, $b = 3$

6. $a = 6$, $b = 2$

7. $a = \frac{16}{3}$, $b = \frac{20}{3}$

8. $a = 30$, $b = 17$

9. $a = \frac{3}{2}$

10. $a = 2$, $b = 2\sqrt{2}$

11. $a = \frac{3}{4}$

12. $a = 5$, $b = 2$

13. $c = 6$, $d = 6\sqrt{2}$

14. $a = 6$, $b = 6$, $c = 2$, $d = 2$

15. $a = 9$, $b = 12$

$a = \frac{9}{7}$, $b = \frac{6}{7}$

More Similar Triangles

Find the area of the following triangles. (Hint: $A = \frac{1}{2}bh$)

1. 6 2. 24 3. 9 4. 4

5. What is the ratio of the sides in #1 and #2? $1:2$
6. What is the ratio of the sides in #3 and #4? $3:2$ 7. $1:4$
7. What is the ratio of the areas in #1 and #2?
8. What is the ratio of the areas in #3 and #4? $9:4$
9. What can you conclude about this? 9. ratios of areas = (rat. of sides)^2

Find the ratio of the areas in the following sets of similar triangles with corresponding sides labeled.

10. $9:1$ 11. $4:1$ 12. $25:9$

13. $16:9$ 14. $9:4$ 15. $4:1$

16. $25:4$ 17. $9:4$ 18. $1:4$

Two Column Proofs

Complete the following proofs

Given: AB > AC, BD = EC
Prove: BE > CD

Statements	Reasons
1. AB > AC, BD = EC	1. Given
2. m∠ACB > m∠ABC	2. In a △, if two ∠s are not ≅, then the bigger side is opposite the bigger ∠.
3. $\overline{BC} \cong \overline{BC}$	3. Reflexive Property
4. $\overline{BD} \cong \overline{EC}$	4. If =, then ≅.
5. BE > CD	5. Hinge Theorem

Given: m∠ABD > m∠DBC
Prove: AD > BD

Statements	Reasons
1. m∠ABD > m∠DBC	1. Given
2. m∠DBC = m∠DAB	2.
3. m∠ABD > m∠DAB	3.
4. AD > BD	4. In a △, if 2 ∠'s are not ≅ then the bigger side is opp bigger ∠. Ext ∠ greater than either remote int. ∠.

Given: $\overline{BO} \cong \overline{HN}$, $\overline{OH} \cong \overline{BN}$
Prove: ∠O ≅ ∠N

Statements	Reasons
1. Construct $\overline{BH}$	1. Two pts determine a line.
2. $\overline{BO} \cong \overline{HN}$, $\overline{OH} \cong \overline{BN}$	2.
3. $\overline{BH} \cong \overline{BH}$	3. Reflexive Property
4. △BOH ≅ △HNB	4. SSS
	CPCTC

More Two Column Proofs

Given: $\overline{CT} \parallel \overline{BG}$
Prove: △CAT ~ △BAG

Statements	Reasons
1. $\overline{CT} \parallel \overline{BG}$	1. Given
2. ∠4 ≅ ∠2	2. If ∥ lines, then corresponding ∠s are ≅.
3. ∠A ≅ ∠A	3. Reflexive Property
4. △CAT ~ △BAG	4. AA

Given: $\overline{AC} \cong \overline{AT}$, $\overline{OD} \cong \overline{OG}$, $\overline{AC} \parallel \overline{OD}$
Prove: △CAT ~ △DOG

Statements	Reasons
1. $\overline{AC} \cong \overline{AT}$, $\overline{OD} \cong \overline{OG}$, $\overline{AC} \parallel \overline{OD}$	1. Given
2. ∠ACT ≅ ∠ATC, ∠ODG ≅ ∠OGD	2. In a △ ∠'s opp ≅ sides are ≅.
3. ∠ACT ≅ ∠ODG, ∠ATC ≅ ∠OGD	3. If ∥ lines, then corr. ∠'s are ≅.
4. △CAT ~ △DOG	4. AA

Given: ∠BAD ≅ ∠CDA, ∠1 ≅ ∠4
Prove: ∠2 ≅ ∠3

Statements	Reasons
1. ∠BAD ≅ ∠CDA, ∠1 ≅ ∠4	1. Given
2. m∠BAD = m∠1 + m∠2, m∠CDA = m∠3 + m∠4	2. AAP
3. m∠BAD = m∠CDA	3. If ≅, then =.
4. m∠4 + m∠2 = m∠3 + m∠4	4. Substitution
5. m∠2 = m∠3	5. APOE, If =, then ≅.

117

Answer Key

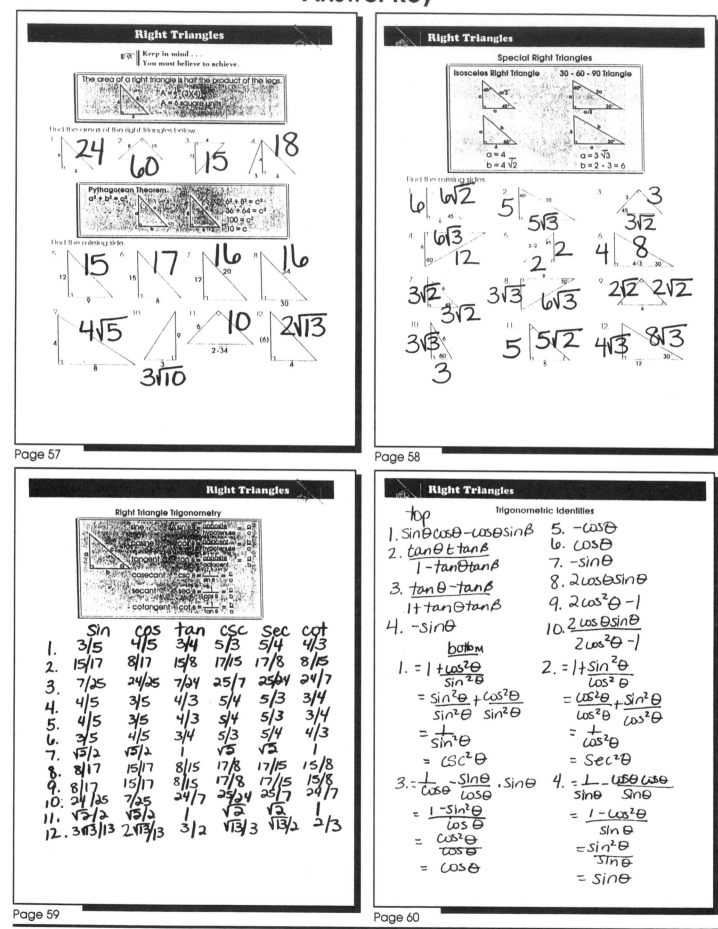

Right Triangles

Keep in mind . . .
You must believe to achieve.

The area of a right triangle is half the product of the legs.

$A = \frac{1}{2}(3)(4)$
$A = 6$ square units

Find the areas of the right triangles below.

1. 24 2. 60 3. 15 4. 18

Pythagorean Theorem
$a^2 + b^2 = c^2$
$6^2 + 8^2 = c^2$
$36 + 64 = c^2$
$100 = c^2$
$10 = c$

Find the missing side.

5. 15 6. 17 7. 16 8. 16
9. $4\sqrt{5}$ 10. $3\sqrt{10}$ 11. 10 12. $2\sqrt{13}$

Right Triangles

Special Right Triangles

Isosceles Right Triangle   30 - 60 - 90 Triangle

$a = 4$
$b = 4\sqrt{2}$

$a = 3\sqrt{3}$
$b = 2 \cdot 3 = 6$

Find the missing sides.

1. $6\sqrt{2}$ 2. 5 ; $5\sqrt{3}$ 3. 3 ; $3\sqrt{2}$
4. $6\sqrt{3}$; 12 5. 2 6. 4 ; 8
7. $3\sqrt{2}$; $3\sqrt{2}$ 8. $3\sqrt{3}$; $6\sqrt{3}$ 9. $2\sqrt{2}$; $2\sqrt{2}$
10. $3\sqrt{3}$; 3 11. 5 ; $5\sqrt{2}$ 12. $4\sqrt{3}$; $8\sqrt{3}$

Right Triangles

Right Triangle Trigonometry

sine $\sin\theta = \frac{\text{opposite}}{\text{hypotenuse}} = \frac{a}{c}$
cosine $\cos\theta = \frac{\text{adjacent}}{\text{hypotenuse}} = \frac{b}{c}$
tangent $\tan\theta = \frac{\text{opposite}}{\text{adjacent}} = \frac{a}{b}$
cosecant $\csc\theta = \frac{c}{a}$
secant $\sec\theta = \frac{c}{b}$
cotangent $\cot\theta = \frac{b}{a}$

	Sin	cos	tan	csc	sec	cot
1.	3/5	4/5	3/4	5/3	5/4	4/3
2.	15/17	8/17	15/8	17/15	17/8	8/15
3.	7/25	24/25	7/24	25/7	25/24	24/7
4.	4/5	3/5	4/3	5/4	5/3	3/4
5.	4/5	3/5	4/3	5/4	5/3	3/4
6.	3/5	4/5	3/4	5/3	5/4	4/3
7.	$\sqrt{2}/2$	$\sqrt{2}/2$	1	$\sqrt{2}$	$\sqrt{2}$	1
8.	8/17	15/17	8/15	17/8	17/15	15/8
9.	8/17	15/17	8/15	17/8	17/15	15/8
10.	24/25	7/25	24/7	25/24	25/7	24/7
11.	$\sqrt{2}/2$	$\sqrt{2}/2$	1	$\sqrt{2}$	$\sqrt{2}$	1
12.	$3\sqrt{13}/13$	$2\sqrt{13}/13$	3/2	$\sqrt{13}/3$	$\sqrt{13}/2$	2/3

Right Triangles

Trigonometric Identities

top

1. $\sin\theta\cos\theta - \cos\theta\sin\beta$
2. $\dfrac{\tan\theta + \tan\beta}{1 - \tan\theta\tan\beta}$
3. $\dfrac{\tan\theta - \tan\beta}{1 + \tan\theta\tan\beta}$
4. $-\sin\theta$
5. $-\cos\theta$
6. $\cos\theta$
7. $-\sin\theta$
8. $2\cos\theta\sin\theta$
9. $2\cos^2\theta - 1$
10. $\dfrac{2\cos\theta\sin\theta}{2\cos^2\theta - 1}$

bottom

1. $= 1 + \dfrac{\cos^2\theta}{\sin^2\theta}$
$= \dfrac{\sin^2\theta}{\sin^2\theta} + \dfrac{\cos^2\theta}{\sin^2\theta}$
$= \dfrac{1}{\sin^2\theta}$
$= \csc^2\theta$

2. $= 1 + \dfrac{\sin^2\theta}{\cos^2\theta}$
$= \dfrac{\cos^2\theta}{\cos^2\theta} + \dfrac{\sin^2\theta}{\cos^2\theta}$
$= \dfrac{1}{\cos^2\theta}$
$= \sec^2\theta$

3. $= \dfrac{1}{\cos\theta} - \dfrac{\sin\theta}{\cos\theta} \cdot \sin\theta$
$= \dfrac{1 - \sin^2\theta}{\cos\theta}$
$= \dfrac{\cos^2\theta}{\cos\theta}$
$= \cos\theta$

4. $= \dfrac{1}{\sin\theta} - \dfrac{\cos\theta}{\sin\theta}\cos\theta$
$= \dfrac{1 - \cos^2\theta}{\sin\theta}$
$= \dfrac{\sin^2\theta}{\sin\theta}$
$= \sin\theta$

Answer Key

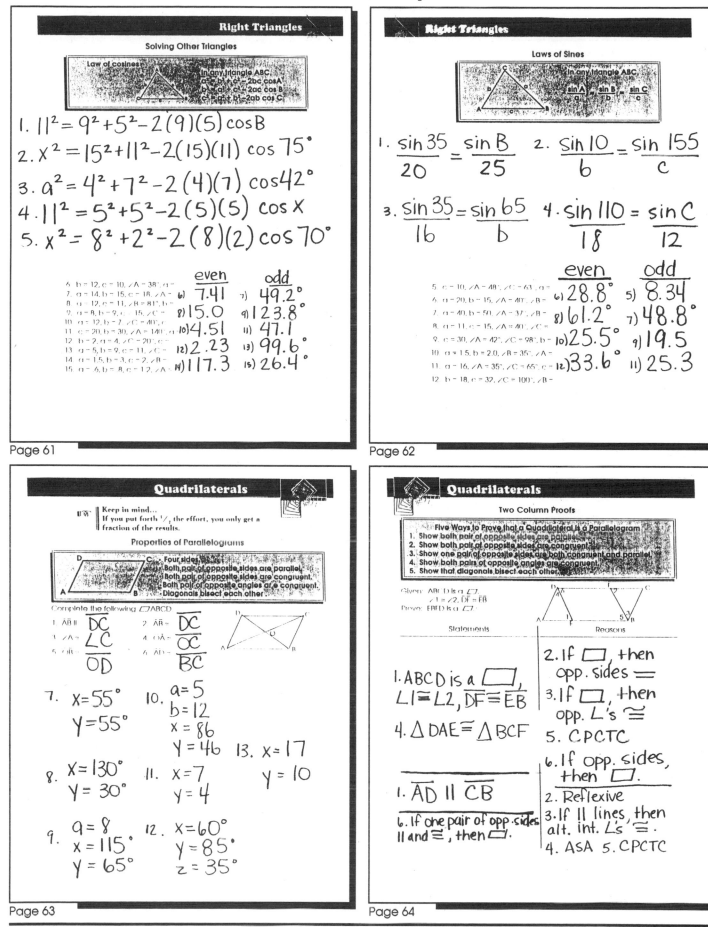

Page 61 — Right Triangles: Solving Other Triangles

Law of cosines: In any triangle ABC,
$a^2 = b^2 + c^2 - 2bc\cos A$
$b^2 = a^2 + c^2 - 2ac\cos B$
$c^2 = a^2 + b^2 - 2ab\cos C$

1. $11^2 = 9^2 + 5^2 - 2(9)(5)\cos B$
2. $x^2 = 15^2 + 11^2 - 2(15)(11)\cos 75°$
3. $a^2 = 4^2 + 7^2 - 2(4)(7)\cos 42°$
4. $11^2 = 5^2 + 5^2 - 2(5)(5)\cos X$
5. $x^2 = 8^2 + 2^2 - 2(8)(2)\cos 70°$

even / odd
6) 7.41   7) 49.2°
8) 15.0   9) 123.8°
10) 4.51   11) 47.1
12) 2.23   13) 99.6°
14) 117.3 15) 26.4°

Page 62 — Right Triangles: Laws of Sines

In any triangle ABC,
$\dfrac{\sin A}{a} = \dfrac{\sin B}{b} = \dfrac{\sin C}{c}$

1. $\dfrac{\sin 35}{20} = \dfrac{\sin B}{25}$
2. $\dfrac{\sin 10}{b} = \dfrac{\sin 155}{c}$
3. $\dfrac{\sin 35}{16} = \dfrac{\sin 65}{b}$
4. $\dfrac{\sin 110}{18} = \dfrac{\sin C}{12}$

even / odd
6) 28.8°   5) 8.34
8) 61.2°   7) 48.8°
10) 25.5° 9) 19.5
12) 33.6° 11) 25.3

Page 63 — Quadrilaterals

Keep in mind... If you put forth ½ the effort, you only get a fraction of the results.

Properties of Parallelograms

Complete the following ▱ABCD

1. $\overline{AB} \parallel$ $\overline{DC}$
2. $\overline{AB} \cong$ $\overline{DC}$
3. $\angle A \cong$ $\angle C$
4. $\overline{OA} \cong$ $\overline{OC}$
5. $\overline{OB} \cong$ $\overline{OD}$
6. $\overline{AD} \cong$ $\overline{BC}$

7. $x = 55°$ $y = 55°$
8. $x = 130°$ $y = 30°$
9. $a = 8$ $x = 115°$ $y = 65°$
10. $a = 5$ $b = 12$ $x = 86$ $y = 46$
11. $x = 7$ $y = 4$
12. $x = 60°$ $y = 85°$ $z = 35°$
13. $x = 17$ $y = 10$

Page 64 — Quadrilaterals: Two Column Proofs

Five Ways to Prove that a Quadrilateral is a Parallelogram
1. Show both pair of opposite sides are parallel.
2. Show both pair of opposite sides are congruent.
3. Show one pair of opposite sides are both congruent and parallel.
4. Show both pairs of opposite angles are congruent.
5. Show that diagonals bisect each other.

Given: ABCD is a ▱.
∠1 ≅ ∠2, $\overline{DF} \cong \overline{EB}$
Prove: EBFD is a ▱.

Statements

1. ABCD is a ▱, $\angle 1 \cong \angle 2$, $\overline{DF} \cong \overline{EB}$
4. $\triangle DAE \cong \triangle BCF$

1. $\overline{AD} \parallel \overline{CB}$

Reasons

2. If ▱, then opp. sides =
3. If ▱, then opp. ∠'s ≅
5. CPCTC
6. If opp. sides, then ▱.

6. If one pair of opp. sides ∥ and ≅, then ▱.

2. Reflexive
3. If ∥ lines, then alt. int. ∠'s ≅.
4. ASA   5. CPCTC

Answer Key

Quadrilaterals — More Two Column Proofs

Given: ABCE is a ▱.
FB ⊥ AD; DC ⊥ BC
Prove: FBCD is a ▱.

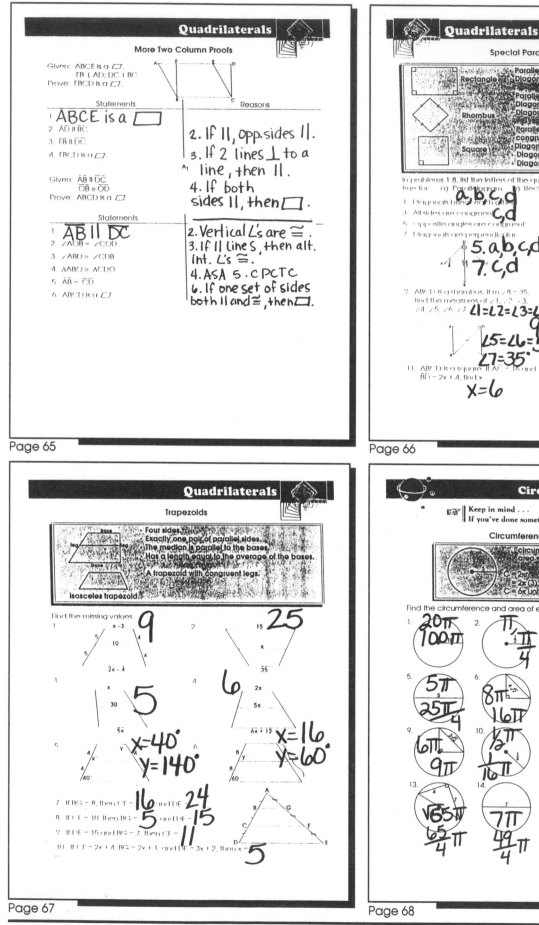

Statements	Reasons
1. ABCE is a ▱	
2. AD ∥ BC	2. If ∥, opp. sides ∥.
3. FB ∥ DC	3. If 2 lines ⊥ to a line, then ∥.
4. FBCD is a ▱.	4. If both sides ∥, then ▱.

Given: AB ∥ DC
OB ≅ OD
Prove: ABCD is a ▱.

Statements	Reasons
1. AB ∥ DC	
2. ∠AOB ≅ ∠COD	2. Vertical ∠'s are ≅.
3. ∠ABD ≅ ∠CDB	3. If ∥ lines, then alt. int. ∠'s ≅.
4. △AOB ≅ △CDO	4. ASA 5. CPCTC
5. AB ≅ CD	6. If one set of sides both ∥ and ≅, then ▱.
6. ABCD is a ▱	

Page 65

Quadrilaterals — Special Parallelograms

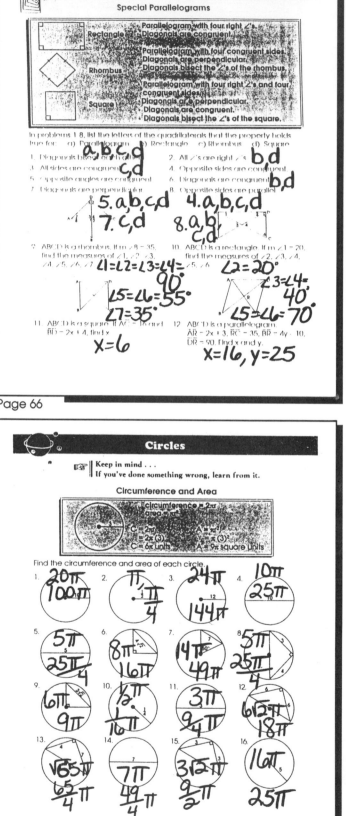

Rectangle — Parallelogram with four right ∠'s. Diagonals are congruent.

Rhombus — Parallelogram with four congruent sides. Diagonals are perpendicular. Diagonals bisect the ∠'s of the rhombus.

Square — Parallelogram with four right ∠'s and four congruent sides. Diagonals are perpendicular. Diagonals are congruent. Diagonals bisect the ∠'s of the square.

In problems 1-8, list the letters of the quadrilaterals that the property holds true for: a) Parallelogram b) Rectangle c) Rhombus d) Square

1. Diagonals bisect each other. a,b,c,d
2. All ∠'s are right ∠'s. b,d
3. All sides are congruent. c,d
4. Opposite sides are congruent. a,b,c,d
5. Opposite angles are congruent. a,b,c,d
6. Diagonals are congruent. b,d
7. Diagonals are perpendicular. c,d
8. Opposite sides are parallel. a,b,c,d

9. ABCD is a rhombus. If m∠8 = 35, find the measures of ∠1, ∠2, ∠3, ∠4, ∠5, ∠6, ∠7.
∠1=∠2=∠3=∠4=90°
∠5=∠6=55°
∠7=35°

10. ABCD is a rectangle. If m∠1 = 20, find the measures of ∠2, ∠3, ∠4, ∠5, ∠6.
∠2=20°
∠3=∠4=40°
∠5=∠6=70°

11. ABCD is a square. If AC = 19 and BD = 2x + 4, find x.
x=6

12. ABCD is a parallelogram. AR = 2x + 3, RC = 35, BR = 4y - 10, DR = 90. Find x and y.
x=16, y=25

Page 66

Quadrilaterals — Trapezoids

Four sides.
Exactly one pair of parallel sides.
The median is parallel to the bases. Has a length equal to the average of the bases.
isosceles trapezoid — A trapezoid with congruent legs.

Find the missing values.

1. 9
2. 25
3. 5
4. 6
5. x=40°, y=140°
6. x=16, y=60°
7. If BG = 8, then CF = 16 and DE = 24.
8. If CF = 10, then BG = 5 and DE = 15.
9. If DE = 15 and BG = 7, then CF = 11.
10. If CF = 2x + 4, BG = 2x + 1, and DE = 3x + 2, then x = 5.

Page 67

Circles

☞ Keep in mind . . .
If you've done something wrong, learn from it.

Circumference and Area

Circumference = 2πr
area = πr²

C = 2πr
C = 2π(3)
C = 6π units

A = πr²
A = π(3)²
A = 9π square units

Find the circumference and area of each circle.

1. 20π / 100π
2. π / π/4
3. 24π / 144π
4. 10π / 25π
5. 5π / 25π
6. 8π / 16π
7. 14π / 49π
8. 5π / 25π/4
9. 6π / 9π
10. ½π / 1/16π
11. 3π / 9/4π
12. 6√2π / 18π
13. √65π / 65/4π
14. 7π / 49/4π
15. 3√2π / 9/2π
16. 16π / 25π

Page 68

Answer Key

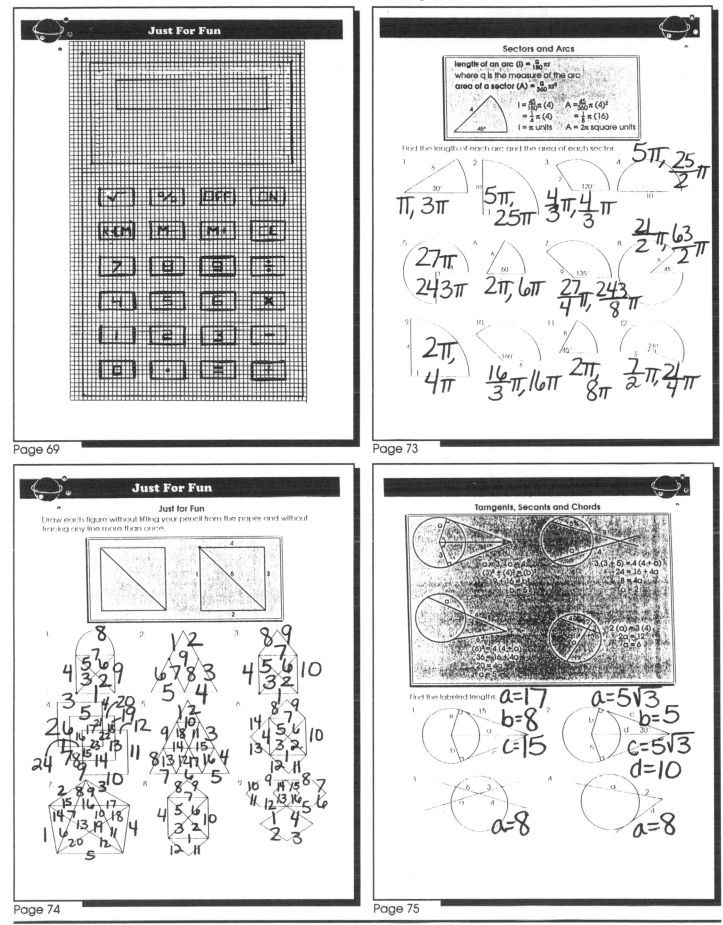

Answer Key

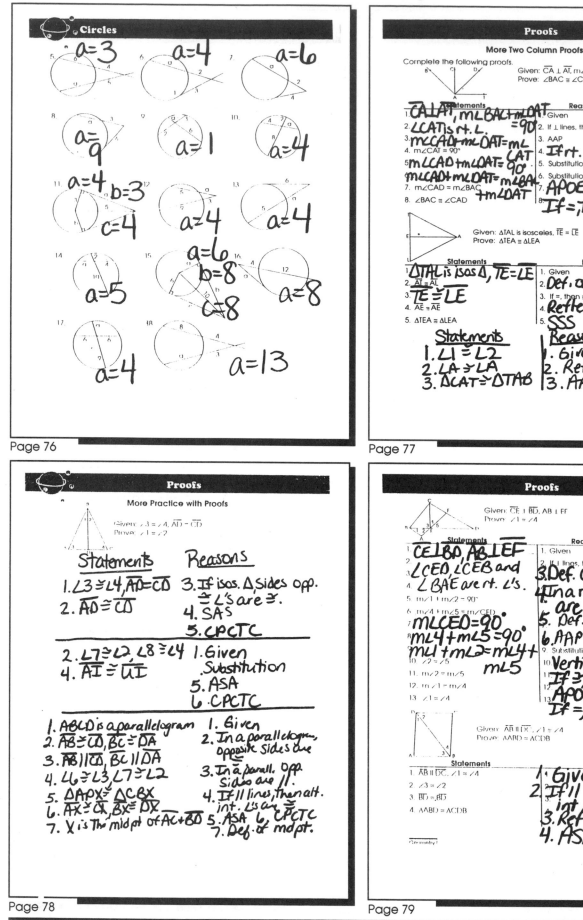

Answer Key

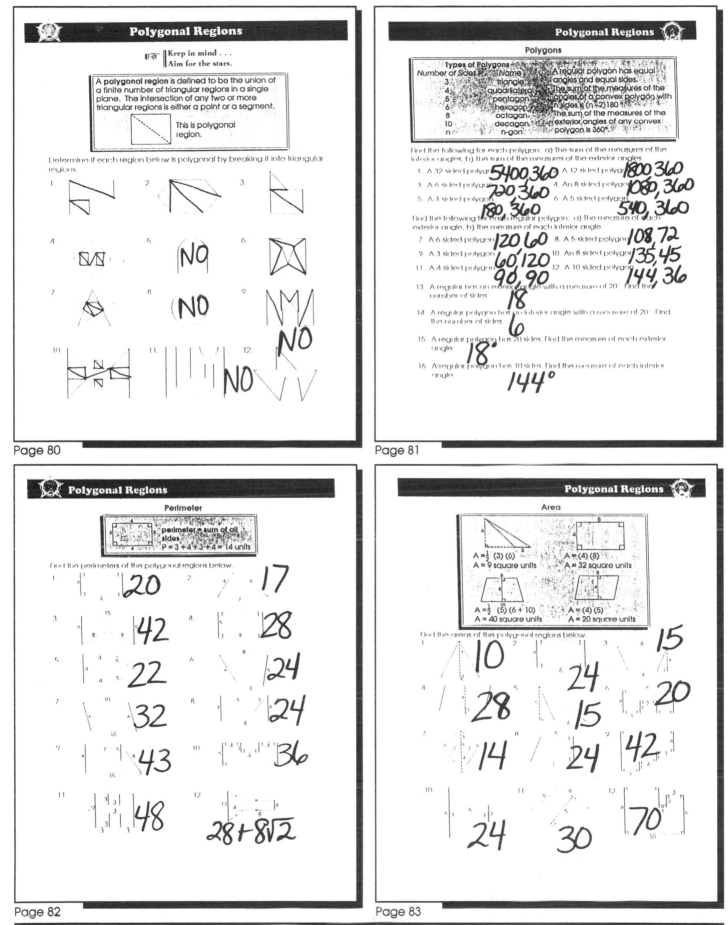

Polygonal Regions

Keep in mind . . . Aim for the stars.

A **polygonal region** is defined to be the union of a finite number of triangular regions in a single plane. The intersection of any two or more triangular regions is either a point or a segment.

This is polygonal region.

Determine if each region below is polygonal by breaking it into triangular regions.

1. 2. 3.

4. 5. NO 6.

7. 8. NO 9.

NO

10. 11. 12. NO

Page 80

Polygonal Regions

Polygons

Types of Polygons		
Number of Sides	Name	A regular polygon has equal angles and equal sides.
3	triangle	The sum of the measures of the angles of a convex polygon with n sides is (n−2)180°.
4	quadrilateral	
5	pentagon	
6	hexagon	
8	octagon	The sum of the measures of the exterior angles of any convex polygon is 360°.
10	decagon	
n	n-gon	

Find the following for each polygon: a) the sum of the measures of the interior angles, b) the sum of the measures of the exterior angles.

1. A 32-sided polygon **5400, 360**   A 12 sided polygon **1800, 360**
3. A 6-sided polygon **720, 360**   4. An 8 sided polygon **1080, 360**
5. A 3 sided polygon **180, 360**   6. A 5 sided polygon **540, 360**

Find the following for each regular polygon: a) the measure of each exterior angle, b) the measure of each interior angle.

7. A 6-sided polygon **120, 60**   8. A 5-sided polygon **108, 72**
9. A 3 sided polygon **60, 120**   10. An 8-sided polygon **135, 45**
11. A 4-sided polygon **90, 90**   12. A 10 sided polygon **144, 36**

13. A regular has an exterior angle with a measure of 20°. Find the number of sides. **18**

14. A regular polygon has an interior angle with a measure of 20°. Find the number of sides. **6**

15. A regular polygon has 20 sides. Find the measure of each exterior angle. **18°**

16. A regular polygon has 10 sides. Find the measure of each interior angle. **144°**

Page 81

Polygonal Regions

Perimeter

perimeter = sum of all sides
P = 3 + 4 + 3 + 4 = 14 units

Find the perimeters of the polygonal regions below.

1. **20**   2. **17**
3. **42**   4. **28**
5. **22**   6. **24**
7. **32**   8. **24**
9. **43**   10. **36**
11. **48**   12. **28 + 8√2**

Page 82

Polygonal Regions

Area

$A = \frac{1}{2}$ (3) (6)
A = 9 square units

A = (4) (8)
A = 32 square units

$A = \frac{1}{2}$ (5) (6 + 10)
A = 40 square units

A = (4) (5)
A = 20 square units

Find the areas of the polygonal regions below.

1. **10**   2. **24**   3. **15**
4. **28**   5. **15**   6. **20**
7. **14**   8. **24**   9. **42**
10. **24**   11. **30**   12. **70**

Page 83

Geometry IF8764   123   © MCMXCIV Instructional Fair, Inc.

Answer Key

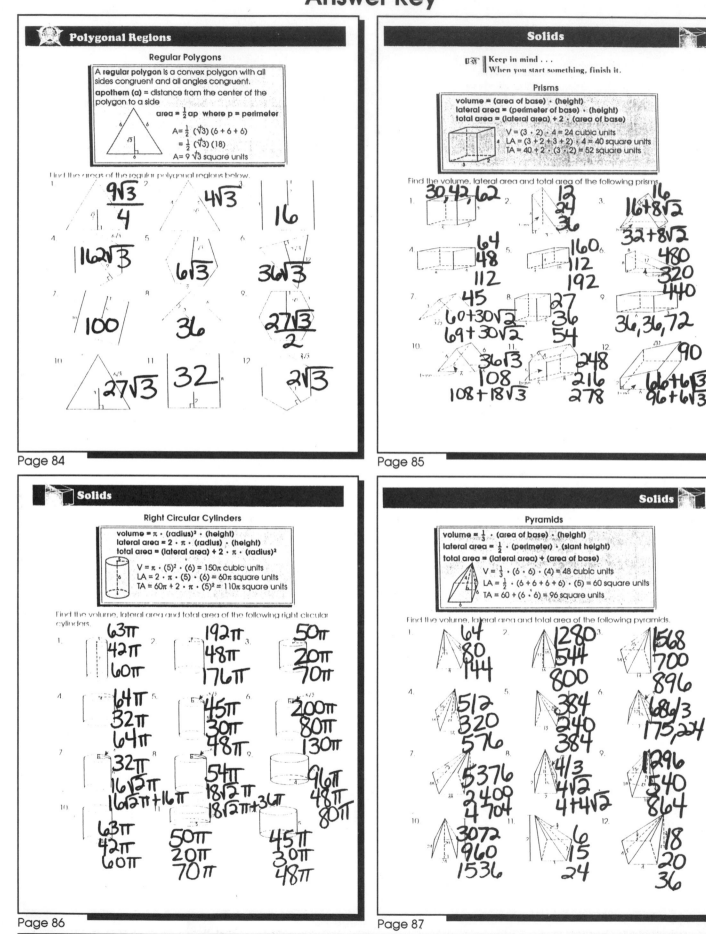

Polygonal Regions

Regular Polygons

A **regular polygon** is a convex polygon with all sides congruent and all angles congruent.

apothem (a) = distance from the center of the polygon to a side

$area = \frac{1}{2}ap$ where p = perimeter

$A = \frac{1}{2}(\sqrt{3})(6+6+6)$
$= \frac{1}{2}(\sqrt{3})(18)$
$A = 9\sqrt{3}$ square units

Find the areas of the regular polygonal regions below.

1. $\dfrac{9\sqrt{3}}{4}$ 2. $4\sqrt{3}$ 3. 16

4. $162\sqrt{3}$ 5. $6\sqrt{3}$ 6. $36\sqrt{3}$

7. 100 8. 36 9. $\dfrac{27\sqrt{3}}{2}$

10. $27\sqrt{3}$ 11. 32 12. $2\sqrt{3}$

Page 84

Solids

☞ Keep in mind . . .
When you start something, finish it.

Prisms

volume = (area of base) · (height)
lateral area = (perimeter of base) · (height)
total area = (lateral area) + 2 · (area of base)

$V = (3 \cdot 2) \cdot 4 = 24$ cubic units
$LA = (3+2+3+2) \cdot 4 = 40$ square units
$TA = 40 + 2 \cdot (3 \cdot 2) = 52$ square units

Find the volume, lateral area and total area of the following prisms.

1. $30, 42, 62$ 2. $12, 27, 36$ 3. $16, 16+8\sqrt{2}, 32+8\sqrt{2}$

4. $64, 48, 112$ 5. $160, 112, 192$ 6. $480, 320, 440$

7. $45, 60+30\sqrt{2}, 69+30\sqrt{2}$ 8. $27, 36, 54$ 9. $36, 36, 72$

10. $36\sqrt{3}, 108, 108+18\sqrt{3}$ 11. $248, 216, 278$ 12. $90, 60+6\sqrt{37}, 96+6\sqrt{37}$

Page 85

Solids

Right Circular Cylinders

volume = π · (radius)² · (height)
lateral area = 2 · π · (radius) · (height)
total area = (lateral area) + 2 · π · (radius)²

$V = \pi \cdot (5)^2 \cdot (6) = 150\pi$ cubic units
$LA = 2 \cdot \pi \cdot (5) \cdot (6) = 60\pi$ square units
$TA = 60\pi + 2 \cdot \pi \cdot (5)^2 = 110\pi$ square units

Find the volume, lateral area and total area of the following right circular cylinders.

1. $63\pi, 42\pi, 60\pi$ 2. $192\pi, 48\pi, 176\pi$ 3. $50\pi, 20\pi, 70\pi$

4. $64\pi, 32\pi, 64\pi$ 5. $45\pi, 30\pi, 48\pi$ 6. $200\pi, 80\pi, 130\pi$

7. $32\pi, 16\sqrt{2}\pi, 16\sqrt{2}\pi+16\pi$ 8. $54\pi, 18\sqrt{2}\pi, 18\sqrt{2}\pi+36\pi$ 9. $96\pi, 48\pi, 80\pi$

10. $63\pi, 42\pi, 60\pi$ 11. $50\pi, 20\pi, 70\pi$ 12. $45\pi, 30\pi, 48\pi$

Page 86

Solids

Pyramids

volume = $\frac{1}{3}$ · (area of base) · (height)
lateral area = $\frac{1}{2}$ · (perimeter) · (slant height)
total area = (lateral area) + (area of base)

$V = \frac{1}{3} \cdot (6 \cdot 6) \cdot (4) = 48$ cubic units
$LA = \frac{1}{2} \cdot (6+6+6+6) \cdot (5) = 60$ square units
$TA = 60 + (6 \cdot 6) = 96$ square units

Find the volume, lateral area and total area of the following pyramids.

1. $64, 80, 144$ 2. $1280, 544, 800$ 3. $1568, 700, 896$

4. $512, 320, 576$ 5. $384, 240, 384$ 6. $168\sqrt{3}, 175, 204$

7. $5376, 3400, 4704$ 8. $4/3, 4\sqrt{2}, 4+4\sqrt{2}$ 9. $1296, 540, 864$

10. $3072, 960, 1536$ 11. $6, 15, 24$ 12. $18, 20, 36$

Page 87

Geometry IF8764

124

© MCMXCIV Instructional Fair, Inc.

Answer Key

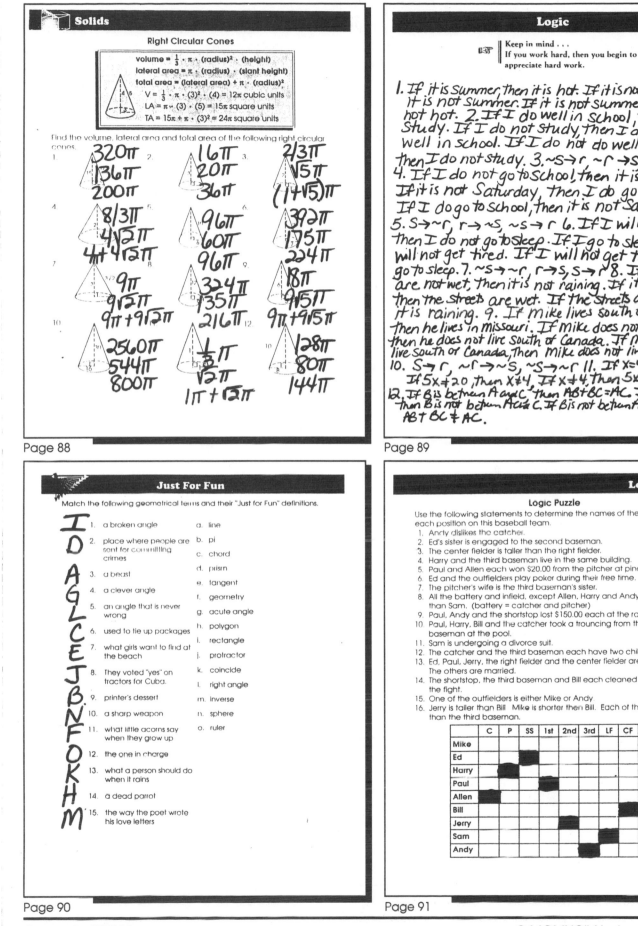

Solids

Right Circular Cones

volume = $\frac{1}{3} \cdot \pi \cdot (radius)^2 \cdot (height)$
lateral area = $\pi \cdot (radius) \cdot (slant\ height)$
total area = $(lateral\ area) + \pi \cdot (radius)^2$
$V = \frac{1}{3} \cdot \pi \cdot (3)^2 \cdot (4) = 12\pi$ cubic units
$LA = \pi \cdot (3) \cdot (5) = 15\pi$ square units
$TA = 15\pi + \pi \cdot (3)^2 = 24\pi$ square units

Find the volume, lateral area and total area of the following right circular cones.

1. 320π
   136π
   200π

2. 16π
   20π
   36π

3. $\frac{2}{3}\pi$
   $\sqrt{5}\pi$
   $(1+\sqrt{5})\pi$

4. $\frac{8}{3}\pi$
   $4\sqrt{2}\pi$
   $4\pi + 4\sqrt{2}\pi$

5. 96π
   60π
   96π

6. 392π
   175π
   224π

7. 9π
   $9\sqrt{2}\pi$
   $9\pi + 9\sqrt{2}\pi$

8. 324π
   135π
   216π

9. 18π
   $9\sqrt{5}\pi$
   $9\pi + 9\sqrt{5}\pi$

10. 2560π
    544π
    800π

11. $\frac{1}{3}\pi$
    $\sqrt{2}\pi$
    $1\pi + \sqrt{2}\pi$

12. 128π
    80π
    144π

Page 88

Logic

☞ Keep in mind . . .
If you work hard, then you begin to appreciate hard work.

1. If it is summer, then it is hot. If it is not hot, then it is not summer. If it is not summer, then it is not hot hot.
2. If I do well in school, then I study. If I do not study, then I do not do well in school. If I do not do well in school, then I do not study.
3. $\sim S \to r$, $\sim r \to S$, $S \to \sim r$
4. If I do not go to school, then it is Saturday. If it is not Saturday, then I do go to school. If I do go to school, then it is not Saturday.
5. $S \to \sim r$, $r \to \sim S$, $\sim S \to r$
6. If I will get tired, then I do not go to sleep. If I go to sleep, then I will not get tired. If I will not get tired, then I go to sleep.
7. $\sim S \to \sim r$, $r \to S$, $S \to r$
8. If the streets are not wet, then it is not raining. If it is raining, then the streets are wet. If the streets are wet, then it is raining.
9. If Mike lives south of Canada, then he lives in Missouri. If Mike does not live in Missouri, then he does not live south of Canada. If Mike does not live south of Canada, then Mike does not live in MO.
10. $S \to r$, $\sim r \to \sim S$, $\sim S \to \sim r$
11. If $x=4$, then $5x=20$. If $5x \neq 20$, then $x \neq 4$. If $x \neq 4$, then $5x \neq 20$.
12. If B is between A and C, then $AB + BC = AC$. If $AB + BC \neq AC$, then B is not between A and C. If B is not between A and C, then $AB + BC \neq AC$.

Page 89

Just For Fun

Match the following geometrical terms and their "Just for Fun" definitions.

1. a broken angle — I
2. place where people are sent for committing crimes — D
3. a beast — A
4. a clever angle — G
5. an angle that is never wrong — L
6. used to tie up packages — C
7. what girls want to find at the beach — E
8. They voted "yes" on tractors for Cuba. — J
9. printer's dessert — B
10. a sharp weapon — N
11. what little acorns say when they grow up — F
12. the one in charge — O
13. what a person should do when it rains — K
14. a dead parrot — H
15. the way the poet wrote his love letters — M

a. line
b. pi
c. chord
d. prism
e. tangent
f. geometry
g. acute angle
h. polygon
i. rectangle
j. protractor
k. coincide
l. right angle
m. inverse
n. sphere
o. ruler

Page 90

Logic

Logic Puzzle

Use the following statements to determine the names of the men playing each position on this baseball team.
1. Andy dislikes the catcher.
2. Ed's sister is engaged to the second baseman.
3. The center fielder is taller than the right fielder.
4. Harry and the third baseman live in the same building.
5. Paul and Allen each won $20.00 from the pitcher at pinochle.
6. Ed and the outfielders play poker during their free time.
7. The pitcher's wife is the third baseman's sister.
8. All the battery and infield, except Allen, Harry and Andy, are shorter than Sam. (battery = catcher and pitcher)
9. Paul, Andy and the shortstop lost $150.00 each at the racetrack.
10. Paul, Harry, Bill and the catcher took a trouncing from the second baseman at the pool.
11. Sam is undergoing a divorce suit.
12. The catcher and the third baseman each have two children.
13. Ed, Paul, Jerry, the right fielder and the center fielder are bachelors. The others are married.
14. The shortstop, the third baseman and Bill each cleaned up betting on the fight.
15. One of the outfielders is either Mike or Andy.
16. Jerry is taller than Bill. Mike is shorter than Bill. Each of them is heavier than the third baseman.

	C	P	SS	1st	2nd	3rd	LF	CF	RF
Mike									■
Ed			■						
Harry		■							
Paul				■					
Allen	■								
Bill								■	
Jerry						■			
Sam					■				
Andy							■		

Page 91

Answer Key

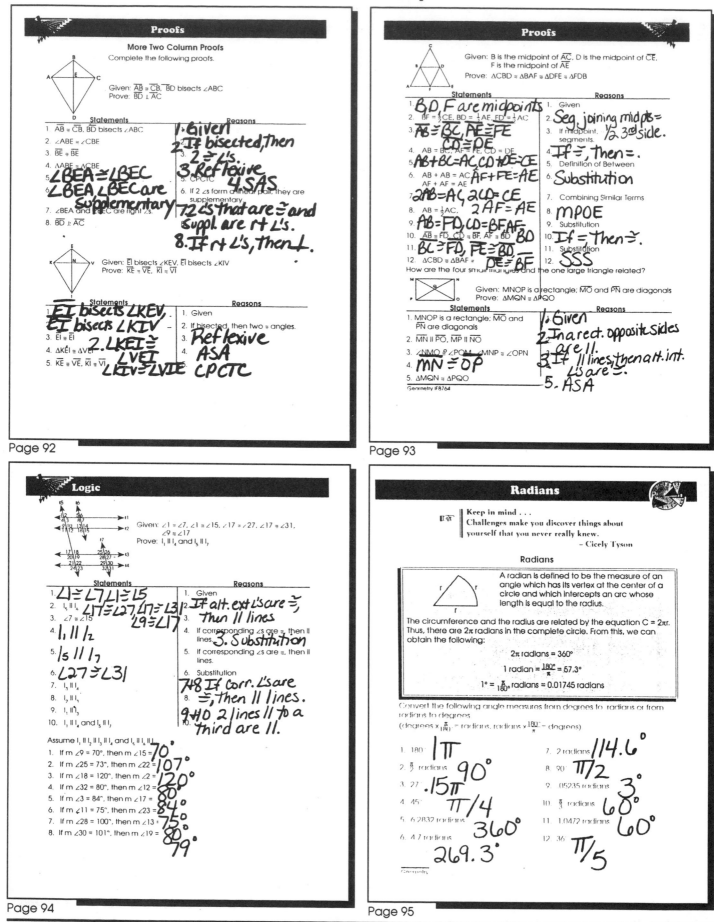

Page 92

Proofs
More Two Column Proofs
Complete the following proofs.

Given: $\overline{AB} \cong \overline{CB}$, $\overline{BD}$ bisects $\angle ABC$
Prove: $\overline{BD} \perp \overline{AC}$

Statements	Reasons
1. $\overline{AB} \cong \overline{CB}$, $\overline{BD}$ bisects $\angle ABC$	1. Given
2. $\angle ABE \cong \angle CBE$	2. If bisected, then 2 ≅ ∠'s
3. $\overline{BE} \cong \overline{BE}$	3. Reflexive
4. $\triangle ABE \cong \triangle CBE$	4. SAS
5. $\angle BEA \cong \angle BEC$	5. CPCTC
6. $\angle BEA$, $\angle BEC$ are supplementary	6. If 2 ∠s form a linear pair, they are supplementary
7. $\angle BEA$ and $\angle BEC$ are right ∠s.	7. 2 ∠s that are ≅ and suppl. are rt ∠'s.
8. $\overline{BD} \perp \overline{AC}$	8. If rt ∠'s, then ⊥.

Given: $\overline{EI}$ bisects $\angle KEV$, $\overline{EI}$ bisects $\angle KIV$
Prove: $\overline{KE} \cong \overline{VE}$, $\overline{KI} \cong \overline{VI}$

Statements	Reasons
1. $\overline{EI}$ bisects $\angle KEV$, $\overline{EI}$ bisects $\angle KIV$	1. Given
2. $\angle KEI \cong \angle VEI$, $\angle KIV \cong \angle VIE$	2. If bisected, then two ≅ angles.
3. $\overline{EI} \cong \overline{EI}$	3. Reflexive
4. $\triangle KEI \cong \triangle VEI$	4. ASA
5. $\overline{KE} \cong \overline{VE}$, $\overline{KI} \cong \overline{VI}$	5. CPCTC

Page 93

Proofs

Given: B is the midpoint of $\overline{AC}$, D is the midpoint of $\overline{CE}$. F is the midpoint of $\overline{AE}$
Prove: $\triangle CBD \cong \triangle BAF \cong \triangle DFE \cong \triangle FDB$

Statements	Reasons
1. B, D, F are midpoints	1. Given
2. $BF = \frac{1}{2}CE$, $BD = \frac{1}{2}AE$, $FD = \frac{1}{2}AC$	2. Seg. joining midpts = ½ 3rd side.
3. $\overline{AB} \cong \overline{BC}$, $\overline{AF} \cong \overline{FE}$, $\overline{CD} \cong \overline{DE}$	3. If midpoint, segments ≅.
4. $AB = BC$, $AF = FE$, $CD = DE$	4. If ≅, then =.
5. $AB + BC = AC$, $CD + DE = CE$	5. Definition of Between
6. $AB + AB = AC$, $AF + FE = AE$, $AF + AF = AE$	6. Substitution
7. $2AB = AC$, $2CD = CE$, $2AF = AE$	7. Combining Similar Terms
8. $AB = \frac{1}{2}AC$, $2AF = AE$	8. MPOE
9. $AB = FD$, $CD = BF$, $AF = BD$	9. Substitution
10. $\overline{AB} \cong \overline{FD}$, $\overline{CD} \cong \overline{BF}$, $\overline{AF} \cong \overline{BD}$	10. If = then ≅.
11. $\overline{BC} \cong \overline{FD}$, $\overline{FE} \cong \overline{BD}$	11. Substitution
12. $\triangle CBD \cong \triangle BAF$, $\overline{DE} \cong \overline{BF}$	12. SSS

How are the four small triangles and the one large triangle related?

Given: MNOP is a rectangle; $\overline{MO}$ and $\overline{PN}$ are diagonals
Prove: $\triangle MQN \cong \triangle PQO$

Statements	Reasons
1. MNOP is a rectangle; $\overline{MO}$ and $\overline{PN}$ are diagonals	1. Given
2. $\overline{MN} \parallel \overline{PO}$, $\overline{MP} \parallel \overline{NO}$	2. In a rect. opposite sides are ∥.
3. $\angle NMO \cong \angle POM$, $\angle MNP \cong \angle OPN$	3. If ∥ lines, then alt. int. ∠s are ≅.
4. $\overline{MN} \cong \overline{OP}$	4.
5. $\triangle MQN \cong \triangle PQO$	5. ASA

Geometry IF8764

Page 94

Logic

Given: $\angle 1 \cong \angle 7$, $\angle 1 \cong \angle 15$, $\angle 17 \cong \angle 27$, $\angle 17 \cong \angle 31$, $\angle 9 \cong \angle 17$
Prove: $l_1 \parallel l_4$ and $l_5 \parallel l_7$

Statements	Reasons
1. $\angle 1 \cong \angle 7$, $\angle 1 \cong \angle 15$	1. Given
2. $l_5 \parallel l_4$, $\angle 17 \cong \angle 27$, $\angle 17 \cong \angle 31$, $\angle 9 \cong \angle 17$	2. If alt. ext. ∠'s are ≅, then ∥ lines.
3. $\angle 7 \cong \angle 15$	3. Substitution
4. $l_1 \parallel l_2$	4. If corresponding ∠s are ≅, then ∥ lines.
5. $l_5 \parallel l_7$	5. If corresponding ∠s are ≅, then ∥ lines.
6. $\angle 27 \cong \angle 31$	6. Substitution
7. $l_1 \parallel l_3$	7&8. If corr. ∠'s are ≅, then ∥ lines.
8. $l_5 \parallel l_4$	8.
9. $l_1 \parallel l_3$	9&10. 2 lines ∥ to a third are ∥.
10. $l_1 \parallel l_4$ and $l_5 \parallel l_7$	10.

Assume $l_1 \parallel l_2 \parallel l_3 \parallel l_4$ and $l_5 \parallel l_6 \parallel l_7$
1. If m$\angle 9 = 70°$, then m$\angle 15 =$ **70°**
2. If m$\angle 25 = 73°$, then m$\angle 22 =$ **107°**
3. If m$\angle 18 = 120°$, then m$\angle 12 =$ **120°**
4. If m$\angle 32 = 80°$, then m$\angle 12 =$ **80°**
5. If m$\angle 3 = 84°$, then m$\angle 17 =$ **84°**
6. If m$\angle 11 = 75°$, then m$\angle 23 =$ **75°**
7. If m$\angle 28 = 100°$, then m$\angle 13 =$ **80°**
8. If m$\angle 30 = 101°$, then m$\angle 19 =$ **79°**

Page 95

Radians

Keep in mind . . .
Challenges make you discover things about yourself that you never really knew.
– Cicely Tyson

Radians

A radian is defined to be the measure of an angle which has its vertex at the center of a circle and which intercepts an arc whose length is equal to the radius.

The circumference and the radius are related by the equation $C = 2\pi r$. Thus, there are 2π radians in the complete circle. From this, we can obtain the following:

$$2\pi \text{ radians} = 360°$$
$$1 \text{ radian} = \frac{180°}{\pi} = 57.3°$$
$$1° = \frac{\pi}{180°} \text{ radians} = 0.01745 \text{ radians}$$

Convert the following angle measures from degrees to radians or from radians to degrees.
(degrees $\times \frac{\pi}{180°}$ = radians, radians $\times \frac{180°}{\pi}$ = degrees)

1. 180° — 1π
2. $\frac{\pi}{2}$ radians — $90°$
3. 27° — $.15\pi$
4. 45° — $\pi/4$
5. 6.2832 radians — $360°$
6. 4.7 radians — $269.3°$
7. 2 radians — $114.6°$
8. 90° — $\pi/2$
9. .05235 radians — $3°$
10. $\frac{\pi}{3}$ radians — $60°$
11. 1.0472 radians — $60°$
12. 36° — $\pi/5$

Geometry

Answer Key

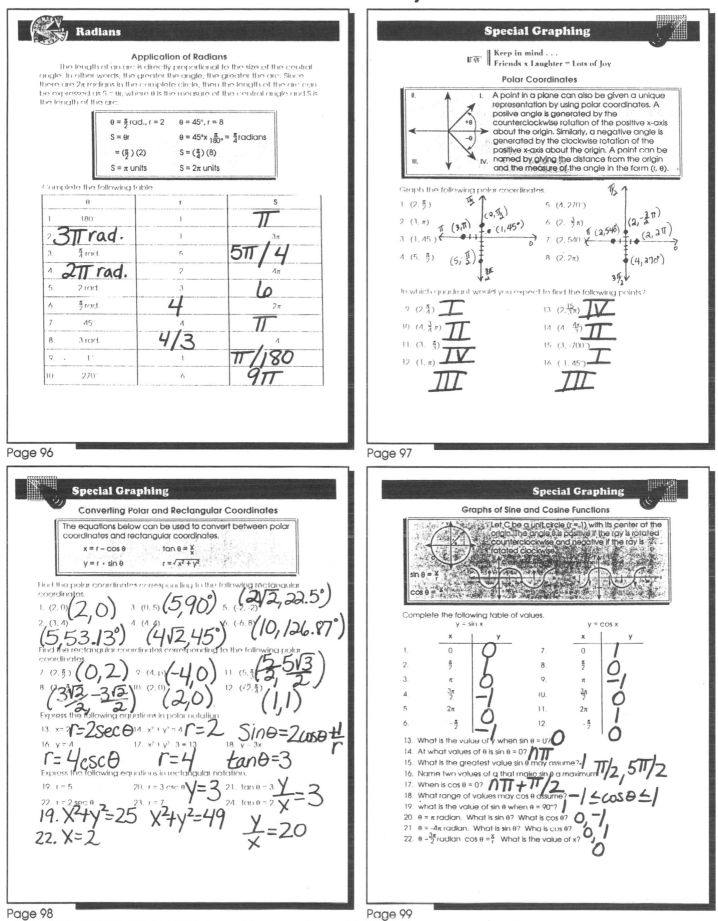

Radians

Application of Radians

The length of an arc is directly proportional to the size of the central angle. In other words, the greater the angle, the greater the arc. Since there are 2π radians in the complete circle, then the length of the arc can be expressed as $S = \theta r$, where θ is the measure of the central angle and S is the length of the arc.

$\theta = \frac{\pi}{2}$ rad., $r = 2$	$\theta = 45°$, $r = 8$
$S = \theta r$	$\theta = 45° \times \frac{\pi}{180°} = \frac{\pi}{4}$ radians
$= (\frac{\pi}{2})(2)$	$S = (\frac{\pi}{4})(8)$
$S = \pi$ units	$S = 2\pi$ units

Complete the following table.

	θ	r	S
1.	180°	1	π
2.	3π rad.	1	3π
3.	$\frac{\pi}{4}$ rad.	5	$5\pi/4$
4.	2π rad.	2	4π
5.	2 rad.	3	6
6.	$\frac{\pi}{2}$ rad.	4	2π
7.	45°	4	π
8.	3 rad.	4/3	4
9.	1°	1	$\pi/180$
10.	270°	6	9π

Special Graphing

Keep in mind . . .
Friends x Laughter = Lots of Joy

Polar Coordinates

I. A point in a plane can also be given a unique representation by using polar coordinates. A positive angle is generated by the counterclockwise rotation of the positive x-axis about the origin. Similarly, a negative angle is generated by the clockwise rotation of the positive x-axis about the origin. A point can be named by giving the distance from the origin and the measure of the angle in the form (r, θ).

Graph the following polar coordinates.

1. $(2, \frac{\pi}{2})$
2. $(3, \pi)$
3. $(1, 45°)$
4. $(5, \frac{\pi}{2})$
5. $(4, 270°)$
6. $(2, \frac{3\pi}{2})$
7. $(2, 540°)$
8. $(2, 2\pi)$

In which quadrant would you expect to find the following points?

9. $(2, \frac{\pi}{4})$ **I**
10. $(4, \frac{3}{4}\pi)$ **II**
11. $(3, \frac{\pi}{4})$ **IV**
12. $(1, \pi)$ **III**
13. $(2, \frac{15}{8}\pi)$ **IV**
14. $(4, \frac{4\pi}{5})$ **II**
15. $(3, -700°)$ **I**
16. $(1, 45°)$ **III**

Special Graphing

Converting Polar and Rectangular Coordinates

The equations below can be used to convert between polar coordinates and rectangular coordinates.

$x = r \cdot \cos\theta$ $\tan\theta = \frac{y}{x}$

$y = r \cdot \sin\theta$ $r = \sqrt{x^2 + y^2}$

Find the polar coordinates corresponding to the following rectangular coordinates.

1. $(2, 0)$ $(2, 0)$
2. $(3, 4)$ $(5, 53.13°)$
3. $(0, 5)$ $(5, 90°)$
4. $(4, 4)$ $(4\sqrt{2}, 45°)$
5. $(-2, -2)$ $(2\sqrt{2}, 22.5°)$
6. $(-6, 8)$ $(10, 126.87°)$

Find the rectangular coordinates corresponding to the following polar coordinates.

7. $(2, \frac{\pi}{2})$ $(0, 2)$
8. $(3, \frac{7\pi}{4})$ $(\frac{3\sqrt{2}}{2}, -\frac{3\sqrt{2}}{2})$
9. $(4, \pi)$ $(-4, 0)$
10. $(2, 0)$ $(2, 0)$
11. $(5, \frac{\pi}{3})$ $(\frac{5}{2}, \frac{5\sqrt{3}}{2})$
12. $(\sqrt{2}, \frac{\pi}{4})$ $(1, 1)$

Express the following equations in polar notation.

13. $x = 2$ $r = 2\sec\theta$
14. $x^2 + y^2 = 4$ $r = 2$
15. $x^2 + y^2 = 13$ $\sin\theta = 2\cos\theta \pm \frac{1}{r}$
16. $y = 4$ $r = 4\csc\theta$
17. $x^2 + y^2 = 13$ $r = 4$
18. $y = 3x$ $\tan\theta = 3$

Express the following equations in rectangular notation.

19. $r = 5$ $x^2 + y^2 = 25$
20. $r = 3\csc\theta$ $y = 3$
21. $\tan\theta = 3$ $\frac{y}{x} = 3$
22. $r = 2\sec\theta$ $x = 2$
23. $r = 7$ $x^2 + y^2 = 49$
24. $\tan\theta = 2$ $\frac{y}{x} = 20$

Special Graphing

Graphs of Sine and Cosine Functions

Let C be a unit circle ($r = 1$) with its center at the origin. The angle is positive if the ray is rotated counterclockwise and negative if the ray is rotated clockwise.

$\sin\theta = \frac{y}{r}$

$\cos\theta = \frac{x}{r}$

Complete the following table of values.

	$y = \sin x$				$y = \cos x$	
	x	y			x	y
1.	0	0	7.		0	1
2.	$\frac{\pi}{2}$	1	8.		$\frac{\pi}{2}$	0
3.	π	0	9.		π	-1
4.	$\frac{3\pi}{2}$	-1	10.		$\frac{3\pi}{2}$	0
5.	2π	0	11.		2π	1
6.	$-\frac{\pi}{2}$	-1	12.		$-\frac{\pi}{2}$	0

13. What is the value of y when $\sin\theta = 0$? 0
14. At what values of θ is $\sin\theta = 0$? $n\pi$
15. What is the greatest value $\sin\theta$ may assume? 1
16. Name two values of θ that make $\sin\theta$ a maximum. $\pi/2, 5\pi/2$
17. When is $\cos\theta = 0$? $n\pi + \pi/2$
18. What range of values may $\cos\theta$ assume? $-1 \le \cos\theta \le 1$
19. What is the value of $\sin\theta$ when $\theta = 90°$? 1
20. $\theta = \pi$ radian. What is $\sin\theta$? What is $\cos\theta$? 0, -1
21. $\theta = -4\pi$ radian. What is $\sin\theta$? What is $\cos\theta$? 0, 1
22. $\theta = \frac{3\pi}{2}$ radian. $\cos\theta = \frac{x}{r}$. What is the value of x? 0

Answer Key

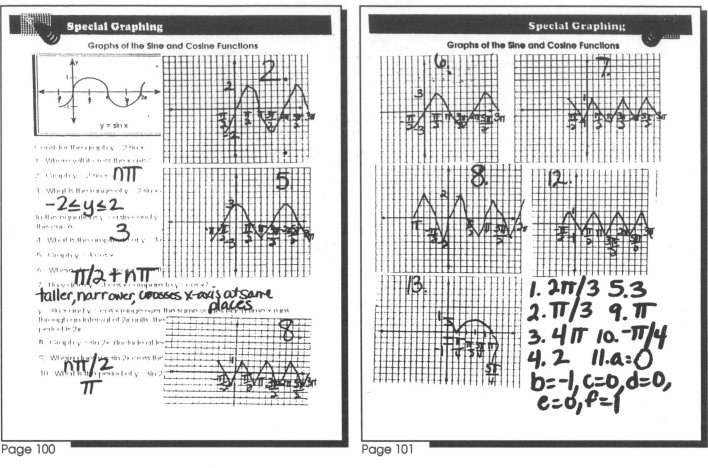

Page 100

Page 101

About the Book . . .

This book has been designed to provide your child with practice in the skill areas required for understanding geometry concepts. The approach is basic with no formal proofs demonstrated. An introduction to basic ideas and terminology in presented in the first part of the book. Definitions, formulas and basic facts are provided where needed to introduce topics. Examples are given where appropriate. Each skill addressed is identified on all of the activity pages.

About the Authors . . .

Mary Lee Vivian has helped many secondary students master a variety of mathematical skills during her 10 years of teaching in the Parkway School District in St. Louis, Missouri. She holds a Bachelor of Arts Degree in Mathematics from Central Methodist College and a Masters Degree in Business Administration from the University of Missouri – St. Louis. Currently taking time off to be at home with her two children, Mary Lee tutors students in secondary math.

Tammy Bohn-Voepel is currently working on a Master of Science and a Doctor of Philosophy in Mathematics at the University of Missouri-Columbia. She holds a Bachelor of Science and a Bachelor of Arts degree in Mathematics and a Master of Arts in Education, each from Northeast Missouri State University.

Credits . . .

Authors: Mary Lee Vivian, Tammy Bohn-Voepel
Artist/Production: Emily Georg-Smith
Project Director: Mina McMullin
Editor: Julie Moore
Cover Design: Annette Hollister-Papp
